# Using Flume

*Mike
Hope you find
this useful!*  *Hari Shreedharan*

Beijing · Cambridge · Farnham · Köln · Sebastopol · Tokyo    O'REILLY®

**Using Flume**

by Hari Shreedharan

Printed in the United States of America.

Published by O'Reilly Media, Inc., 1005 Gravenstein Highway North, Sebastopol, CA 95472.

O'Reilly books may be purchased for educational, business, or sales promotional use. Online editions are also available for most titles (*https://www.safaribooksonline.com/* (*https://www.safaribooksonline.com/?portal=oreilly*)). For more information, contact our corporate/institutional sales department: 800-998-9938 or *corporate@oreilly.com*.

**Editor:** Ann Spencer
**Production Editor:** Kara Ebrahim
**Copyeditor:** Charles Roumeliotis
**Proofreader:** Rachel Head

**Indexer:** Meghan Jones
**Interior Designer:** David Futato
**Cover Designer:** Ellie Volckhausen
**Illustrator:** Rebecca Demarest

October 2014:     First Edition

**Revision History for the First Edition**

2014-09-15:   First Release

See *http://oreilly.com/catalog/errata.csp?isbn=9781449368302* for release details.

978-1-449-36830-2

[LSI]

# Table of Contents

# Foreword

The past few years have seen tremendous growth in the development and adoption of Big Data technologies. Hadoop and related platforms are powering the next wave of data analytics over increasingly large amounts of data. The data produced today will be dwarfed by what is expected tomorrow, growing at an ever-increasing rate as the digital revolution engulfs all aspects of our existence. The barrier to entry in this new age of massive data volumes is of course the obvious one: *how do you get all this data in your cluster to begin with*? Clearly, this data is produced in a wide spectrum of sources spread across the enterprise, and has an interesting mix of interaction, machine, sensor, and social data among others. Any operator who has dealt with similar challenges would no doubt agree that it is nontrivial, if not downright hard, to build a system that can route this data into your clusters in a cost-effective manner.

Apache Flume is exactly built to handle this challenge.

Back in 2011 when Flume went into Incubation at The Apache Software Foundation, it was a project built by Cloudera engineers to address large-scale log data aggregation on Hadoop. Being a popular project from the beginning, it had seen a large number of new requirements ranging from event-ordering to guaranteed-delivery semantics, that came up over its initial releases. Given its popularity and high demand for complex requirements, we decided to refactor the project entirely and make it simpler, more powerful in its applicability and manageability, and allow for easy extensions where necessary. Hari and I were in the Incubator project along with a handful of other engineers who were working around the clock with the Flume community to drive this vision and implementation forward. From that time until now, Flume has graduated into its own top-level Apache project, made several stable releases, and has grown significantly rich in functionality.

Today, Flume is actively deployed and in use across the world in large numbers of data centers, sometimes spanning continental boundaries. It continues to effectively provide a super-resilient, fault-tolerant, reliable, fast, and efficient mechanism to move massive amounts of data from a variety of sources over to destination systems such as HBase, HDFS, etc. A well-planned Flume topology operates with minimal or no intervention, practically running itself indefinitely. It provides contextual routing and is able to work through downtimes, network outages, and other unpredictable/ unplanned interruptions by providing the capacity to reliably store and retransmit messages when connectivity is restored. It does all of this out of the box, and yet provides the flexibility to customize any component within its implementation using fairly stable and intuitive interfaces that are widely in use.

In *Using Flume*, Hari provides an overview of various components within Flume, diving into details where necessary. Operators will find this book immensely valuable for understanding how to easily set up and deploy Flume pipelines. Developers will find it a handy reference to build or customize components within Flume, and to better understand its architecture and component designs. Above all, this book will give you the necessary insights for setting up continuous ingestion for HDFS and HBase—the two most popular storage systems today.

With Flume deployed, you can be sure that data—no matter where it's produced in your enterprise, or how large its volume is—will make it safely and timely into your Big Data platforms. And you can then focus your energy on getting the right insights out of your data. Good luck!

—*Arvind Prabhakar, CTO, StreamSets*

# Preface

Today, developers are able to write and deploy applications on a large number of servers in the "cloud" very easily. These applications are producing more data than ever, which when stored and analyzed gives valuable insights that can improve the applications themselves and the businesses that the applications are a part of. The data generated by such applications is often analyzed using systems like Hadoop and HBase.

Analyzing this data is really possible only if you can get the data into these systems from frontend servers. Often, the validity of such analysis becomes less valid as the data becomes older. To get the data into the processing system in near real time, systems like Apache Flume are used. Apache Flume is a system for moving large amounts of data from large numbers of data producers to systems that store, index, or analyze that data. Such systems also decouple the producers from the consumers of the data, making it easy to change either side without the other knowing about it. In addition to decoupling, they also provide failure isolation and an added buffer between the producer and the storage system. The data producers will not know about the storage or indexing system being inaccessible until all of the Flume buffers also fill up—this provides an additional buffer, which might be enough for the storage system to come back online and clear up the backlog of events in the Flume buffers.

In this book, we will discuss in detail why systems like Flume are needed, the internals of a Flume agent, and how to configure and deploy Flume agents. We will also discuss the various ways in which Flume deployments can be customized and how to write plug-ins for Flume.

Chapter 1 gives a basic introduction to Apache Hadoop and Apache HBase. This chapter is only meant to introduce the reader to Hadoop and HBase and give some details of their internals. This can be skipped if the reader is already familiar with Hadoop and HBase.

Chapter 2 introduces Flume, its major components, and its configuration, and also explains how to deploy Flume to push data from data-generating servers to storage and indexing systems.

Chapter 3, Chapter 4, Chapter 5, and Chapter 6 explain the various sources, channels, and sinks that come packaged with Flume and how to write custom plug-ins to customize the way Flume receives, modifies, formats, and writes data.

In Chapter 7, we discuss the various ways to send data from your own applications to Flume agents. This chapter is primarily meant for developers writing applications that push data to Flume agents.

We will also discuss how to plan, deploy, and monitor Flume deployments in Chapter 8.

## Conventions Used in This Book

The following typographical conventions are used in this book:

*Italic*
> Indicates new terms, URLs, email addresses, filenames, and file extensions.

`Constant width`
> Used for program listings, as well as within paragraphs to refer to program elements such as variable or function names, databases, data types, environment variables, statements, and keywords.

**`Constant width bold`**
> Shows commands or other text that should be typed literally by the user.

*`Constant width italic`*
> Shows text that should be replaced with user-supplied values or by values determined by context.

**Bold in configuration listings**
> Indicates mandatory parameters in configuration parameter listings.

*Writing custom code\**
> Certain chapter and section names end with an asterisk (\*). This indicates that they cover advanced or developer topics related to design aspects of Flume components or explain how to write custom components that can be plugged into Flume.

This element signifies a tip or suggestion.

 This element signifies a general note.

 This element indicates a warning or caution.

# Using Code Examples

Supplemental material (code examples, exercises, etc.) is available for download at *https://github.com/harishreedharan/usingflumecode*.

 **Code in the Book**

The code shown in the book has been edited to make it as clear as possible, and may not compile or run as is. The full working version of the code can be found at the GitHub repository shown above. Please be aware that the companion code is meant to illustrate key Flume concepts and may not handle all edge or error cases.

This book is here to help you get your job done. In general, if example code is offered with this book, you may use it in your programs and documentation. You do not need to contact us for permission unless you're reproducing a significant portion of the code. For example, writing a program that uses several chunks of code from this book does not require permission. Selling or distributing a CD-ROM of examples from O'Reilly books does require permission. Answering a question by citing this book and quoting example code does not require permission. Incorporating a significant amount of example code from this book into your product's documentation does require permission.

We appreciate, but do not require, attribution. An attribution usually includes the title, author, publisher, and ISBN. For example: "*Using Flume* by Hari Shreedharan (O'Reilly). Copyright 2015 Hari Shreedharan, 978-1-449-36830-2."

If you feel your use of code examples falls outside fair use or the permission given above, feel free to contact us at *permissions@oreilly.com*.

## Safari® Books Online

 Safari Books Online is an on-demand digital library that delivers expert content in both book and video form from the world's leading authors in technology and business.

Technology professionals, software developers, web designers, and business and creative professionals use Safari Books Online as their primary resource for research, problem solving, learning, and certification training.

Safari Books Online offers a range of plans and pricing for enterprise, government, education, and individuals.

Members have access to thousands of books, training videos, and prepublication manuscripts in one fully searchable database from publishers like O'Reilly Media, Prentice Hall Professional, Addison-Wesley Professional, Microsoft Press, Sams, Que, Peachpit Press, Focal Press, Cisco Press, John Wiley & Sons, Syngress, Morgan Kaufmann, IBM Redbooks, Packt, Adobe Press, FT Press, Apress, Manning, New Riders, McGraw-Hill, Jones & Bartlett, Course Technology, and hundreds more. For more information about Safari Books Online, please visit us online.

## How to Contact Us

Please address comments and questions concerning this book to the publisher:

O'Reilly Media, Inc.
1005 Gravenstein Highway North
Sebastopol, CA 95472
800-998-9938 (in the United States or Canada)
707-829-0515 (international or local)
707-829-0104 (fax)

We have a web page for this book, where we list errata, examples, and any additional information. You can access this page at *http://bit.ly/using-flume*.

To comment or ask technical questions about this book, send email to *bookquestions@oreilly.com*.

For more information about our books, courses, conferences, and news, see our website at *http://www.oreilly.com*.

Find us on Facebook: *http://facebook.com/oreilly*

Follow us on Twitter: *http://twitter.com/oreillymedia*

Watch us on YouTube: *http://www.youtube.com/oreillymedia*

# Acknowledgments

I gratefully dedicate this book to my parents, Dr. M. Shreedharan and Usha Shreedharan, without whose efforts and encouragement I would not have been able to become an engineer and eventually write this book.

I am also grateful to my sister, Lakshmi Shreedharan, and brother-in-law, Dinakar Kesavapillai, for all their help and support during my college and grad school days. I also want to thank my niece, Dhwani, for all the fun she adds to my life.

I am really thankful to my wife, Archana Sastry, for her support and the late nights during the early days of Flume development.

I thank Arvind Prabhakar for being a mentor and friend whose guidance has always helped me choose the right path.

Mike Percy, Brock Noland, Jarcec Cecho, Kathleen Ting, Jeff Lord, Prasad Mujumdar, Will McQueen, and Ken Choy have all helped me grow as an engineer and a person and I am thankful for that.

I also take this opportunity to thank Jon Hsieh for starting the Flume project, and the Apache Flume community for building and maintaining it.

# CHAPTER 1

# Apache Hadoop and Apache HBase: An Introduction

Apache Hadoop is a highly scalable, fault-tolerant distributed system meant to store large amounts of data and process it in place. Hadoop is designed to run large-scale processing systems on the same cluster that stores the data. The philosophy of Hadoop is to store all the data in one place and process the data in the same place— that is, move the processing to the data store and not move the data to the processing system. Apache HBase is a database system that is built on top of Hadoop to provide a key-value store that benefits from the distributed framework that Hadoop provides.

Data, once written to the *Hadoop Distributed File System* (HDFS), is immutable. Each file on HDFS is append-only. Once a file is created and written to, the file can either be appended to or deleted. It is not possible to change the data in the file. Though HBase runs on top of HDFS, HBase supports updating any data written to it, just like a normal database system.

This chapter will provide a brief introduction to Apache Hadoop and Apache HBase, though we will not go into too much detail.

## HDFS

At the core of Hadoop is a distributed file system referred to as HDFS. HDFS is a highly distributed, fault-tolerant file system that is specifically built to run on commodity hardware and to scale as more data is added by simply adding more hardware. HDFS can be configured to replicate data several times on different machines to ensure that there is no data loss, even if a machine holding the data fails. Replicating data also allows the system to be highly available even if machines holding a copy of the data are disconnected from the network or go down. This section will briefly cover the design of HDFS and the various processing systems that run on top of HDFS.

HDFS was originally designed on the basis of the Google File System [gfs]. HDFS is a distributed system that can store data on thousands of off-the-shelf servers, with no special requirements for hardware configuration. This means HDFS does not require the use of storage area networks (SANs), expensive network configuration, or any special disks. HDFS can be run on any run-of-the-mill data center setup. HDFS replicates all data written to it, based on the replication factor configured by the user. The default replication factor is 3, which ensures that any data written to HDFS is replicated on three different servers within the cluster. This greatly reduces the possibility that any data written to HDFS will be lost.

HDFS, like any other file system, writes data to individual *blocks*. Each HDFS file consists of at least one block. Each file consists of multiple blocks, based on the size of the file. HDFS is designed to hold very large files. Therefore, HDFS block sizes are also usually pretty large compared to other file systems. HDFS block sizes are configurable, and in most cases range between 128 MB to 512 MB. HDFS tries to ensure that each block is replicated based on the replication factor, thus ensuring the file itself is replicated as much as the replication factor. HDFS is rack-aware, and the default block placement policy tries to ensure that each replica of a block is on a different rack.

HDFS consists of two types of servers: *name nodes* and *data nodes*. Most Hadoop clusters generally have two name nodes and several data nodes. Data nodes are the nodes on which the data is stored. At any point in time, there is one *active* name node and an optional *standby* name node. The active name node is the currently active name node that serves client and other data nodes. The standby name node is an active backup to the primary, and takes over if the active name node goes down or is no longer accessible for some reason. Name nodes are responsible for storing metadata about files and blocks on the file system. The name node maps every file to the list of blocks that the file consists of. The name node also holds information about each block's location—which data nodes the block is stored on and where on the data node it is.

Each client write is initially written to a local file on the client machine, until the client flushes the file or closes it or the size of the temporary file exceeds a block boundary. At this point, the file is created (or a new block is added if new data is being written once a block boundary is crossed or an existing file is reopened for append) and the name node assigns blocks to it. Then the data is written to each block, which is replicated to multiple data nodes, one after another. The operation is successful only if all the data nodes succesfully replicate the blocks.

HDFS files cannot be edited and are append-only. Each file, once closed, can be opened only to append data to it. HDFS also does not guarantee that writes to a file are visible to other clients until the client writing the data flushes the data to data node memory, or closes the file. Each time a new block is required, the name node allocates a new block to the file and keeps track of it. For each read, the client gets the locations of the blocks that represent the file from the name node and directly reads the data from the data node. From the user's point of view, HDFS is a single storage system and the fact that each file is replicated and stored on multiple systems is completely transparent to the user. So, user code need not worry about any of the failure tolerance or replication aspects of HDFS. Even the client API writing to a file on the local machine before a flush or close call is transparent to the user code.

The client API is one way of interacting with HDFS. HDFS also provides a set of shell commands that can be used to perform many common file operations. HDFS commands are of the form:

```
hdfs dfs -<command> <options>
```

For example, to get a listing of files in the */Data/* directory on HDFS, the following command can be used:

```
hdfs dfs -ls /Data
```

The list of supported commands can be found in the Hadoop documentation [commands]. Running these commands requires that HDFS be configured correctly on the system, with *HADOOP_HOME* or *HADOOP_PREFIX* set correctly with the Hadoop configuration files correctly in *HADOOP_CLASSPATH*. For more details on HDFS architecture and configuration, refer to *Hadoop: The Definitive Guide* [hdfs-architecture].

## HDFS Data Formats

In general, data formats in HDFS are classified into *splittable* and *unsplittable* formats. A splittable format is one in which a file can be reliably split into multiple pieces called *splits* at record boundaries. A splittable file format can seek to the start of a record from any point. Splittable file formats are MapReduce-friendly, since MapReduce splits files to read data from a file in parallel from different mappers.

It is always better to use binary formats rather than text to write to HDFS. This is because most binary formats have some way of indicating corruption or incompleteness in a record. Failures can cause incomplete records to be written to files. An example is if the HDFS cluster runs out of space, or has connectivity issues: there could be a block allocation failure, which can cause the file to contain incomplete or corrupt records. Binary records help ensure that such incorrect records are detected and ignored. An example of a binary format that is used commonly in Hadoop is the *Avro* container file format. This format is splittable, and can detect corrupt or incomplete records in a file. MapReduce, Hive, Pig, etc. support Avro as an input format.

Avro also supports compression using the *Snappy* and *Deflate/bz2* compression codecs.

There are several data formats that are typically used on HDFS. One of the most common data formats on HDFS is a *sequence file*. A sequence file is a splittable file format that is typically used with MapReduce jobs. It is represented as a list of keys and values, each of which is an instance of a *Writable*, which basically represents a serializable class.

There are compression formats that are splittable, like bz2, preprocessed LZO, etc. More details on file formats in the Hadoop ecosystem can be found in *Hadoop: The Definitive Guide* [serialization].

Flume supports writing several of the built-in formats out of the box, and also allows users to plug in their own *serializers* that can write data in any format of their own choosing to HDFS. We will discuss this in Chapter 5, in "Controlling the Data Format Using Serializers*" on page 108.

## Processing Data on HDFS

As we discussed, Hadoop brings the processing systems to the data store. As a result, the same nodes that host the data also run systems that can process the data stored on HDFS. MapReduce has long been the classical system that processes data on HDFS.

MapReduce is a distributed processing framework that allows the user to write Java code that reads data from HDFS and processes it. Each MapReduce program runs on multiple nodes, each processing a part of the input data. MapReduce programs have two phases: the *Map* phase and the *Reduce* phase. Each phase runs a piece of Java code on multiple nodes simultaneously, thus processing huge amounts of data in parallel. Each *mapper* reads an input split (a fixed subset of the inputs) from a specific directory on HDFS and processes the inputs as keys and corresponding values.

How the data in the files in the directory are mapped to keys and values depends on the format being used and the *input format* that processes it [input-format]. The Map phase processes the inputs and produces intermediate key-value pairs. All key-value pairs with the same intermediate key are then processed by the same *reducer*. Finally, the reducer eventually writes out final outputs as key-value pairs to a configured output directory. You can read more about MapReduce in *Hadoop: A Definitive Guide* [mr].

Apache Hive and Cloudera Impala provide SQL interfaces (really subsets of SQL) to process data on HDFS. Hive parses the SQL query to generate a MapReduce job that processes the data, while Impala has its own processing engine that reads the data and applies transformations based on the query to process the data. These systems map flat files on HDFS to *tables* on which the queries are run. Such systems provide an easy migration path for users who have been using SQL-based database systems to process and store their data. There are several other systems, like Apache Pig, Apache Spark, etc., that can be used to process data stored on HDFS.

## Apache HBase

Apache HBase is the Hadoop Ecosystem's key-value store. HBase is often used to write and update data in real time. It is also used to serve data in real time, in places where a traditional database could be used. HBase is built on top of HDFS and relies on HDFS for replication. Logically, the HBase data model is similar to a database with data being written to tables that have several rows and columns, though the columns are not fixed in the schema and can be created dynamically by a client (each row can have a different set of columns and there is no fixed schema representing a fixed set of columns).

Each row is accessed with a key known as the *row key*, which is very similar to the primary key in a standard database system. There can be as many columns for a row key as required, but there can be exactly one value per row for every column (though HBase can keep multiple "versions"—the last *n* values of the column for that row). HBase groups columns into *column families*, which are stored together on HDFS. Therefore, it is usually a good idea to group columns whose data is written and accessed in a similar pattern.

The HBase client API allows Java programs to interact with an HBase cluster. Writes to HBase are in the form of *Puts*, which represent writes to a single row. A single Put represents a single remote procedure call (RPC) call that can write to multiple columns within the same row. HBase also supports *Increments*, which can be used to increment values in columns that can be used as counters. Just like Puts, Increments can also update multiple columns in the same row in a single RPC call.

In the context of Flume's HBase interaction, we are only concerned with Puts and Increments, though HBase provides RPC calls to update or delete data. More details on HBase operations can be found in *HBase: The Definitive Guide* [hbase-client]. To interact with HBase from languages other than Java, HBase provides a Thrift API, which you can read about on the Apache HBase wiki [hbase-thrift].

In addition to the client API, HBase provides a shell to interact with the HBase cluster. The HBase shell has commands to do Puts, Gets, Increments, Deletes, Scans, and so on, and also to create, disable, truncate, and delete tables [hbase-shell]. To start an HBase shell, use the following command:

```
hbase shell
```

HBase provides row-level atomicity. If a writer writes to multiple columns within the same row in a single Put, then it is guaranteed that a reader will read either old values of all columns or the new values of all columns and not old values of some columns and new values of others. HBase, though, provides no transactions or ACID

(Atomicity, Consistency, Isolation, Durability) compliance. Since there are no transactions over multiple rows, there are no guarantees of consistency for clients reading multiple rows.

As mentioned earlier, HBase is built on top of HDFS. As a result, data on HBase is automatically replicated. HBase divides rows on HBase into *Regions*. A region is simply the set of rows with row keys between two fixed values. HBase partitions the entire dataset into multiple regions, each of which is hosted by a server known as a *Region Server*. At any point in time, there is exactly one region server hosting a particular region, though a single server can host more than one region. Every read or write to a row belonging to a region goes through the region server hosting that region. The server that decides which server hosts which region is the *HBase Master*. The Master is HBase's version of the HDFS name node. The master also decides when a region becomes too big and has to be split, etc.

Flume allows users to *Put* data or *Increment* counters on HBase. The user can plug in custom pieces of code to do the translation from Flume events to HBase Puts or Increments. We will cover this in "Translating Flume Events to HBase Puts and Increments Using Serializers*" on page 117.

## Summary

In this chapter, we discussed the basics of HDFS and HBase. Though Flume supports other systems, these are the most important and commonly used systems. In Chapter 5, we will discuss how to write data to these systems in a scalable way using Flume.

## References

- *http://research.google.com/archive/gfs.html*
- [hdfs-architecture] HDFS architecture, *Hadoop: The Definitive Guide, 3rd Edition*, Chapter 3
- [serialization] Hadoop serialization, *Hadoop: The Definitive Guide, 3rd Edition*, Chapter 4
- [hbase-client] HBase operationsn, *HBase: The Definitive Guide*, Chapter 3
- [commands] Hadoop commands, *http://bit.ly/1p9jalP*
- [hbase-thrift] HBase Thrift API, *http://wiki.apache.org/hadoop/Hbase/ThriftApi*
- [hbase-shell] HBase shell, *http://wiki.apache.org/hadoop/Hbase/Shell*
- [input-format] Hadoop input format, *Hadoop: The Definitive Guide*, Chapter 7
- [mr] MapReduce, *Hadoop: The Definitive Guide*, Chapter 2

# Streaming Data Using Apache Flume

Pushing data to HDFS and similar storage systems using an intermediate system is a very common use case. There are several systems, like Apache Flume, Apache Kafka, Facebook's Scribe, etc., that support this use case. Such systems allow HDFS and HBase clusters to handle sporadic bursts of data without necessarily having the capacity to handle that rate of writes continuously. These systems act as a buffer between the data producers and the final destination. By virtue of being buffers, they are able to balance out the impedance mismatch between the producers and consumers, thus providing a steady state of flow. Scaling these systems is often far easier than scaling HDFS or HBase clusters. Such systems also allow the applications to push data without worrying about having to buffer the data and retry in case of HDFS downtime, etc.

Most such systems have some fundamental similarities. Usually, these systems have components that are responsible for accepting the data from the producer, through an RPC call or HTTP (which may be exposed via a client API). They also have components that act as buffers where the data is stored until it is removed by the components that move the data to the next hop or destination. In this chapter, we will discuss the basic architecture of a Flume agent and how to configure Flume agents to move data from various applications to HDFS or HBase.

Apache Hadoop is becoming a standard data processing framework in large enterprises. Applications often produce massive amounts of data that get written to HDFS, the distributed file system that forms the base of Hadoop. Apache Flume was conceived as a system to write data to Apache Hadoop and Apache HBase in a reliable and scalable fashion. As a result, Flume's HDFS and HBase Sinks provide a very rich set of features that makes it possible to write data in any format that is supported by these systems and in a MapReduce/Hive/Impala/Pig–friendly way. In this book, we will discuss why we need a system like Flume, its design and implementation, and the various features of Flume that make it highly scalable, flexible, and reliable.

# The Need for Flume

Why do we really need a system like Flume? Why not simply write data directly to HDFS from every application server that produces data? In this section, we will discuss why we need such a system, and what it adds to the architecture.

Messaging systems that isolate systems from each other have existed for a long time—Flume does this in the Hadoop context. Flume is specifically designed to push data from a massive number of sources to the various storage systems in the Hadoop ecosystem, like HDFS and HBase.

In general, when there is enough data to be processed on a Hadoop cluster, there is usually a large number of servers producing the data. This number could be in the hundreds or even thousands of servers. Such a huge number of servers trying to write data to an HDFS or HBase cluster can cause major problems, for multiple reasons.

HDFS requires that exactly one client writes to a file—as a result, there could be thousands of files being written to at the same time. Each time a file is created or a new block is allocated, there is a complex set of operations that takes place on the name node. Such a huge number of operations happening simultaneously on a single server can cause the server to come under severe stress. Also, when thousands of machines are writing a large amount of data to a small number of machines, the network connecting these machines may get overwhelmed and start experiencing severe latency.

In many cases, application servers residing in multiple data centers aggregate data in a single data center that hosts the Hadoop cluster, which means the applications have to write data over a wide area network (WAN). In all these cases, applications might experience severe latency when attempting to write to HDFS or HBase. If the number of servers hosting the applications or the number of applications writing data increases, the latency and failure rate are likely to increase. As a result, considering HDFS cluster and network latencies becomes an additional concern while designing the software that is writing to HDFS.

Most applications see production traffic in predictable patterns, with a few hours of peak traffic per day and much less traffic during the rest of the day. To ensure an application that is writing directly to HDFS or HBase does not lose data or need to buffer a lot of data, the HDFS or HBase cluster needs to be configured to be able to handle peak traffic with little or no latency. All these cases make it clear that it is important to isolate the production applications from HDFS or HBase and ensure that production applications push data to these systems in a controlled and organized fashion.

Flume is designed to be a flexible distributed system that can scale out very easily and is highly customizable. A correctly configured Flume agent and a pipeline of Flume agents created by connecting agents with each other is guaranteed to not lose data, provided durable channels are used.

The simplest unit of Flume deployment is a Flume *agent*. It is possible to connect one Flume agent to one or more other agents. It is also possible for an agent to receive data from one or more agents. By connecting multiple Flume agents to each other, a *flow* is established. This chain of Flume agents can be used to move data from one location to another—specifically, from applications producing data to HDFS, HBase, etc.

By having a number of Flume agents receive data from application servers, which then write the data to HDFS or HBase (either directly or via other Flume agents), it is possible to scale the number of servers and the amount of data that can be written to HDFS by simply adding more Flume agents.

Each Flume agent has three components: the *source*, the *channel*, and the *sink*. The *source* is responsible for getting events into the Flume agent, while the *sink* is responsible for removing the events from the agent and forwarding them to the next agent in the topology, or to HDFS, HBase, Solr, etc. The *channel* is a buffer that stores data that the source has received, until a sink has successfully written the data out to the next hop or the eventual destination.

In effect, the data flow in a Flume agent works in the following way: the source produces/receives the data and writes it to one or more channels, and one or more sinks read these events from the channels and push them out to the next agent or to a storage or indexing system.

Flume agents can be configured to send data from one agent to another to form a *pipeline* before the data is written out to the destination. The durability of the data once the data has reached a Flume agent depends completely upon the durability guarantees of the channel used by the agent. In general, when a Flume agent is configured to use any of the built-in sources or sinks together with one of the durable channels, the agent is guaranteed to not lose data. By virtue of individual agents not losing data, it is guaranteed that a Flume pipeline will not lose data either.

Flume, though, can cause duplicate data to eventually be written out, if there are unexpected errors/timeouts and retries in the Flume pipeline. If disks that hold the durable channel fail irrecoverably, Flume might lose data because of the disk failures. Flume does allow users to replicate events across redundant flows to ensure that disk and agent failures are handled, though this might cause duplicates. Therefore, users might have to do some post-processing to ensure that duplicates are taken care of.

# Is Flume a Good Fit?

Flume represents data as *events*. Events are very simple data structures, with a body and a set of headers. The body of the event is a byte array that usually is the payload that Flume is transporting. The headers are represented as a map with string keys and string values. Headers are not meant to transfer data, but for routing purposes and to keep track of priority, severity of events being sent, etc. The headers can be used to add event IDs or UUIDs to events as well.

Each event must essentially be an independent record, rather than a part of a record. This also imposes the requirement that each event be able to fit in the memory of the Flume agent JVM. If a File Channel is being used, then there should be enough disk space to accommodate this. If data cannot be represented as multiple individual records, Flume might not be a good fit for the use case.

Flume is primarily meant to push data from a large number of production servers to HDFS, HBase, etc. In cases where Flume is not a good fit, there is often an easier method, like Web HDFS or the HBase HTTP API, that can be used to write data. If there are only a handful of production servers producing data and the data does not need to be written out in real time, then it might also make sense to just move the data to HDFS via Web HDFS or NFS, especially if the amount of data being written out is relatively small—a few files of a few GB every few hours will not hurt HDFS. In this case, planning, configuring, and deploying Flume may not be worth it. Flume is really meant to push events in real time where the stream of data is continuous and its volume reasonably large.

As noted earlier, the simplest unit of deployment of Flume is called a *Flume agent*. An agent is a Java application that receives or generates data and buffers it until it is eventually written to the next agent or to a storage or indexing system. We will discuss the three main components of Flume agents (sources, channels, and sinks) in the next section.

# Inside a Flume Agent

As discussed earlier, each Flume agent consists of three major components: sources, channels, and sinks. In this section, we will describe these and other components and how they work together.

Sources are active components that receive data from some other application that is producing the data. There are sources that produce data themselves, though such sources are mostly used for testing purposes. Sources can listen to one or more network ports to receive data or can read data from the local file system. Each source must be *connected* to at least one channel. A source can write to several channels, replicating the events to all or some of the channels, based on some criteria.

Channels are, in general, passive components (though they may run their own threads for cleanup or garbage collection) that buffer data that has been received by the agent, but not yet written out to another agent or to a storage system. Channels behave like queues, with sources writing to them and sinks reading from them. Multiple sources can write to the same channel safely, and multiple sinks can read from the same channel. Each sink, though, can read from only exactly one channel. If multiple sinks read from the same channel, it is guaranteed that exactly one sink will read (and commit—more about this in Chapter 4) a specific event from the channel.

Sinks poll their respective channels continuously to read and remove events. The sinks push events to the next hop (in the case of RPC sinks), or to the final destination. Once the data is safely at the next hop or at its destination, the sinks inform the channels, via transaction commits, that those events can now be deleted from the channels.

Figure 2-1 shows a simple Flume agent with a single source, channel, and sink.

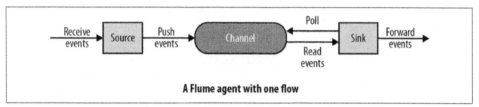

A Flume agent with one flow

*Figure 2-1. A simple Flume agent with one source, channel, and sink*

Flume itself does not restrict the number of sources, channels, and sinks in an agent. Therefore, it is possible for Flume sources to receive events and, through configuration, replicate the events to multiple destinations. This is made possible by the fact that sources actually write data to channels via channel processors, interceptors, and channel selectors.

Each source has its own *channel processor*. Each time the source writes data to the channels, it does so by delegating this task to its channel processor. The channel processor then passes these events to one or more *interceptors* configured for the source.

An interceptor is a piece of code that can read the event and modify or drop the event based on some processing it does. Interceptors can be used to drop events based on some criteria, like a regex, add new headers to events or remove existing ones, etc. Each source can be configured to use multiple interceptors, which are called in the order defined by the configuration, with the result of one interceptor passed to the next in the chain. This is called the *chain-of-responsibility* design pattern. Once the interceptors are done processing the events, the list of events returned by the interceptor chain is passed to the list of channels selected for every event in the list by the *channel selector*.

A source can write to multiple channels via the processor-interceptor-selector route. Channel selectors are the components that decide which channels attached to this source each event must be written to. Interceptors can thus be used to insert or remove data from events so that channel selectors may apply some criteria on these events to decide which channels the events must be written to. Channel selectors can apply arbitrary filtering criteria to events to decide which channels each event must be written to, and which channels are required and optional.

A failure to write to a required channel causes the channel processor to throw a Chan nelException to indicate that the source must retry the event (all events that are in that transaction, actually), while a failure to write to an optional channel is simply ignored. Once the events are written out, the processor indicates success to the source, which may send out an acknowledgment (ACK) to the system that sent the event and continue accepting more events. Figure 2-2 shows this workflow.

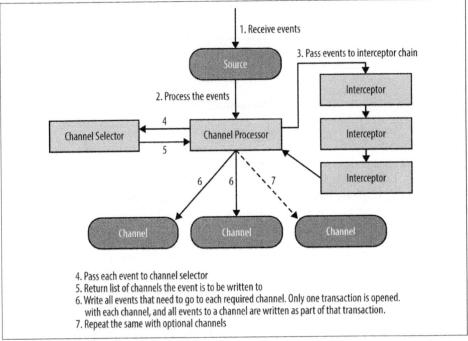

*Figure 2-2. Interaction between sources, channel processors, interceptors, and channel selectors*

*Sink runners* run a *sink group*, which may contain one or more sinks. If there is only one sink in a group, it is more efficient to not have a group at all. The sink runner is simply a thread that asks the sink group (or the sink) to process the next batch of events. Each sink group has a *sink processor* that selects one of the sinks in the group to process the next set of events. Each sink can take data from exactly one channel, though multiple sinks could take data from the same channel. The sink selected (or the lone sink, if there is no group) takes events from the channel and writes them to the next hop or final destination. This is shown in Figure 2-3.

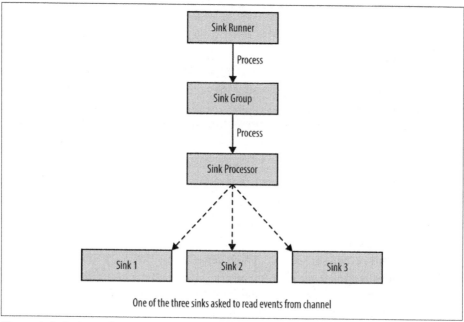

Figure 2-3. Sinks, sink runners, sink groups, and sink processors

# Configuring Flume Agents

Flume agents are configured using plain-text configuration files. Flume configuration uses the *properties file format*, which is simply a plain-text file with newline-separated key-value pairs. An example of a properties file is shown here:

```
key1 = value1
key2 = value2
```

By using this format, Flume makes it easy to pass configuration into an agent and its various components. In the configuration file, Flume follows a hierarchical structure. Each Flume agent has a name, which is set when the Flume agent is started using the flume-ng command (described in "Running a Flume Agent" on page 29). The configuration file can contain configurations for several Flume agents, but only the configuration of the agent whose name is specified in the flume-ng command is actually loaded.

There are some components that can have several instances of that type in a Flume agent, like sources, sinks, channels, etc. To be able to identify the configuration of each of these components, they are *named*. The configuration file must list the names of the sources, sinks, channels, and sink groups in an agent in the following format, called the *active list*:

```
agent1.sources = source1 source2
agent1.sinks = sink1 sink2 sink3 sink4
agent1.sinkgroups = sg1 sg2
agent1.channels = channel1 channel2
```

This configuration snippet represents a Flume agent named `agent1`, with two sources, two sink groups, two channels, and four sinks. Even if there are configuration parameters listed for some component, if they are not in the active list for that agent they are not created, configured, or started. Other components, such as interceptors and channel selectors, need not be present in the active list. They are automatically created and activated when the component (source, sink, etc.) they're associated with is activated.

For each component to be configured, the configuration for that component is passed in with a prefix in the following format:

```
<agent-name>.<component-type>.<component-name>.<configuration-parameter> = \
<value>
```

The `<component-type>` for sources is `sources`, sinks is `sinks`, channels is `channels`, and sinkgroups is `sinkgroups`. Components such as interceptors, channel selectors, and sink processors are tied to a single top-level component and are anchored to these components in the same configuration pattern.

Component names are namespaced based on their component type. Therefore, it is possible to have multiple components with the same name, as long as their component type is different. Components like interceptors are also namespaced to individual sources, so it is possible, though not recommended, to have multiple interceptors with the same name as long as each one is configured to a different source.

For example, configuration could be passed to `source1` in the following format:

```
agent1.sources.source1.port = 4144
agent1.sources.source1.bind = avro.domain.com
```

For each component, the prefix of the configuration parameter key is removed (including the component name). Only the actual parameter and its value are passed in, via a `Context` class instance passed in to the `configure` method. `Context` is a Map-like key-value store, with some slightly more complex methods. So, in this case the source gets only two parameters with keys `port` and `bind` and values `4144` and `avro.domain.com`, respectively, in the `Context` instance (and not the entire configuration line). When we discuss the configuration for each component, the tables will show only the actual parameters passed to the components and not the entire lines from the configuration file.

The Flume configuration uses the `type` parameter for all sources, sinks, channels, and interceptors to instantiate the component. The `type` parameter can be the fully qualified class name (FQCN), or the alias for built-in components. An example of specifying the `type` parameter follows:

```
agent1.sources.source1.type = avro
```

The Flume configuration system also ensures that the correct channels are set for each source, by creating the channel processor and setting the correct channels for each source's processor. It also handles interceptor initialization so that the correct channel processors from the correct sources pass the events to the correct interceptors (though from the configuration, it might seem like interceptors are subcomponents of sources—the sources actually don't need to create or configure interceptors). Similarly, the channel for each sink is also set by the configuration system. The configuration system adds sinks to the correct sink groups and also configures the sink processors for the groups.

Any component that needs to get a configuration from the Flume configuration system must implement the `Configurable` interface, shown in Example 2-1.

*Example 2-1. Configurable interface*

```
package org.apache.flume.conf;
public interface Configurable {
  public void configure(Context context);
}
```

Components can have subcomponents, which can also be configurable. Each component must either configure its subcomponents or pass the subcomponent configuration to the subcomponents, which must then configure themselves. Though each subcomponent can be configured in any way that the component implementation specifies, it is a good practice to implement the `Configurable` interface. Using the `Context` class method `getSubProperties`, subproperties specific to the subcomponent can be passed to it.

An example of configurable subcomponents is HDFS serializers, which are described in detail in "Controlling the Data Format Using Serializers*" on page 108. Serializers are configured by the HDFS Sink, using the `Configurable` interface and the `getSub Properties` method. Serializers can be configured using the suffix `serializer.` to the `hdfsSink`, and the serializer gets the key as the substring following the `serial izer.` in the configuration. In the following example, the serializer would get a `Con text` instance with one key-value pair. The key would be `bufferSize` and the value would be `4096`:

```
agent.sinks.hdfsSink.serializer.bufferSize = 4096
```

All Flume components with configurable subcomponents follow this pattern, with each subcomponent getting just its own parameters with all prefixes removed. This is true for even subcomponents of subcomponents, if any exist.

Example 2-2 shows an example of a Flume agent that has multiple components, with some of them having subcomponents. In this agent there is one source, two channels, and two sinks. The source is an HTTP Source, which is named `httpSrc`. This source writes to two memory channels, `memory1` and `memory2`—this is set by the configuration system in the channel processor, and source implementations need not worry about setting the channels. Multiple parameters—`bind`, `port`, `ssl`, `keystore`, `keystore-password`, `handler`, and `handler.insertTimestamp`—and their values are available in the `Context` instance passed to the `configure` method. It is up to the source implementation to decide what to do with any configuration parameters passed to it.

For this configuration file, the configuration system also creates an interceptor to which all events received by the HTTP Source are forwarded. In this example, the HTTP Source does not need to bother about any special handling of the interceptor creation or configuration. Creation and configuration of interceptors is handled by the channel processor. Similarly, all other components get the parameters and their values via the `configure` method, including the ones meant for subcomponents.

*Example 2-2. A typical Flume agent configuration*

```
agent.sources = httpSrc
agent.channels = memory1 memory2
agent.sinks = hdfsSink hbaseSink

agent.sources.httpSrc.type = http
agent.sources.httpSrc.channels = memory1 memory2

# Bind to all interfaces
agent.sources.httpSrc.bind = 0.0.0.0
agent.sources.httpSrc.port = 4353

# Removing this line will disable SSL
agent.sources.httpSrc.ssl = true
agent.sources.httpSrc.keystore = /tmp/keystore
agent.sources.httpSrc.keystore-password = UsingFlume

agent.sources.httpSrc.handler = usingflume.ch03.HTTPSourceXMLHandler
agent.sources.httpSrc.handler.insertTimestamp = true

agent.sources.httpSrc.interceptors = hostInterceptor
agent.sources.httpSrc.interceptors.hostInterceptor.type = host

# Initializes a memory channel with default configuration
agent.channels.memory1.type = memory
```

```
# Initializes a memory channel with default configuration
agent.channels.memory2.type = memory

# HDFS Sink
agent.sinks.hdfsSink.type = hdfs
agent.sinks.hdfsSink.channel = memory1
agent.sinks.hdfsSink.hdfs.path = /Data/UsingFlume/%{topic}/%Y/%m/%d/%H/%M
agent.sinks.hdfsSink.hdfs.filePrefix = UsingFlumeData

agent.sinks.hbaseSink.type = asynchbase
agent.sinks.hbaseSink.channel = memory2
agent.sinks.hbaseSink.serializer = usingflume.ch05.AsyncHBaseDirectSerializer
agent.sinks.hbaseSink.table = usingFlumeTable
```

# Getting Flume Agents to Talk to Each Other

As we will see in the following sections, there is almost always a need for one Flume agent to send data to another. To achieve this goal, specialized RPC sink–source pairs come bundled with Flume. The preferred RPC sink–RPC source pair for agent-to-agent communication is the Avro Sink–Avro Source pair.

To receive data from other Flume agents or from clients, the agents receiving the data can be configured to use Avro Sources and the agents sending the data must be configured to run Avro Sinks. The Avro Sink is a specialized sink that can send events to the Avro Source. In addition to the Avro Sink, the Flume RPC client can also send events to the Avro Source. Avro Sources receive data from other Flume agents or applications running Flume RPC clients via the Avro RPC protocol. A single Avro Source can receive data from a large number of clients or Flume agents. Even though a single Avro Sink can send data to only one Avro Source, it is possible to send data from one agent to many other agents, using sink groups and sink processors we will discuss in "Sink Groups and Sink Processors" on page 157.

We will discuss this in more detail in "Sink-to-Source Communication" on page 36. For now, it is just important to understand that it is possible to send data from one Flume agent to another and from custom applications to Flume agents via a client API (which we will discuss in Chapter 7).

# Complex Flows

As explained earlier, it is possible for Flume agents to have several sources, sinks, and channels, though the number of these components in a single agent must be carefully managed to ensure that hardware is not overwhelmed. Since each source can actually write to multiple channels, events can easily be replicated to make sure that each event goes to more than one destination. Sinks can then remove data from channels to push data to various destinations.

A *flow* is a series of one or more agents that push data to one another and eventually to a storage or indexing system. In reality, flows can be arbitrarily more complex, with each of the three components being part of multiple flows, and flows including multiple source-channel-sink triplets.

In general, Flume is meant to push data in from a very large number of servers to send data to a single HDFS cluster. Flume comes bundled with Avro and Thrift sink–source pairs, which can be used to send data from one Flume agent to another. This allows the user to design a fan-in–style flow from a large number of data-producing applications. It is important to restrict the number of applications writing data to any storage system to ensure that the storage system scales with the amount of data being written and can handle bursty data writes.

There are multiple ways in which Flume agents can be organized within a cluster. The first and the simplest one is to deploy a single tier of Flume agents to receive data from the application servers and have the same agents write the data directly to the storage system. Such a system isolates applications from a storage system failure and allows the storage system to handle periodic bursts by absorbing the increasing input rate. Flume will adjust the rate of writes to the storage system by backing off for increasing amounts of time every time a write fails (up to some maximum period), so as to not overwhelm the storage system if the capacity is lower than what is required to handle the current write rate.

The number of Flume agents within this single tier usually needs to be only a fraction of the total number of application servers, since Flume's Avro Source and Thrift Source are designed to receive a large amount of data from a large number of servers, though each agent will have a maximum capacity that depends on the exact hardware deployed, the network, the latency requirements, etc. Such a topology can be designed as shown in Figure 2-4.

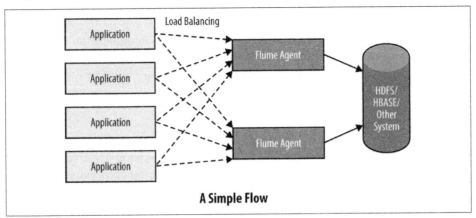

*Figure 2-4. Aggregating data from a large number of application servers to HDFS using Flume*

To design a fan-in topology, there needs to be a number of Flume agents receiving data from the applications producing the data while a few agents write data to the storage system. Depending on how many servers are producing how much data, the agents could be organized into one, two, or more tiers, with agents from each tier forwarding data from one tier to the next using an RPC sink–RPC source combination.

As shown in Figure 2-5, the outermost tier has the maximum number of agents to receive data from the application, though the number of Flume agents is usually only a small fraction of the number of application servers; the exact number depends on a variety of factors including the network, the hardware, and the amount of data. When the application produces more data or more servers are added, it is easy to scale out by simply adding more agents to the outermost tier and having them configured to write data to the machines in the second tier.

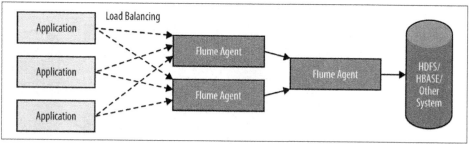

*Figure 2-5. A fan-in flow*

Often the second tier can be scaled out with more agents much more slowly than the outermost tier, since the number of servers writing the data to the second tier (the number of Flume agents in the outermost tier) needs to grow much more slowly than the number of application servers. This is because the first tier of Flume agents will absorb much of the impact caused by the increase in application servers.

This kind of topology allows Flume to control the rate of writes to the storage system by backing off as needed, while also allowing the application to write data without any worry. Such a topology is also often used when the application producing the data is deployed in many different data centers, and data is being aggregated to one cluster. By writing to a Flume agent within the same data center, the application can avoid having to write data across a cross–data center WAN link, yet ensure that the data will eventually get persisted to the storage system. The communication between Flume agents can be configured to allow higher cross–data center latency to ensure that the agent-to-agent communication can complete successfully without timeouts.

Having more tiers allows for absorbing longer and larger spikes in load, by not overwhelming any one agent or tier and draining out data from each tier as soon as possible. Therefore, the number of tiers required is primarily decided by the amount of data being pushed into the Flume deployment. Since the outermost tier receives data from the largest number of machines, this tier should have the maximum number of agents to scale the networking architecture. As we move further into the Flume topology, the number of agents can reduce significantly.

If the number of servers producing data consistently increases, the number of Flume agents in the tier receiving data from the application servers also needs to increase. This means that at some point, it may be required to increase subsequent tiers, though the number of agents in subsequent tiers can be increased at a far slower rate than in the outer tiers. This also ensures increased buffering capacity within the Flume setup, to accommodate the increase in data production. An example of such a flow is shown in Figure 2-6.

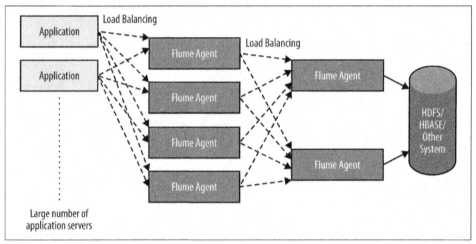

*Figure 2-6. A large, complex topology supporting a large number of application servers and providing a lot of buffering*

In most cases, communications between applications and Flume agents and between Flume agents themselves have to be resilient to agent or machine failure. Even if data on a failed machine is unavailable while the machine is still down, this should not cause backlogs if capacity has not been exhausted. Flume has features allowing applications that use the Flume API to automatically load balance between multiple Flume agents (this would be a subset of the outermost tier of Flume agents), and also allows sinks to load balance between multiple agents in the next tier via a sink processor. These two combined ensure that data flow continues if there is capacity remaining in tiers following the failed agent.

# Replicating Data to Various Destinations

Very often, event counters are aggregated in HBase together with some metadata for real-time querying from user applications, while the actual data is written to HDFS for detailed processing and analysis. Flume allows such topologies, too. An example of this is shown in Figure 2-7.

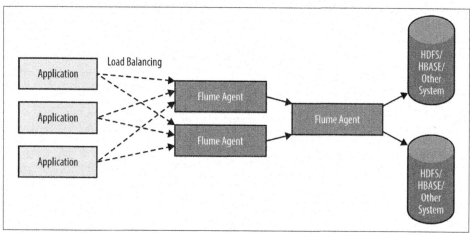

*Figure 2-7. Replicating data to various destinations*

Accomplishing this is fairly simple. To do this, the Avro Source should be configured to write to the channels that the HDFS and HBase Sinks read from. Since more than one sink can read from a single channel, more HDFS and HBase Sinks can be configured, each reading from the channels feeding HDFS and HBase, respectively. A sample configuration for such an agent is shown here (configuration parameters specific to each component are omitted for clarity):

```
agent.sources.avro.type = avro
# The following line causes the Avro Source
# to replicate data to channels feeding HDFS and HBase
agent.sources.avro.channels = hdfsChannel hbaseChannel
agent.channels.hdfsChannel.type = file
agent.channels.hbaseChannel.type = file
agent.sinks.hdfsSink1.type = hdfs
agent.sinks.hdfsSink1.channel = hdfsChannel
agent.sinks.hdfsSink2.type = hdfs
agent.sinks.hdfsSink2.channel = hdfsChannel
agent.sinks.hbaseSink2.type = hbase
agent.sinks.hbaseSink2.channel = hbaseChannel
```

# Dynamic Routing

An important feature of Flume is *dynamic routing*. Event data coming in is often not of the same priority, or does not need to go to the same data store—some might need to go to HDFS only, while other events may be destined for HDFS and HBase, or the data may go to different clusters based on the priority or some other criterion. In any of these cases, events must be routed based on some criteria. Flume supports this using the *multiplexing channel selector*. The multiplexing channel selector is a channel selector that inspects every event that passes through it for the value of a specific header; based on this value, it selects a set of channels that the event has to get written to, as illustrated in Figure 2-8. This is built into Flume, and the header, the values, and the channels to select are configurable. Configuring dynamic routing is a bit more involved, so we will discuss it in more detail in "Channel Selectors" on page 150.

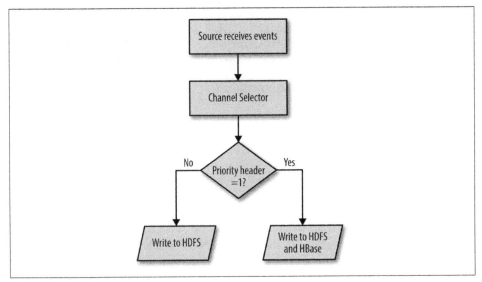

*Figure 2-8. Dynamic routing*

Intermediate tiers are important when dynamic routing is being configured. Having an additional tier after the tier that does the dynamic routing ensures that once the flow is bifurcated, each new flow does not hit the destination directly and gets buffered on one more tier.

# Flume's No Data Loss Guarantee, Channels, and Transactions

Flume provides guarantees of no data loss, if configured properly. Of course, once the combined capacity of all Flume agents in the pipeline is used up, Flume will no longer accept data from clients. At this point, the client needs to buffer the data, or else data could be lost. Thus, it is extremely important to configure the pipeline to be able to handle the maximum expected downtime. We will discuss configuring Flume pipelines in Chapter 8.

Flume's durability guarantees depend on the durability guarantees of the channel used. Flume comes bundled with two channels: the *Memory Channel* and the *File Channel*. The Memory Channel is an in-memory buffer, and thus any data in the buffer will be lost if the Java Virtual Machine (JVM) or the machine is restarted. The File Channel, on the other hand, is on disk. The File Channel does not lose data even when the JVM or machine is restarted, as long as the disk(s) on which the data is stored is still functioning and accessible. Any data stored on the File Channel will eventually be accessible once the machine and the agent start running.

Channels are *transactional* in nature. A transaction in this context is different from a database transaction. Each Flume transaction represents a batch of events written to or removed from a channel atomically. Whenever a source writes events to the channel or a sink takes events from a channel, it must do so within the purview of a transaction.

Flume guarantees that the events will reach their destination at least once. Flume strives to write data only once, and in the absence of any kind of failure the events are only written once. Errors like network timeouts or partial writes to storage systems could cause events to get written more than once, though, since Flume will retry writes until they are completely successful. A network timeout might indicate a failure to write or just a slow machine. If it is a slow machine, when Flume retries this will cause duplicates. Therefore, it is often a good idea to make sure each event has some sort of unique identifier that can eventually be used to deduplicate the event data, if required.

## Transactions in Flume Channels

Transactional semantics are key to the "no data loss" guarantees made by Flume. When each source (or sink) writes or reads data to or from a channel, it starts a transaction with the channel. For all channels that come bundled with Flume, each transaction is thread-local. For this reason, transaction handling in different types of sources and sinks differs slightly, though the basic idea is the same: each thread should run its own transaction. For all pollable sources and all sinks—which, as described earlier, are driven by runner threads—each process call should start only one transaction and throw an exception if the transaction is rolled back, to inform the runner thread to back off for a bit. Even if the source or sink spawns multiple new threads for I/O, it is best to follow this protocol, to avoid ambiguity if one of the many transactions initiated from the process method fails.

When sources write events to a channel, the transactions are handled by the channel processor, so sources don't have to handle the transactions by themselves. The channel processor commits the transaction only when the events are successfully written out to the channel; otherwise, it rolls back the transaction and closes it. Since it is possible for each source to write to multiple channels, the channel processor for the source writes events and commits them to one channel at a time. Therefore, it is possible for the data to be written out and committed to some channels but not others. In this case, Flume cannot roll back the transactions that were committed, but to ensure that the data is written out to all channels successfully, Flume will retry writes to all channels, including the ones where the writes were successful previously; this may cause duplicates.

In the case of terminal sinks, a transaction should be committed only when the data is safely written out to the storage system. Once the data is safe at the eventual destination, the transaction can be committed and the channel can delete the events in that transaction. If the write fails, the sink must roll back the transaction to ensure that the events are not lost. All sinks bundled with Flume work this way, and ensure that the data is on HDFS, HBase, Solr, Elastic Search, etc. before the transaction is committed. If the write fails or times out, the transaction is rolled back, and then this or another sink reading from the channel will try to write the events again.

The technique discussed earlier ensures that the data is written out by the terminal sinks in a durable way, but what about an agent-to-Flume agent or a client-to-Flume agent communication? For communication between RPC sinks and RPC sources, the RPC sink sends events out in a batch—these are all read as part of the same transaction from the channel, which are written to its channel(s) by the source in a single transaction. Once the source successfully commits the transaction with its channel(s), it sends an acknowledgment (ACK) to the sink that sent the events indicating that the events are now safe in the receiving agent's channels. When the sink receives this ACK, the sink commits the transaction it opened when it reads the events from the channel, indicating that the events can now be removed from the channel.

If the source takes too long to send the ACK or there is some network issue that causes the sink to time out, then the sink assumes that the write failed, and it rolls back the transaction and repeats the whole process again (this or another sink connected to this channel could read the same events). This method of overlapping transactions guarantees that events are safely in one of the channels at any point in time. Figure 2-9 shows the timeline of how the RPC sinks and RPC sources guarantee that the events are safely in at least one of the agents at any point.

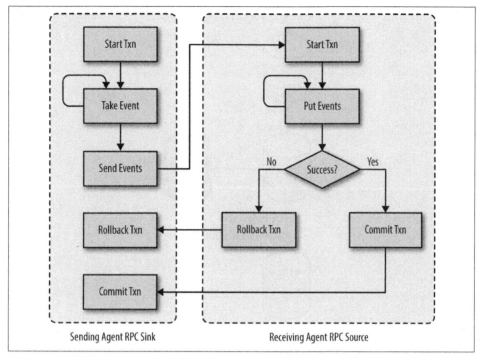

Figure 2-9. RPC sinks and sources guarantee that each event is at least in one agent's channel by overlapping transactions

# Agent Failure and Data Loss

What happens if one of the agents fails, or if the storage system becomes unreachable? When an agent or the eventual destination becomes unreachable, the agent(s) writing to that location will end up seeing errors at the sink. The sink will either see connection failures or missing ACKs from the next hop or the storage system (or the storage system's client API throwing exceptions). When the sink hits an exception that indicates that the data *may not* have been written, the sink rolls back the transaction with the channel. Since the incoming data flow has not stopped, this causes the channel size to increase, eventually filling up the channel. When this agent's channel fills up, the Avro Source (or any other source writing the data to this channel) starts getting `ChannelExceptions` on Puts to the channel, causing the source to push back to the previous hop by returning an error. This in turn causes the previous hop's sink to roll back its transaction, causing the channel size on that hop to grow. This scenario is shown in Figure 2-10.

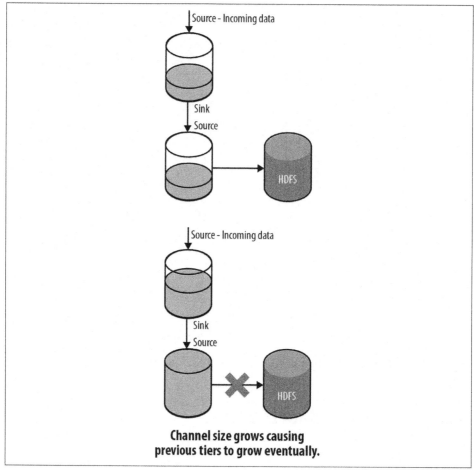

*Figure 2-10. Failure causes channels to fill up*

As is evident, the failure now causes each tier to buffer data until the channels are full, at which point it starts pushing back on the previous tier, until all tiers are full. At this point, the client starts seeing errors, which the client must now handle by buffering the data or dropping it, causing data loss. Capacity must be planned in such a way that downtime should never create a situation where this happens. We will talk about planning capacity in Chapter 8.

# The Importance of Batching

When events are sent to a source that receives data over the network from an RPC sink or a remote client, *the source writes out all events in this batch in a single transaction by delegating this task to the channel processor.*

In case of the File Channel, which is the persistent channel implementation, each transaction commit causes an `fsync` [fsync]. `fsync` is a system call defined by the POSIX standard that tells the operating system to flush all of its internal buffers for a specific file descriptor to disk. If the amount of data written per transaction is small, the overhead cost (in terms of time taken and resources consumed) of initiating a system call, switching to kernel space, and flushing all buffers before actually syncing to disk becomes a very high fraction of the total cost of the `fsync` call itself.

In the case of the Memory Channel, which is the in-memory channel implementation, there is a cost with regard to synchronization across the channel that comes into play during a commit, but this is far smaller than the overhead of an `fsync` call.

RPC calls have an additional overhead due to metadata associated with the actual call and all of the additional TCP overheads. When the amount of data sent is really small, these overheads end up being a large fraction of the cost of each RPC call, causing unnecessary network utilization, etc. To avoid such overhead, it is always a good idea to batch several events (unless of course each event is large by itself) into a single RPC call or write from a remote client.

Even though Flume's RPC client and RPC sinks support writing events without batching or with a batch size of 1, it is almost always a good idea to bundle events into reasonably sized batches to avoid paying the additional overhead cost more times than necessary. The ideal batch size would depend on the specific use case, but for events of up to a few kilobytes, batch sizes between 100 and 1,000 usually work well (though specific hardware, network, and other considerations affect this value, and it should be finally set after testing various values and finding one that matches the performance requirements).

Batching affects the performance of RPC sinks and any other sinks that write data over the network. RPC sink performance is affected for multiple reasons, as mentioned earlier. Even for the HDFS Sink, Flume flushes events to the memory of all data nodes when each batch gets committed. Therefore, it is always a good idea to use reasonably large batch sizes for all sinks.

There are sources that control batch sizes, like the Exec Source, JMS Source, etc. These sources should also batch events for performance, for the same reasons. Sources write events to channels, and they should be written out in reasonably large batches to avoid the `fsync` or synchronization issues discussed earlier in this section. So, even for sources that control their own batch sizes, it is important that they be configured to use batch sizes that are reasonably large.

### What Is a Reasonable Batch Size?

Well, it depends on the deployment, hardware, and several other factors. Batch sizes should not be finalized without a good deal of trial-and-error testing, since having batches that are huge also causes its own problems—like too much fragmentation over the network, etc. Also, having batches that are too large increases the risk of duplication of events, because each batch failing could end up causing a massive number of events to get written again, and if some of the events were successfully written out to HDFS, these events will end up getting written all over again.

To choose the correct batch size for RPC and terminal sinks, start with something like the equivalent of a few hundred KB to 1 MB, and then work up or down from there based on what timeouts you see, and what rate of duplicates you see. If there are too many duplicates or many timeouts, you have to reduce your batch size; in the opposite case, increase it until timeouts start appearing. Once you see the timeouts, you have hit the threshold, and you should reduce it a few percentage points from there.

## What About Duplicates?

Flume provides at-least-once guarantees, which basically means that any event sent via Flume to a storage system will get stored at least once. Flume, though, may end up storing the data more than once. There are numerous scenarios that can cause duplicates, some due to errors, others due to configuration.

Since each agent-to-agent RPC call has a configurable timeout, it is possible that even though an RPC did not fail, the sending agent might think it failed if it did not get a response within the timeout, triggering a retry. If the RPC did not fail, this retry will cause the same event to be sent again, causing duplicates. Such a scenario could happen on terminal sinks, such as the HDFS or HBase Sink.

Also, since Flume sources can write to more than one channel, the same event can essentially get duplicated if multiple channels are configured for the same source. If the sinks reading from the channels eventually push the events to the same storage system, this can cause duplicates.

If the use case is duplicate-sensitive, it is usually a good idea to insert unique identifiers in events. These identifiers can be used by a post-processing job to remove duplicates, using Spark, MapReduce, etc.

# Running a Flume Agent

This section assumes that the Flume directory structure is not changed and the current working directory is the top level of the Flume directory structure. Each Flume agent is started from the command line using the `flume-ng` command. This command takes in several parameters—the name of the Flume agent being started, the configuration file to use, and the configuration directory to use.

The Flume configuration file can contain configuration for multiple Flume agents, each identified by a unique name. When a Flume agent is started, this name is passed in to the `flume-ng` script as the value of the `-n` command-line switch. Flume's configuration system will load the configuration parameters associated with the specific agent's own name only. Because the configuration of multiple agents can be in a single file, it is easy to deploy the same file to multiple tiers, each with a different configuration. In most cases, since all agents in one tier communicate with the same set of agents in the next tier, each agent in that tier can have an identical configuration. Using the same name and the same configuration file for all agents in a tier makes deployment of tiers extremely easy to automate. The configuration file is passed to the Flume agent using the `-f` command-line switch.

The *configuration* directory, whose path can be passed to the Flume agent using the `-c` command-line switch, is home to two important files: *flume-env.sh* and *log4j.properties*. When a Flume agent is started, the agent initialization script will source the *flume-env.sh* script. This file must contain any environment variables that need to be passed to the `flume-ng` script. The most common environment variables that are initialized using the *flume-env.sh* file are listed in Table 2-1.

*Table 2-1. Environment variables initialized using flume-env.sh*

| Environment variable | Description |
| --- | --- |
| FLUME_CLASSPATH | Classpath to be passed to the Flume agent in addition to the Flume *lib* and *plugins.d* directories, which are automatically added |
| JAVA_OPTS | Any Java-specific options to be passed to the JVM, including the `-XX` and `-D` parameters to control memory and pass in parameters from the command line |
| HADOOP_PREFIX (or) HADOOP_HOME | Directory where Hadoop is installed (*$HADOOP_PREFIX/bin* contains the Hadoop executable) |
| HBASE_HOME | Directory where HBase is installed (*$HBASE_HOME/bin* contains the HBase executable) |

The `FLUME_CLASSPATH` environment variable is a list of directories (separated by :) in addition to Flume's *lib* and *plugins.d* directories, which are added to the classpath for the Flume agent. The *plugins.d* directory is the directory where custom component

JARs (Java Archive files) can be dropped in, so Flume can use those to load the custom components.

JAVA_OPTS is a set of arguments that are to be passed directly to the JVM. The most commonly used are the parameters used to modify the heap size allocated to the JVM: -Xms and -Xmx. You can read about them and the other options that can go into JAVA_OPTS in the Java documentation [java-commandline].

HADOOP_PREFIX (and equivalently HADOOP_HOME in the older Hadoop version 1) is the directory where Hadoop is installed. If the hadoop command is the PATH, Flume will simply use that if HADOOP_PREFIX is not set. HBASE_HOME accomplishes the same for HBase.

To run a Flume agent named usingFlumeAgent, which uses a Flume configuration /home/usingflume/flume/flume.conf and a configuration directory /home/usingflume/flume/conf, the following command can be used (assuming that the current working directory is the directory in which Flume is installed):

```
bin/flume-ng agent -n usingFlumeAgent -f /home/usingflume/flume/flume.conf
-c /home/usingflume/flume/conf
```

The agent will read the *log4j.properties* file in the configuration directory and log according to the specification in that file. log4j configuration details can be found in the log4j documentation [log4j]. Once the agent starts, it keeps running until it is killed by a SIGTERM or its equivalent, causing the agent to shut down. The agent does all the logging to the log4j logs (it might look like the agent is *stuck*, even though it is actually running and doing what it is supposed to; nothing gets logged to the console).

The flume-ng script accepts a lot more parameters, which are described in Table 2-2.

*Table 2-2. Command-line parameters accepted by flume-ng script*

| Parameter | Description |
| --- | --- |
| -n | Agent name to use. This must be placed after flume-ng agent on the command line. |
| -f | Configuration file (without this the agent will not run). |
| -c | Configuration directory to use (if not specified, ./conf is used). |
| -C | List of directories to be appended to the classpath. These can be specifed in FLUME_CLASSPATH as well. |
| -d | Dry run only. This will print out the entire command that Flume will use if run without this switch. |

| Parameter | Description |
| --- | --- |
| `--plugins-path` | If *./plugins.d* is not to be used as the directory where JARs containing custom classes are, the value of this parameter is checked for the plug-ins. |
| `-h` | This will print out detailed help. |

Even though Flume can accept parameters to pass to the JVM via the command line, it is recommended to use `JAVA_OPTS` to set these parameters, and thus they are not listed here.

To find out the exact version and revision information for the version of Flume that is being used, run:

```
bin/flume-ng version
```

# Summary

In this chapter, we discussed the basics of Flume and its design, its various components, and how to configure it. Finally, we looked at how to run a Flume agent once its configuration and components have been decided.

Chapter 3, Chapter 4, and Chapter 5 will cover sources, channels, and sinks, respectively. Chapter 6 will cover other components—interceptors, channel selectors, sink groups, and sink processors. Chapter 7 will explain how to get data into Flume using the Flume software development kit (SDK) and the Embedded Agent API. The last chapter, Chapter 8, will cover details on how to plan with, deploy, and monitor Flume.

# References

- [java-commandline] Java command-line arguments, *http://bit.ly/1p9NzQX*
- [log4j] log4j documentation, *https://logging.apache.org/log4j/1.2/manual.html*
- [fsync] `fsync` system call, *http://bit.ly/1p9Nzk3*

CHAPTER 3

# Sources

*Sources* are the components responsible for accepting data into a Flume agent. Sources can accept data from other systems, like the Java Message Service (JMS), or the output of other processes. Sources are also used to receive data from other Flume agents whose sinks send data via RPC. There are even sources that can produce data. It is possible to write sources to accept data from pretty much anything!

The data sources receive from an external system or from other agents (or produce by themselves) is then written out to one or more channels configured for the source. This is the basic responsibility of a source.

In this chapter, we will discuss the design and working of various sources that come packaged with Flume and how to configure them optimally for use; we will also look at how to write a custom source.

## Lifecycle of a Source

Sources are named components that are configured like any other component through the configuration file. Flume's configuration system validates each source's configuration and discards sources that are incorrectly configured. The validation done by the configuration system is pretty minimal, though. The Flume configuration system ensures that:

* Each source has at least one properly configured channel "connected" to it.
* Each source has a `type` parameter defined.
* The source is in the active list of sources for the agent.

Once the configuration system *approves* a source, it is then instantiated and configured by the `ConfigurationProvider`. If the source is misconfigured or is missing required parameters, this source is discarded. Once the source is successfully configured, Flume's lifecycle management system will attempt to start the source. The source is then stopped only if the agent itself is stopped or killed, or if the agent is reconfigured by the user.

Sources, like all Flume components, require their type to be specified in the configuration. This can be the fully qualified class name (FQCN), or the alias for built-in sources. All sources require at least one properly configured channel to write to. Therefore, a list of channels is also a mandatory parameter for the source to be considered properly configured. The required parameters are shown in Table 3-1.

*Table 3-1. Mandatory configuration parameters for all sources*

| Parameter | Description |
| --- | --- |
| type | The type of the source. This can be the FQCN or the alias of the source (only for sources that are part of Flume itself). The class must be installed using the *plugins.d* framework described in "Deploying Custom Code" on page 204. The alias for each of Flume's built-in sources is mentioned in the relevant section. |
| channels | A space-separated list of channels the source should write events to. For all channels selected for writes by the channel selector based on the event and the routing parameters, the source will write events to the channels in the order specified in the configuration file. More details on this are in "Channel Selectors" on page 150. |

A source named `usingFlumeSource` of type `avro`, running in an agent started with the name `usingFlume`, would be configured with a file that looks like:

```
usingFlume.sources = usingFlumeSource
usingFlume.channels = memory

usingFlume.sources.usingFlumeSource.type = avro
usingFlume.sources.usingFlumeSource.channels = memory
usingFlume.sources.usingFlumeSource.port = 7877
usingFlume.sources.usingFlumeSource.bind = 0.0.0.0
```

There are a few parameters that can optionally be passed to all sources. These are meant to configure interceptors and channel selectors for the source. They are shown in Table 3-2. These parameters are passed to the source just as any other configuration parameters are passed in.

*Table 3-2. Optional configuration parameters for all sources*

| Parameter | Description |
| --- | --- |
| interceptors | A list of names that represent a chain of interceptors |
| interceptors.<interceptor_name>.* | Parameters to pass to the interceptor with the specific name |

| Parameter | Description |
|-----------|-------------|
| selector | The alias or FQCN of the channel selector to use; if no selectors are specified, the *replicating channel selector* is used |
| selector.* | Configuration parameters to pass to the channel selector |

An example configuration for two interceptors for a source named avro is shown in Example 3-1. Two interceptors, *host* and *static* (named i1 and i2, respectively), are configured to intercept events being received by the source. As you can see, interceptors can accept configuration with the interceptors.<interceptor_name>. prefix.

*Example 3-1. Configuring interceptors*

```
agent.sources.avro.interceptors = i1 i2
agent.sources.avro.interceptors.i1.type = host
agent.sources.avro.interceptors.i1.preserveExsiting = true
agent.sources.avro.interceptors.i2.type = static
agent.sources.avro.interceptors.i2.key = header
agent.sources.avro.interceptors.i2.value = staticValue
```

Each source has exactly one channel selector (which is why it is not a named component and can be configured using the selector configuration suffix). Though the channel selector configuration looks like the configuration of a source subcomponent, the source does not need to configure the selector—this is done by the configuration system. In Example 3-2, the channel processor for the source named avro configures a *multiplexing channel selector* to bifurcate the flow of events from the source. We will discuss the specific configuration parameters for a multiplexing channel selector in Chapter 6, but as this example demonstrates, selectors can accept configuration parameters based on which they can return the channels to which the source should write specific events.

*Example 3-2. Channel selector configuration*

```
agent.sources.avro.selector.type = multiplexing
agent.sources.avro.selector.header = priority
agent.sources.avro.selector.mapping.1 = channel1
agent.sources.avro.selector.mapping.2 = channel2
agent.sources.avro.selector.default = channel2
```

If an agent is reconfigured, the same instance of the source class will not be reused. Therefore, all sources packaged with Flume are stateless. It is expected that any custom sources that are plugged into Flume are also stateless to avoid data loss.

Now that we have covered the basic concepts of sources, let's discuss the various sources that come packaged with Flume.

# Sink-to-Source Communication

One of the most important features of Flume is the ease of horizontally scaling a Flume deployment. The reason this can be done easily is that it's trivial to add new agents to a Flume deployment and configure them to send data to other Flume agents. Similarly, once a new agent is added, it is fairly easy to configure the agents that are already running to write to this agent by simply updating the configuration file.

At the center of this flexibility is Flume's RPC sink–source combination. As discussed in "Getting Flume Agents to Talk to Each Other" on page 17, RPC sinks are designed to send events to RPC sources—Thrift Sink to Thrift Source and Avro Sink to Avro Source. RPC sinks and sources are highly scalable, with the sources being able to receive data from a large number of sinks or RPC clients. Even though each RPC sink can send data only to one RPC source, each agent can be configured to send data to multiple other agents using sink groups and sink processors; see "Sink Groups and Sink Processors" on page 157.

In this section, we will discuss Flume's RPC sources and the various aspects of configuring and deploying them.

## Avro Source

Flume's primary RPC source is the *Avro Source*. The Avro Source is designed to be a highly scalable RPC server that accepts data into a Flume agent, from another Flume agent's Avro Sink or from a client application that uses Flume's SDK to send data. The Avro Source together with the Avro Sink represents Flume's internal communication mechanism (between Flume agents). With the scalability of the Avro Source combined with the channels that act as a buffer, Flume agents can handle significant load spikes.

Flume's Avro Source uses the Netty-Avro inter-process communication (IPC) protocol to communicate. As a result, it is possible to send data to the Avro Source from Java or JVM languages. To send events from your application to an agent with an Avro Source, you can make use of the Flume SDK (see "Flume Client SDK" on page 168) or the embedded agent (see "Embedded Agent" on page 185).

An Avro Source can be configured to accept compressed events from an Avro Sink that is configured to output them. It can also be configured to make sure that any clients or sinks sending data to it encrypt the data using SSL. An Avro Source's configuration parameters are detailed in Table 3-3.

*Table 3-3. Avro Source configuration*

| Config parameter | Default value | Description |
| --- | --- | --- |
| **type** | - | The alias for an Avro Source is `avro`. The FQCN, which is `org.apache.flume.source.AvroSource` (case sensitive), can also be used. |
| **bind** | - | The IP address/hostname to bind to. To bind to all interfaces on the machine, use 0.0.0.0. |
| **port** | - | The port to bind to. |
| threads | `infinity` | The maxmium number of worker threads to accept incoming data from clients/Avro Sinks. |
| ssl | `false` | Should SSL be enabled? If this is set to `true`, all clients connecting to this source are required to use SSL. If SSL is enabled, the `keystore` and `keystore-password` parameters are required. |
| keystore | - | The path to the keystore to use for SSL. This is a required parameter if SSL is enabled. |
| keystore-password | - | The password to be used to open the keystore. This is a required parameter if SSL is enabled. |
| keystore-type | JKS | The type of keystore that is being used. |
| compression-type | - | The compression format used to decompress the incoming data. The only compression format supported is zlib [zlib_ch3]. To accept zlib-compressed data, set this parameter to `deflate`. |

Configuring the Avro Source in the simplest way requires a minimal set of parameters. Minimally, the source requires two mandatory parameters other than the `type` parameter itself: `bind` and `port`. These two parameters define the socket address that the source uses. If there are multiple network interfaces, the Avro Source can bind to one or all of them. To bind to just one of the interfaces, simply set the IP address/domain address of that interface as the value of the `bind` parameter. To bind to all interfaces, use 0.0.0.0 as the value of the `bind` parameter. The `port` parameter defines the port number the source should listen on, for the configured bind address(es).

The Avro Source uses a Netty server [netty] to serve incoming requests. The Netty server uses Java's nonblocking I/O (NIO) [nio], which allows it to be highly performant while using a relatively small number of threads to handle the requests. The Avro Source allows the user to configure the maximum number of threads that the source should use to handle incoming data using the `threads` parameter. This allows the user to keep a check on the resources consumed by the source. Though there is no theoretical maximum on the number of threads, the actual number is limited by the JVM, the OS, and the hardware.

### SSL Keystores

A *keystore* is a collection of cryptographic keys and certificates, as defined by the Java standard [keystore]. Each keystore is protected by a password, which can be used load the keystore. In Flume's case, this password is stored in the Flume configuration file as plain text; the configuration file must be guarded by the correct permissions to avoid this password falling into the wrong hands.

If the Avro Sink(s) or RPC clients sending data to Flume are configured to use SSL to send the events to the Avro Source, the Avro Source must be configured with the SSL-related parameters. The `ssl` parameter must be set to `true` and the `keystore` and `keystore-password` parameters must be set. The `keystore` parameter must point to a valid keystore file, and `keystore-password` is the password that is to be used to open the keystore.

The `keystore-type` parameter is optional and can be set to an alternate keystore type, if needed [keystore-type]. The cryptographic algorithm used is defined by `ssl.KeyManagerFactory.algorithm` in the Java security properties file. If this parameter is not set in the Java security properties file, then the *SunX509* algorithm is used. More details about the Java security properties file can be found in the Java Security Guide [java-security].

Avro Sinks and Flume's RPC clients can be configured to compress data before sending it to the Avro Source. This is especially useful if the data is sent over a WAN, between data centers, etc. to reduce bandwidth usage. Currently, the Avro Source only supports zlib compression for RPC. To enable the Avro Source to receive data in compressed form, set the `compression-type` parameter to `deflate`. If this parameter is not set or is set to `none`, Flume will not attempt to decompress the data; this might cause the events to get backlogged at the previous hop, since the source will not be able to parse the compressed data and will return an error to the previous hop, causing that hop to retry forever.

**Avro Sources and Compression**

If the `compression-type` parameter is set to `deflate`, the incoming data must be compressed, or else the source will not be able to parse the incoming data. The sink or Flume client sending the data must be configured to compress the data being sent. Therefore, if both compressed and uncompressed data will be sent to the same Flume agent, the agent should run two Avro Sources, one for receiving compressed data and another for receiving uncompressed data.

Also note that when the Avro Sink/Flume RPC client sends data to the Avro Source, it compresses the data batch by batch, not event by event, since this may provide a better compression ratio and reduce the CPU usage for compression.

Here is an example of an Avro Source configured with SSL and compression. To disable SSL, simply remove the `ssl` parameter, and the remaining SSL-related parameters will be ignored:

```
agent.sources = avroSrc
agent.channels = memChannel

agent.sources.avroSrc.type = avro
agent.sources.avroSrc.channels = memChannel

# Bind to all interfaces
agent.sources.avroSrc.bind = 0.0.0.0
agent.sources.avroSrc.port = 4353

# Removing the next line will disable SSL
agent.sources.avroSrc.ssl = true
agent.sources.avroSrc.keystore = /tmp/keystore.jks
agent.sources.avroSrc.keystore-password = UsingFlume
agent.sources.avroSrc.keystore-type = jks

agent.sources.avroSrc.compression-type = deflate

# Initializes a memory channel with default configuration
agent.channels.memChannel.type = memory
```

An Avro Sink that writes to this source would have a configuration similar to the following:

```
agent.channels = avroSinkChannel
agent.sinks = avroSink

agent.channels.avroSinkChannel.type = memory

agent.sinks.avroSink.type = avro
agent.sinks.avroSink.channel = memory
```

```
agent.sinks.avroSink.hostname = avrosrchost.example.com
agent.sinks.avroSink.port = 4353

# SSL properties
agent.sinks.avroSink.ssl = true
agent.sinks.avroSink.trust-all-certs = true
agent.sinks.avroSink.truststore = /path/to/keystore
agent.sinks.avroSink.truststore-password = UsingFlume
agent.sinks.avroSink.truststore-type = JKS

agent.sources.avroSink.compression-type = deflate
```

# Thrift Source

As mentioned in "Avro Source" on page 36, Flume's use of Avro's Java-specific RPC mechanism makes the Avro Source unable to accept data from non-JVM languages. As Flume became more popular, this use case had to be addressed. Therefore, Apache Thrift RPC support [thrift_ch3] was added to Flume. Thrift is a top-level project at the Apache Software Foundation that enables cross-language communication, which is extremely popular. The Thrift Sink–Thrift Source combination in Flume is designed to work pretty much exactly like the Avro Sink–Avro Source combination. Flume also has a Java Thrift RPC client that is part of the Flume SDK. The Thrift Source, in the simplest terms, is a multithreaded high-performance Thrift server. The Thrift interface definition language (IDL) that Flume uses is shown here:

```
namespace java org.apache.flume.thrift

struct ThriftFlumeEvent {
  1: required map <string, string> headers,
  2: required binary body,
}

enum Status {
  OK,
  FAILED,
  ERROR,
  UNKNOWN
}

service ThriftSourceProtocol {
  Status append(1: ThriftFlumeEvent event),
  Status appendBatch(1: list<ThriftFlumeEvent> events),
}
```

This IDL can be used to generate Thrift clients in any language that Thrift supports. The generated code can then be used to send data to Flume's Thrift Source.

The configuration of the Thrift Source is extremely simple and mimics that of the Avro Source (see Table 3-4).

*Table 3-4. Thrift Source configuration*

| Config parameter | Default value | Description |
|---|---|---|
| **type** | - | The alias for a Thrift Source is `thrift`. The FQCN, which is `org.apache.flume.source.ThriftSource` (case sensitive), can also be used. |
| **bind** | - | The IP address/hostname to bind to. To bind to all interfaces on the machine, use 0.0.0.0. |
| **port** | - | The port to bind to. |
| threads | - | The maximum number of threads this source should use for processing requests. |

The `bind` parameter specifies the hostname/IP address of the interface to bind to; use 0.0.0.0 to bind to all interfaces. The `port` parameter specifies the port to use—this is the port clients would use to send events to this source. These are both mandatory parameters.

The `threads` parameter for a Thrift Source works in a slightly different way than for the Avro Source. Flume (as of version 1.4.0), by default, is built against and includes Thrift version 0.7.0. This was meant to support clients (programs written to use the Flume SDK) that would also write to HBase version 0.92 (or older) from the same process. If there is no requirement to support this version of HBase, then it is recommended that the Thrift version that comes with Flume be replaced with a newer version, though due to incompatibilities in the Thrift-generated code, Flume may also need to be recompiled against the newer version.

When using a version of Thrift lower than 0.8.0, Flume uses Thrift's `TThreadPool Server`, which uses one thread per client connected, and the `threads` parameter controls the maximum number of threads that the source will create, thus indirectly controlling the number of clients that can connect to the agent. It is recommended to not set this parameter in this case. If a newer version of Thrift is being used, then Flume uses Thrift's `TThreadedSelectorServer`, which uses Java's nonblocking I/O and therefore can support more clients than there are threads available. In this case, the `threads` parameter works just like the Avro Source's `threads` parameter and can be used to keep the resource utilization under control.

The Thrift Source, unlike the Avro Source, does not currently support compression or SSL. A Thrift Source should therefore be used only to push data into Flume from systems that are written in non-JVM languages, or if the application that is writing the data already uses Thrift for other purposes. For Flume agent–to–Flume agent communication, it is recommended that the Avro Sink–Avro Source pair be used.

The following is an example of configuration of a Thrift Source:

```
agent.sources = thriftSrc
agent.channels = memChannel

agent.sources.thriftSrc.type = thrift
agent.sources.thriftSrc.channels = memChannel

# Bind to all interfaces
agent.sources.thriftSrc.bind = 0.0.0.0
agent.sources.thriftSrc.port = 4564

# Initializes a memory channel with default configuration
agent.channels.memChannel.type = memory
```

A Thrift Sink that writes to this source would have a configuration similar to the following:

```
agent.channels = memChannel
agent.sinks = thriftSink

agent.channels.memChannel.type = memory

agent.sinks.thriftSink.type = thrift
agent.sinks.thriftSink.channel = memory
agent.sinks.thriftSink.hostname = thriftsrchost.example.com
agent.sinks.thriftSink.port = 4564
```

## Failure Handling in RPC Sources

Failure handling in both the Avro and Thrift Sources is a bit tricky. This is because the RPC sources are invoked by a client or sink on the other side of a network link, though it looks like a local method call. In all cases where the RPC sources cannot start due to some permanent error, like being unable to bind to the port, the source will throw an exception when it tries to start. Since Flume's configuration system will retry every few seconds to restart the component, since it was successfully configured, the source will start up if the condition causing the error no longer exists—for example, if the other process that was bound to the port was killed or released the port.

The trickier part, though, is with respect to the code that actually receives the data and writes the events to the channel. If even one of the channels the source is configured to write to throws a ChannelException due to the channel being full, or if the transaction is too large, the source returns a failure status to the client or sink that called it and expects it to retry. Since RPC sources receives data via threads owned by a thread pool, exceptions would simply cause the thread to die.

In all such cases, the real indication of failure is only in the log files where these exceptions are logged. Sometimes these exceptions may indicate a major problem, like the process running out of resources (as with an OutOfMemoryError). Therefore, it is important to monitor the logs generated by the Flume agent to ensure that things are running smoothly. ChannelExceptions being thrown too often can mean that the channels are too underallocated for the rate of writes, or that the sinks are not clearing the data from the channels fast enough. Increasing the number of sinks can help if too few sinks are reading the data, but if the eventual destination itself cannot handle the load, the capacity needs to be rethought. In all cases, errors may cause duplicates but never actually cause data loss, since events are removed from the channel if and only if the data is actually successfully written out to the next hop.

# HTTP Source

Flume comes bundled with an HTTP Source that can receive events via HTTP POST. For application environments where it might not be possible to deploy the Flume SDK and its dependencies, or in cases where the client code prefers to send data over HTTP rather than over Flume's RPC, the HTTP Source can be used to receive data into Flume. From a client's point of view, an HTTP Source behaves exactly like a web server that accepts Flume events.

The HTTP Source takes in a few configuration parameters, as shown in Table 3-5. The configuration of the source is extremely simple and allows the user to also configure the handler that is plugged in.

*Table 3-5. HTTP Source configuration*

| Config parameter | Default value | Description |
| --- | --- | --- |
| `type` | - | The alias for the HTTP Source is `http`. The FQCN, which is `org.apache.flume.source.http.HttpSource` (case sensitive), can also be used. |
| `bind` | - | The IP address/hostname to bind to. To bind to all interfaces on the machine, use 0.0.0.0. |
| `port` | - | The port to bind to. |
| `enableSSL` | `false` | To enable SSL, this parameter should be set to `true`. |
| `keystore` | - | The path to the keystore file to be used. |
| `keystorePassword` | - | The password to be used for accessing the keystore. |
| `handler` | `JSONHandler` | The FQCN of the handler class that should be used by the HTTP Source to convert the HTTP request into Flume events. See "Writing Handlers for the HTTP Source*" on page 44 to learn how to write handlers for the HTTP Source. |
| `handler.*` | - | Any parameters that have to be passed to the handler can be passed in through the configuration by using the `handler.` prefix. |

As is to be expected, the bind and port parameters define the interface and the port the source binds to. This is the hostname and port that the client sends data to.

The HTTP Source also supports SSL for secure transport. By default, the source does not use SSL. To enable SSL, set the enableSSL parameter to true. If SSL is enabled, the keystore and keystorePassword parameters are mandatory. The keystore parameter is the full path to the keystore to be used for SSL. keystorePassword is the password that is to be used to access the keystore.

An example of how to configure an HTTP Source that uses a custom handler is shown in Example 3-3.

*Example 3-3. HTTP Source configuration example*

```
agent.sources = httpSrc
agent.channels = memChannel

agent.sources.httpSrc.type = http
agent.sources.httpSrc.channels = memChannel

# Bind to all interfaces
agent.sources.httpSrc.bind = 0.0.0.0
agent.sources.httpSrc.port = 4353

# Removing this line will disable SSL
agent.sources.httpSrc.ssl = true
agent.sources.httpSrc.keystore = /tmp/keystore
agent.sources.httpSrc.keystore-password = UsingApacheFlume

agent.sources.httpSrc.handler = usingflume.ch03.HTTPSourceXMLHandler
agent.sources.httpSrc.handler.insertTimestamp = true

# Initializes a memory channel with default configuration
agent.channels.memChannel.type = memory
```

What parameters the handler requires and how they are used by the handler depends on the specific handler implementation. Please consult the handler's documentation for details on this.

## Writing Handlers for the HTTP Source*

It is easy for the user to develop and plug in a *handler* to convert the data received into Flume events. This allows the HTTP Source to accept data from clients in any format that can be processed by the handler. The HTTP Source handler is a class that inherits a very simple interface, HTTPSourceHandler:

```
package org.apache.flume.source.http;
public interface HTTPSourceHandler extends Configurable {
  public List<Event> getEvents(HttpServletRequest request) throws
```

```
    HTTPBadRequestException, Exception;
}
```

The handler interface is extremely simple and has only one method, `getEvents`, which accepts the `HTTPServletRequest` sent by the client and returns a list of Flume events. Even though this handler interface is simple, it can essentially do any arbitrary processing to convert the input data from the `HTTPServletRequest` into Flume events. The amount of processing should be limited, though, or the client sending data to this source might get timed out. The handler is configurable through Flume's standard configuration mechanism. Since the HTTP Source always uses exactly one transaction per request whatever the handler is, the sender has to be careful to send only as many events as the channels support.

The handler is responsible for making sure that the configuration parameters passed to it are valid. The HTTP Source will instantiate and configure the handler on startup. Since the HTTP Source propagates any `Exception` thrown by the handler to the configuration system, the handler must verify the parameters and apply the parameters in the `configure` method. The parameters are passed in to the `configure` method via a `Context` instance. `Context` instances are simply key-value pairs containing various configuration keys and their values. If the configuration passed in is invalid and cannot be applied successfully, the HTTP Source rethrows the exception thrown by the handler to the configuration system, which in turn disables the HTTP Source and removes it from the agent.

While processing incoming data, the HTTP Source handles exceptions thrown by the handler by returning a failure to the client. The HTTP Source expects the handler to throw an `HTTPBadRequestException` if the incoming data was malformed and cannot be converted into Flume events. This operation must be idempotent, and the handler must throw the same exception for the same input every time. If an `HTTPBadReques tException` is thrown by the handler, the HTTP Source returns HTTP error code 400, to inform the client that the request was malformed. If the handler throws any other exception, the source returns HTTP error code 500, to inform the client that there was an internal error in the HTTP Source. It is then up to the client to decide how to retry in such a case. If one of the channels that the source is writing to throws a channel exception, the source returns error code 503, to signal that the channel is temporarily at capacity and the client should retry later.

The JAR file containing the handler (or the handler's *.class* file) and all its dependencies should be added to the Flume classpath via the *plugins.d* mechanism discussed in "Deploying Custom Code" on page 204.

If no handler is specified in the configuration, the HTTP Source uses a handler that comes bundled with Flume, which can handle JSON formatted events. Each request can contain several events represented as an array, though the channel(s) the source writes to might have a limited transaction capacity. The handler accepts JSON-formatted data in the UTF-8, UTF-16, or UTF-32 charset, and converts it into a list of events with the body serialized in the charset of the original HTTP request. The format that the handler accepts is shown here:

```
[{
    "headers" : {
              "event1Header1" : "event1Value1",
              "event1header2" : "event1Value2"
          },
          "body" : "This is the body of the first event."

},
{
          "headers" : {
              "event2Header1" : "event2Value1",
              "event2Header2" : "event2Value2"
          },
          "body" : "This is the body of the second event"
}]
```

HTTPSourceXMLHandler, shown in Example 3-5, is another example of a handler that works with the HTTP Source. This handler converts XML-formatted data into Flume events. The handler is pretty simple and expects the data to be in the XML format shown in Example 3-4. The format expected by this handler is pretty simple. Only data in between <events> and </events> is processed. Each event is expected to be between <event> and </event> tags. The only thing that limits the number of events per request is the transaction capacity of the channel(s) the source writes to. Each event can have one or more sections, enclosed by <headers> and </headers> tags. Each header is denoted by a tag whose name is used as the header name; the value in between the opening header name tag and the closing tag is used as its value. The body is enclosed between <body> and </body> tags.

*Example 3-4. Format expected by HTTPSourceXMLHandler*

```
<events>
  <!-- This can contain as many events
  as the channel can support in a transaction -->

  <event>
    <headers>
      <header1>value1</header1>
      <header2>value2</header2>
    </headers>

    <body>This is a test.
        This input should show up in an event.
    </body>
  </event>
```

```
<event>
  <!-- There can be zero or more headers sections.
   They are merged together, so each header name
   must be unique even between sections. -->
  <headers>
    <event2Header1>event2Value1</event2Header1>
  </headers>

  <!-- Each event can have only one body -->

  <body>This is the 2nd event.</body>

  <headers>
    <event2Header2>event2Value2</event2Header2>
  </headers>
  </event>
</events>
```

The handler parses the XML-formatted events into Flume events and returns them to the HTTP Source, which in turn writes them to the channel(s). While parsing the events, the handler makes sure that each event has at least a header and a body. If not, the handler throws an `HTTPBadRequestException` to inform the client that the incoming data was malformed. It can be configured to insert a timestamp into the Flume event headers, which the HDFS Sink can use for bucketing of events.

*Example 3-5. XML handler for HTTP Source*

```java
package usingflume.ch03;

/**
 * A handler for the HTTP Source that accepts XML-formatted data.
 * Each event can contain multiple header nodes,
 * but exactly one body node. If there is
 * more than one body tag, the first one in the event is picked up.
 */
public class HTTPSourceXMLHandler implements HTTPSourceHandler {

  private final String ROOT = "events";
  private final String EVENT_TAG = "event";
  private final String HEADERS_TAG = "headers";
  private final String BODY_TAG = "body";

  private final String CONF_INSERT_TIMESTAMP = "insertTimestamp";
  private final String TIMESTAMP_HEADER = "timestamp";

  private final DocumentBuilderFactory documentBuilderFactory
    = DocumentBuilderFactory.newInstance();

  private final ThreadLocal<DocumentBuilder> docBuilder
    = new ThreadLocal<DocumentBuilder>();
```

```
private boolean insertTimestamp;

@Override
public List<Event> getEvents(HttpServletRequest
  httpServletRequest) throws HTTPBadRequestException, Exception {
  if (docBuilder.get() == null) {
    docBuilder.set(documentBuilderFactory.newDocumentBuilder());
  }
  Document doc;
  final List<Event> events;
  try {
    doc = docBuilder.get().parse(
      httpServletRequest.getInputStream());
    Element root = doc.getDocumentElement();
    root.normalize();

    // Verify that the root element is "events"
    Preconditions.checkState(
      ROOT.equalsIgnoreCase(root.getTagName()));

    NodeList nodes = root.getElementsByTagName(EVENT_TAG);
    int eventCount = nodes.getLength();
    events = new ArrayList<Event>(eventCount);
    for (int i = 0; i < eventCount; i++) {
      Element event = (Element) nodes.item(i);
      // Get all headers. If there are multiple header sections,
      // combine them.
      NodeList headerNodes
        = event.getElementsByTagName(HEADERS_TAG);
      Map<String, String> eventHeaders
        = new HashMap<String, String>();
      for (int j = 0; j < headerNodes.getLength(); j++) {
        Node headerNode = headerNodes.item(j);
        NodeList headers = headerNode.getChildNodes();
        for (int k = 0; k < headers.getLength(); k++) {
          Node header = headers.item(k);

          // Read only element nodes
          if (header.getNodeType() != Node.ELEMENT_NODE) {
            continue;
          }
          // Make sure a header is inserted only once,
          // else the event is malformed
          Preconditions.checkState(
            !eventHeaders.containsKey(header.getNodeName()),
            "Header expected only once " + header.getNodeName());
          eventHeaders.put(
            header.getNodeName(), header.getTextContent());
        }
      }
      Node body = event.getElementsByTagName(BODY_TAG).item(0);
```

```
        if (insertTimestamp) {
          eventHeaders.put(TIMESTAMP_HEADER, String.valueOf(System
            .currentTimeMillis()));
        }
        events.add(EventBuilder.withBody(
          body.getTextContent().getBytes(
            httpServletRequest.getCharacterEncoding()),
          eventHeaders));
      }
    } catch (SAXException ex) {
      throw new HTTPBadRequestException(
        "Request could not be parsed into valid XML", ex);
    } catch (Exception ex) {
      throw new HTTPBadRequestException(
        "Request is not in expected format. " +
          "Please refer documentation for expected format.", ex);
    }
    return events;
  }

  @Override
  public void configure(Context context) {
    insertTimestamp = context.getBoolean(CONF_INSERT_TIMESTAMP,
      false);
  }
}
```

An example of XML handler configuration is shown in Example 3-3. This configuration instructs the handler to insert the timestamp of processing into each event. In general, any number of parameters can be passed to HTTP Source handlers in this way.

The HTTPHandler interface is part of the flume-ng-core Maven artifact, which can be added to your application by including Example 3-6 in your application's *pom.xml* file's dependency section.

*Example 3-6. Including the flume-ng-core artifact in your application*

```
<dependency>
  <groupId>org.apache.flume</groupId>
  <artifactId>flume-ng-core</artifactId>
  <version>1.5.0</version>
</dependency>
```

Use the *plugins.d* framework shown in "Deploying Custom Code" on page 204 to deploy custom HTTP handlers to Flume agents.

# Spooling Directory Source

In many scenarios, applications generate data that gets written to files. Often, these files are not simply text, or they may not make sense if each line is converted into a single event, but a group of lines together make an event. An example of this is stack traces. It is often difficult or not possible to modify these applications to use the Flume Client API to send data directly to Flume. In such cases, Flume's Spooling Directory Source can be used to read data from each of these files.

A Spooling Directory Source *watches* a directory, from which it reads events. The source expects files in the directory to be immutable, though new files can be added to the directory in real time. Once a file is moved to the directory, it should not be written to. If you're dealing with log files, a good way of doing this is to configure your logging system to move the file when it is being rolled. Also, the source expects that filenames are never reused. If either of these two happens, the source will throw an exception and quit. The only way to restart the source at this point is to restart the agent itself.

The Spooling Directory Source is a good alternative to using an Exec Source with `tail -F`, as discussed later in this chapter, since this source guarantees data delivery and is generally more reliable than using `tail -F` with an Exec Source. The only downside is that the data is not tailed in real time, and is read only once the file is closed and moved to the relevant directory. Once a file is completely consumed by the source and all its events successfully written to the source's channel(s), the source can either rename the file or delete the file, based on the configuration. When the file is renamed, the source simply adds a suffix to the filename, rather than changing it completely. The suffix is configurable as well.

The Spooling Directory Source uses a *tracker* persisted to disk to track the location within each file at which events were successfully written out to the channel, so that the source can start reading data from that position if the agent or machine fails and restarts. This allows the source to track which file it is processing at any point in time and resume processing that file from the last processed location when the source restarts. This is one of the reasons the source does not allow filenames to be reused.

Table 3-6 shows the various configuration parameters accepted by the Spooling Directory Source.

*Table 3-6. Spooling Directory Source configuration*

| Parameter | Default | Description |
|---|---|---|
| **type** | - | The alias for the Spooling Directory Source is spooldir. The FQCN is org.apache.flume.source.SpoolDirectorySource. |
| **spoolDir** | - | The directory to "watch" and read files from. Subdirectories of this directory are not scanned. |
| batchSize | 100 | The maximum number of events to write to the channel per transaction. |
| ignorePattern | ^$ | Files with names matching this regex are ignored and data is not read from them. |
| deletePolicy | never | When to delete ingested files—must be never or immediate. |
| fileSuffix | .COMPLETED | The suffix to use for files that have been completely ingested. The "." is *required* if this is to be an extension. |
| fileHeader | false | If set to true, the filename is added to the event headers. |
| fileHeaderKey | file | The key to use in the headers, if the filename is added to headers. |
| trackerDir | .flumespool | The directory where the Spooling Directory Source stores the metadata that is used to restart the source from where it left off. |
| deserializer | line | The alias or FQCN of the Builder class that can be used to build the deserializer that should be used to read custom-formatted data. "Reading Custom Formats Using Deserializers*" on page 53 explains how to write deserializers. |
| deserializer.* | - | Any parameters to be passed to the deserializer. |
| inputCharset | UTF-8 | The character set to use when the deserializer calls readChar. |

The type of the Spooling Directory Source is spooldir. As mentioned earlier, this source reads all files in a given directory and processes them one by one. The full path to the directory to process should be passed in via the spoolDir parameter. For performance reasons, the source writes events in batches. The maximum size of each batch is defined by the batchSize parameter. The source attempts to read as many events as it can from the file until the specified batch size is reached. If there are fewer events available in the files, it will commit the transaction as soon as all events are read from the files.

Sometimes, there are files that get written to the same directory that may actually not contain data, like metadata files. To avoid ingesting such files, which are known to not contain valid data, an *ignore* pattern can be specified via the ignorePattern parameter. This parameter takes a regex, and any files with filenames matching this regex are ignored.

As mentioned earlier, once the files are completely ingested, Flume can either rename or delete the files. To delete the files immediately, set the value of the deletePolicy parameter to immediate. If deletePolicy is set to never (the default), the file is renamed once ingested with the suffix specified by the fileSuffix parameter appended to the original name of the file. Any files that use this suffix for completed files are ignored, so be careful to not use a file suffix that could be the suffix of new files that get written to the directory.

When a file is processed and events are generated from the file, it is often beneficial for processing systems to know which file the events came from (for example, showing the filename a stack trace belongs to in a search UI). The full path and the filename can be included by setting the fileHeader parameter to true. The key to use in the headers can be set using the fileHeaderKey parameter (this defaults to file).

The Spooling Directory Source is able to recover from where it left off, so as to avoid duplicates but still consume all data from the file. This is made possible by persisting information to disk about the file it is processing and reading this information when the source starts up. This information is persisted in the tracker directory. The tracker directory is *always* inside the directory that this source is watching. The default name of the tracker directory is *.flumespool*. This can be changed using the trackerDir parameter. Note that the directory is created inside the directory that is being read, and the value of the trackerDir parameter is used as a relative path to the directory that the source is watching. Once the name of the tracker directory is set, if the value of this parameter is changed (even after shutting down Flume), the source will no longer be able to track the location of the file it was processing and might end up being processed again from the beginning, causing duplicates. So, once this is set, it should not be changed.

Example 3-7 shows an example of an agent configured to use the Spooling Directory Source to read data from a directory on disk in batches of 250 events each. The source deletes files as soon as they are completely ingested. It also inserts a header with the filename, with the key usingFlumeFiles.

*Example 3-7. Spooling Directory Source configuration example*

```
agent.sources = spool
agent.channels = memChannel

agent.sources.spool.type = spooldir
agent.sources.spool.channels = memChannel

agent.sources.spool.spoolDir = /data/flume/spool
agent.sources.spool.batchSize = 250
```

```
agent.sources.spool.deletePolicy = immediate
agent.sources.spool.fileHeader = true
agent.sources.spool.fileHeaderKey = usingFlumeFiles
agent.sources.spool.deserializer = \
usingflume.ch03.ProtobufDeserializer$ProtobufDeserializerBuilder

agent.channels.memChannel.type = memory
agent.channels.memChannel.capacity = 10000
agent.channels.memChannel.transactionCapacity = 500
```

## Reading Custom Formats Using Deserializers*

The source *deserializes* data in the files in the directory using a pluggable *deserializer*, allowing the source to read and interpret the data from these files into events in different ways. For example, a deserializer that "understands" Avro could read Avro container formatted files and convert each Avro message to a Flume event, or several lines could be read at once, until an entire stack trace is read and then converted to Flume events. Once all data in a file is read, this source can either delete or rename the file with a new extension so that the same file is not processed again.

To use a custom deserializer, set the value of the deserializer parameter to an implementation of EventDeserializer$Builder that can build the EventDeserial izer implementation to use. The deserializer can be configured by passing in parameters with the deserializer. prefix. Text-based deserializers can call the readChar method to read a character. The way a character is represented differs by character set. To tell the source what character set to use, set inputCharset to the name of the character set, which by default is UTF-8.

Deserializers implement the EventDeserializer interface, and should also provide a Builder class, which must implement the EventDeserializer$Builder interface. The Builder must have a public, no-argument constructor that the Flume framework can use to instantiate the builder. The Builder's build method must create and return a fully configured instance of the deserializer.

A Context instance and an instance of ResettableInputStream are passed to this method. The Context instance can be used to configure the deserializer. The deserializer is expected to deserialize events from the input stream. ResettableInputStream is an interface that is meant to read data from the stream, but also gives the ability to roll back to a previous location in the stream. An instance of the ResettableInput Stream class guarantees that a reset call will reset the reads from this stream to the position in the stream at which the last mark call happened, regardless of how many bytes were read from the stream using the read or readChar methods after the last mark call. This allows the Spooling Directory Source to reread events if writes to a channel failed and the events could not be written. The deserializer can use this functionality in its own mark and reset methods to ensure it rolls back to the correct location within the stream.

The deserializer implements two other methods that are called by the source to read events from the stream—the readEvent and readEvents methods. The readEvent method must return exactly one event from the stream, while the readEvents method takes an argument that is the maximum number of events it must read from the stream.

Example 3-9 shows a deserializer that deserializes messages serialized as Protocol Buffer (Protobuf) messages based on the format shown in Example 3-8. Each Protobuf message is written to the file after its length is written to the file as a 4-byte integer.

*Example 3-8. Protobuf format used by ProtobufDeserializer*

```
option java_package = "usingflume.ch03";
option java_outer_classname = "UsingFlumeEvent";

message Event {
  repeated Header header = 1;
  required bytes body = 2;
}

message Header {
  required string key = 1;
  required string val = 2;
}
```

*Example 3-9. ProtobufDeserializer: a class that deserializes data written as Protobuf messages*

```
package usingflume.ch03;

public class ProtobufDeserializer implements EventDeserializer {
  private final ResettableInputStream stream;
  private boolean isOpen;

  private ProtobufDeserializer(ResettableInputStream stream) {
    // No configuration to do, so ignore the context.
    this.stream = stream;
    isOpen = true;
  }

  @Override
  public Event readEvent() throws IOException {
    throwIfClosed();
    // To not create an array each time or copy arrays multiple times,
    // read the data to an array that backs byte buffers,
```

```
    // then wrap that array in a stream and pass it to the Protobuf
    // parseDelimitedFrom method.
    // The format is expected to be:
    // <length of message> - int
    // <protobuf message (written using writeTo (not delimited)>
    // We assume here that the file is well-formed and the length
    // or the
    // message are not partially cut off.
    byte[] sz = new byte[4];
    if (stream.read(sz, 0, 4) != -1) {
      int length = ByteBuffer.wrap(sz).getInt();
      byte[] data = new byte[length];
      stream.read(data, 0, data.length);
      UsingFlumeEvent.Event protoEvent =
        UsingFlumeEvent.Event.parseFrom(new ByteArrayInputStream(data));
      List<UsingFlumeEvent.Header> headerList
        = protoEvent.getHeaderList();
      Map<String, String> headers = new HashMap<String, String>(
        headerList.size());
      for (UsingFlumeEvent.Header hdr : headerList) {
        headers.put(hdr.getKey(), hdr.getKey());
      }
      return EventBuilder.withBody(protoEvent.getBody().toByteArray(), headers);
    }
    return null;
  }

  @Override
  public List<Event> readEvents(int count) throws IOException {
    throwIfClosed();
    List<Event> events = new ArrayList<Event>(count);
    for (int i = 0; i < count; i++) {
      Event e = readEvent();
      if (e == null) {
        break;
      }
      events.add(e);
    }
    return events;
  }

  @Override
  public void mark() throws IOException {
    throwIfClosed();
    stream.mark();
  }

  @Override
  public void reset() throws IOException {
    throwIfClosed();
    stream.reset();
  }
```

```
@Override
public void close() throws IOException {
  isOpen = false;
  stream.close();
}

private void throwIfClosed() {
  Preconditions.checkState(isOpen, "Serializer is closed!");
}

public static class ProtobufDeserializerBuilder implements Builder {

  @Override
  public EventDeserializer build(Context context,
    ResettableInputStream resettableInputStream) {
    // The serializer does not need any configuration,
    // so ignore the Context instance. If some configuration has
    // to be passed to the serializer, this Context instance can be used.
    return new ProtobufDeserializer(resettableInputStream);
  }
}
}
```

This `ProtobufDeserializer` class reads Protobuf-serialized events from the file and converts them into Flume events in the `readEvent` method, returning `null` when no more events are available to be read. If no events could be read by the `readEvents` method, an empty list is returned, as is mandated by the `EventDeserializer` interface.

Since the file is immutable, once we reach a stage where no more events are available in the file, this means all the events have been read out from the file, at which point the source closes the deserializer by calling the `close` method. If the serializer is maintaining any internal state or has some cleanup to do, this method is expected to do that. In this case, we simply close the stream. The `mark` and `reset` methods simply check that the deserializer is open and forward the calls to the stream. This specific implementation of the serializer does not need any configuration, but deserializers can receive configuration via the `Context` instance passed to the builder, which in turn can be passed through a constructor to the deserializer instance. Example 3-7 showed a Spooling Directory Source configured to use `ProtobufDeserializer`.

Flume comes bundled with a handful of deserializers. The default deserializer is the `LineDeserializer` [line-deserializer]. This is an example of a deserializer that accepts configuration. The line deserializer is enabled if no deserializer is set for the Spooling Directory Source or if the value of the `deserializer` parameter is set to `line`. The line deserializer reads the file line by line, converting each line to an event, based on a configurable character set (UTF-8 by default). Table 3-7 lists the configuration parameters.

*Table 3-7. Line deserializer configuration*

| Parameter | Default | Description |
| --- | --- | --- |
| outputCharset | UTF-8 | The charset to use to convert the characters read from the file to the byte array that is set as the event body. |
| maxLineLength | 2048 | The maximum number of characters to return per line. If the line is longer than this, it is truncated. |

Another deserializer that comes bundled with Flume is the AvroEventDeserializer. To use this deserializer, set the deserializer parameter to avro. The Avro deserializer can read *Avro container files* and send data out as Avro-formatted events. There is only one configuration parameter for this deserializer, as described in Table 3-8.

*Table 3-8. Avro deserializer configuration*

| Parameter | Default | Description |
| --- | --- | --- |
| schemaType | flume.avro.schema.hash | This can be set to either flume.avro.schema.hash or flume.avro.schema.literal. Setting this to flume.avro.schema.hash causes the 64-bit Rabin fingerprint of the schema to be inserted in the headers with the key flume.avro.schema.hash. If the value of this parameter is set to flume.avro.schema.literal, the entire JSONified schema is inserted into the header with the flume.avro.schema.literal key. |

To interpret the data, it is important to know the schema used. Though this information is contained in the file itself, it is important to keep the schema with each event so that it is possible to read the data from the event. So, this deserializer supports inserting the Avro schema in the headers or simply putting the *64-bit Rabin fingerprint* of the schema (as specified in the Avro specification [schema-fp]) in the headers, which can later be used to look up a schema registry that is indexed on the schema fingerprint. (Imagine a situation where there is Avro-formatted data that is going to be in one of several known schemas, which is mostly the case. Using this fingerprint in the headers allows the user to identify which schema should be used to read the message, and thus this can be used by a serializer while writing the data.) To set the fingerprint in the event headers, set the schemaType parameter to flume.avro.schema.hash. The schema fingerprint is written to a header with the key flume.avro.schema.hash.

If the entire JSON-ified schema should be written to every event, set schemaType to flume.avro.schema.literal. In this case, the entire schema is written with the key flume.avro.schema.literal. Writing the schema in every event's header is pretty inefficient since it increases the event size, especially if there are a limited number of schema types.

To read files from a directory as a binary large object (BLOB) [blob], the blob deserializer can be used. The FQCN of the blob deserializer is org.apache.flume.sink.solr.morphline.BlobDeserializer. This deserializer takes the maximum size of a blob it should accept, and for each file attempts to read data from the file in blobs of that many bytes. This serializer takes only one configuration parameter, maxBlobLength, which is the maximum size, in bytes, of each blob. If a file is larger than this, the file is split up into several blobs, each with a size less than equal to the configured maximum. This deserializer buffers all blobs in a batch in memory, so the batch size and maximum blob size should be configured to ensure that the serializer does not end up using more memory than expected.

Since the Spooling Directory Source is also a part of the flume-ng-core artifact, make sure you add the flume-ng-core artifact to your serializer's *pom.xml* file, as shown in Example 3-6. Custom deserializers can be deployed to a Flume agent using the *plugins.d* framework shown in "Deploying Custom Code" on page 204.

## Spooling Directory Source Performance

A Spooling Directory Source is I/O-bound. To avoid complicating deserializer implementations, the source was specifically designed to be single-threaded. This means that it is possible that the performance could be improved by using more threads to read the data and use more of the available CPUs. One way of improving performance of files being read is to write the files alternately to different directories and have one Spooling Directory Source process each of the directories (and write to the same channel, if all the data is going to the same destination). This means more threads read data from the disk and more of the CPUs can be utilized for deserialization.

# Syslog Sources

Syslog is a well-known format that is used by many applications to write log messages. Flume integrates with syslog and can receive syslog messages both in TCP and UDP. Flume provides two syslog sources: the *Syslog UDP Source* and the *Multiport Syslog Source*. The Syslog UDP Source receives syslog messages in UDP, while the Multiport Syslog Source can receive syslog messages on several ports in TCP. Both sources can parse the syslog messages and extract several fields into Flume event headers, which can be used in HDFS Sink bucketing. If the syslog messages do not conform to the Syslog RFCs, RFC-3164 or RFC-5424, the events will contain a header with the key flume.syslog.status with the value Invalid.

The Syslog UDP Source considers an entire UDP datagram to be one syslog event and converts it to a single Flume event, while the Multiport Syslog Source creates a new message each time it encounters a newline (\n) character. These sources create two headers, Facility and Severity, in each Flume event header to indicate the facility and severity of each message. This can be used in bucketing or with the multiplexing channel selector (discussed in Chapter 6).

Table 3-9 lists the configuration parameters that are common to both sources.

*Table 3-9. Syslog Source configuration*

| Parameter | Default | Description |
|---|---|---|
| type | - | The Syslog UDP Source type is syslogudp and the Multiport Syslog Source type is multiport_syslogtcp. |
| host | - | The IP address/hostname to bind to. To bind to all interfaces on the machine, use 0.0.0.0. |
| keepFields | false | If set to true, all fields from the syslog message are left in the event body in addition to having them in the event headers. |

The Syslog UDP Source can be enabled using the syslogudp alias, while the Multiport Syslog Source can be enabled using the multiport_syslogtcp alias. Both sources require the user to specify the hostname to bind to as the value of the host parameter. To bind to all interfaces on the machine, use 0.0.0.0 as the value of host. If keepFields is set to true, fields from the syslog message that are normally moved to the event headers (or removed altogether), such as Priority, Timestamp, and Hostname, are left in the body of the event as well as copied to the event headers. The Multiport Syslog Source also allows syslog messages to be encoded in different character sets on each port it receives the data on. This allows a single source to essentially receive data from various sources, each encoding the message in a different character set.

As well as the common parameters, the Syslog UDP Source has only one additional parameter (see Table 3-10).

*Table 3-10. Syslog UDP Source configuration*

| Parameter | Default | Description |
|---|---|---|
| port | - | The port to bind to. |

The port parameter is used to specify which port the source should bind to.

The Multiport Syslog Source can bind to several ports on the host. In addition to the common parameters, the Multiport Syslog Source defines the parameters listed in Table 3-11.

*Table 3-11. Multiport Syslog Source configuration*

| Parameter | Default | Description |
| --- | --- | --- |
| **ports** | - | A space-separated list of ports to bind to. |
| portHeader | - | The port on which the event was received is included in the headers as the value of the key specified by this header. If this parameter is not configured, the port information is not included. |
| charset.default | UTF-8 | The default character set to use. |
| charset.port.<port> | - | The character set to use for a specific port. |
| eventSize | 2500 | The maximum size of a single event, in bytes. |
| batchSize | 100 | The number of events to buffer in memory before writing to the channel. |
| readBufferSize | 1024 | The buffer size the underlying server should use. |
| numProcessors | - | The number of processors to use. This allows the source to increase the degree of parallelism. |

The Multiport Syslog Source can receive data on multiple ports. The ports should be listed separated by spaces as the value of the ports parameter. Each event received can be annotated with the port number on which the event was received. The value of the configuration parameter portHeader is used as the key for the header in the Flume event, and the value of this header is the port number.

The source also allows syslog messages to be encoded in different character sets on each port it receives data on. To configure the character set per port, use the char set.port. prefix followed by the port number as the configuration parameter, with the value being the character set name. The default character set can be set using the charset.default parameter. The value of this parameter is used when a specific character set has not been set for a port.

As mentioned earlier, the source assumes that each event is delimited by a newline character. Sometimes, it is important to also ensure that each event does not go over some fixed size. This maximum size for each event can be set using the eventSize parameter, which is represented in bytes. If the event's size is greater than this value, the event is truncated to this length, and a header with the key flume.syslog.status is inserted with the value Incomplete. The Multiport Syslog Source also buffers events in memory to avoid affecting channel performance. The batch size can be specified using the batchSize parameter.

This source uses a framework called *Apache MINA* to receive messages. The MINA server uses an internal buffer while reading the data from the network. The size of this buffer is configurable via the configuration parameter readBufferSize, specified in bytes. MINA also supports heavy parallelism. To configure the degree of parallelism, the number of processors that can be used can be passed in using the numProcessors parameter. If this is not defined, the value of the number of processors to be used is autodetected. For each processor that can be used, MINA will spawn up to two threads. To reduce thread usage (not often required), reduce the value specified by numProcessors.

Example 3-10 shows an example of a Multiport Syslog Source configured to receive data on all interfaces and three ports, 4353, 4565, and 4553. The source is configured to process the data received on port 4565 as ISO-8859-1 charset encoded, while all other data received on the other two ports is assumed to be encoded as UTF-8. The source also adds a header to each event with the key port, with the port number where the event was received as the value. The source writes events in batches of 1,000 events each, with a maximum event size of 1,092 bytes. The source also configures MINA to use a buffer of 2,048 bytes while receiving data.

*Example 3-10. Multiport Syslog Source configuration example*

```
agent.sources = syslog
agent.channels = memChannel

agent.sources.syslog.type = multiport_syslogtcp
agent.sources.syslog.channels = memory

# Bind to all interfaces
agent.sources.syslog.host = 0.0.0.0
agent.sources.syslog.ports = 4353 4565 4553

agent.sources.syslog.charset.default = UTF-8
agent.sources.syslog.charset.port.4565 = ISO-8859-1

agent.sources.syslog.batchSize = 1000
agent.sources.syslog.portHeader = port
agent.sources.syslog.readBufferSize = 2048
agent.sources.syslog.eventSize = 1092

agent.channels.memChannel.type = memory
agent.channels.memChannel.capacity = 10000
agent.channels.memChannel.transactioncapacity = 5000
```

**Syslog Data Loss**

Syslog is generally assumed to be a "fire and forget" protocol. The RFCs do not define a way of sending an acknowledgment from the receiver to the sender, nor does it specify a way to retransmit a message after a timeout. Therefore, if the Flume source is unable to write the events to the channel, or if there is some network disruption causing the message to be lost (especially in the UDP case), there is no real way for Flume to inform the sender of failure or for the sender to know that there is an error condition and resend the message. This essentially causes silent data loss, with no possibility of recovering the lost data. This causes Flume's no-data-loss guarantee to not hold true for syslog, and therefore, it is recommended to *only* use syslog if there is no other option and the Flume RPC client or the embedded agent cannot be used at all.

# Exec Source

An Exec Source executes a command configured by the user and generates events based on the standard output of the command. It can also read the error stream from the command, convert the events into Flume events, and write them to the channel. The source expects the command to continuously produce data and ingests its output and error stream. The source runs as long as the process started by the command runs, continuously reading the output stream of the process (and the error stream, if configured).

Each line in the output stream is then encoded as a byte array. The encoding to be used is configurable, and defaults to UTF-8. Each byte array generated as a result is then used as the body of a Flume event. For performance reasons, the source then batches a preconfigured number of events (or until a timeout) and writes them out to the channel. If the channel is full, the source can be configured to stop reading the output and error streams of the process (thus blocking the process temporarily) or to drop the current batch and continue reading the output and error streams (thus letting the process continue). Table 3-12 illustrates the configuration parameters for an Exec Source.

*Table 3-12. Exec Source configuration*

| Config parameter | Default value | Description |
| --- | --- | --- |
| type | - | The alias for an Exec Source is exec. The FQCN is `org.apache.flume.source.ExecSource` (case sensitive). |
| command | - | The command that the source should run. |

| Config parameter | Default value | Description |
|---|---|---|
| restart | false | If set to true, the source will attempt to restart the process if it dies. |
| restartThrottle | 10000 | The time in milliseconds to wait before the process is restarted. This parameter has no effect if restart is false or is not set. |
| logStdErr | false | If set to true, the error stream of the process is also read by the source and converted into Flume events. |
| batchSize | 20 | The maximum number of events to buffer before writing out to the channel(s) configured. |
| batchTimeout | 3000 | The time in milliseconds to wait before writing buffered events to the channel(s) configured. |
| charset | UTF-8 | The character set to use to encode the output and error streams into Flume events. |
| shell | - | The shell or command processor to be used to run the command. |

The command that is to be run is passed in through the command parameter. The Exec Source can be configured to restart the process started by the command, by setting the restart parameter to true. To make sure there is a sufficient time difference between executions of the command, restartThrottle can be set. Once the process dies, the source will wait for this time interval before running the command again.

Exec Source buffers data to ensure good performance when used in conjunction with the File Channel. As mentioned in "File Channel" on page 85, the performance of the channel is better when the number of events per transaction is reasonably high. The batchSize parameter in the Exec Source controls the size of a batch. The source can also be configured to write out the buffered events at the end of a configured time interval, which can be set using the batchTimeout parameter. If both batchSize and batchTimeout are set, the batch is written to the channel as soon as the batch size or batch timeout is met.

The Exec Source can be set to run the configured command in a separate shell, which may be different from the one the Flume process is running in. To run the process in a different shell, pass the full path of the shell executable to the shell parameter. If the command requires shell features like substitution of wildcards or pipes, the shell parameter must be set, since Flume will not perform substitution.

Here is an example of a configuration file where the Exec Source is used for running a complex command using the shell parameter:

```
agent.sources = execSrc
agent.channels = memChannel

agent.sources.execSrc.type = exec
agent.sources.execSrc.shell = /bin/bash -c
agent.sources.execSrc.command = tail -F /var/log/flume/flume.log | grep "error:"

agent.sources.execSrc.channels = memChannel

# Initializes a memory channel with default configuration
agent.channels.memChannel.type = memory
```

**Possibility of Data Loss with Exec Source**

The Exec Source is an example of an asynchronous source, which cannot inform the data producer if there is a failure. As a result, restarting the agent or the machine can result in data loss, as explained here.

The Exec Source is most commonly used to tail files from within Flume. Tailing a file using the Exec Source with the command `tail -F` will get the data into Flume in near real time, but there is risk of data loss. If the Flume agent dies or the machine restarts, the Exec Source will run the command when it starts up; in this case it will run `tail -F <file_name>`. Since the `tail` command will only pull in new data written to the file, any data written to the file between the agent's death and the time the source started up is lost. For this reason, it is recommended to use the Spooling Directory Source discussed earlier in this chapter to handle data written into files. Though slightly more restrictive, this source will not lose data as it tracks the data being read from the file.

Even when used with some other command, the Exec Source does buffer as many events as the batch size before writing the events to the channel. These events will also be lost if the agent or machine restarts before the batch timeout or batch size is reached.

# JMS Source

Flume comes bundled with a source that can fetch data from a Java Message Service queue or topic. Using the JMS Source, it is possible to accept messages from messaging systems that support JMS, like ActiveMQ, as well. Installing and using the JMS Source is slightly trickier than most other sources. Since it is possible to integrate with multiple messaging systems that support JMS, the client libraries supplied by the respective system *must* be installed into the *plugins.d* directory, as discussed in "Deploying Custom Code" on page 204.

The configuration parameters for the JMS Source are shown in Table 3-13.

*Table 3-13. JMS Source configuration*

| Config parameter | Default value | Description |
|---|---|---|
| **type** | - | The alias for the JMS Source is jms. The FQCN is org.apache.flume.source.jms.JMSSource (case sensitive). |
| **initialContextFactory** | - | The class name of the vendor's initial context factory. An example, in the case of ActiveMQ, would be org.apache.activemq.jndi.ActiveMQInitial ContextFactory. |
| **destinationName** | - | The name of the JMS destination from where the messages are consumed. |
| **destinationType** | - | The type of the JMS destination, queue, or topic. |
| **providerURL** | - | The URL of the JMS broker. |
| connectionFactory | ConnectionFactory | The JNDI name the connection factory appears as. |
| messageSelector | - | The FQCN of the message selector class to filter the messages, if needed. |
| userName | - | The username to log in to the JMS provider. |
| passwordFile | - | The file that contains the password to the JMS provider. |
| batchSize | 100 | The number of events to write to the channel per transaction. |
| converter.type | DEFAULT | The FQCN of a class that implements JMSMessage Converter. See "Converting JMS Messages into Flume Events*" on page 67. |
| converter.charset | UTF-8 | The charset that the default converter should use. This parameter may not be accepted by other converters. |
| converter.* | - | Other configuration parameters to be passed to the converter. |

Vendor-supplied libraries to communicate with the JMS broker must be dropped into Flume's *plugins.d* directory. The library's initial context factory and connection factory classes should be passed in as values to the configuration parameters initialCon textFactory and connectionFactory. This information should be available in the documentation of the vendor-supplied libraries. The value of connectionFactory defaults to ConnectionFactory, which should work for popular JMS systems like ActiveMQ. Other JMS-related parameters, such as the destination name, destination type, and message selector (if messages need to be filtered), should also be passed in through the configuration file. The source also requires the URL of the JMS broker as the value of the providerURL parameter.

The source can log in to secure JMS brokers using the username specified by the user Name and the password specified in a file whose path is specified by the passwordFile parameter.

By default, this source will pull up to 100 messages from the broker per JMS session, but this can be adjusted using the batchSize parameter.

The JMS Source can convert data from JMS-style messages into Flume events via a *converter*. The default converter, which is used if no converter is specified in the configuration, can handle most standard JMS messages. If custom or proprietary formats are used, a custom converter can be deployed using the converter.type parameter, whose value should be the FQCN of the converter class. Any parameters that have to be passed to a converter can be passed in using the converter. prefix. For example, to use a character set other than the default UTF-8 character set with the default converter, set the value of converter.charset to the standard name of the character set, like ISO-8859-1. "Converting JMS Messages into Flume Events*" on page 67 discusses in detail how to write custom converters. Example 3-11 presents a sample JMS Source configuration.

*Example 3-11. JMS Source configuration example*

```
agent.sources = jmsSrc
agent.channels = memChannel

agent.sources.jmsSrc.type = jms
agent.sources.jmsSrc.channels = memory

# Bind to all interfaces
agent.sources.jmsSrc.initialContextFactory = \
org.apache.activemq.jndi.ActiveMQInitialContextFactory
agent.sources.jmsSrc.destinationName = UsingFlume

agent.sources.jmsSrc.charset.providerURL = tcp://usingflume.oreilly.com:61616
agent.sources.jmsSrc.destinationType = QUEUE

agent.sources.jmsSrc.batchSize = 1000
agent.sources.jmsSrc.converter.type = usingflume.ch03.JsonMessageConverter
agent.sources.jmsSrc.converter.charset = iso-8859-1

agent.channels.memChannel.type = memory
agent.channels.memChannel.capacity = 10000
agent.channels.memChannel.transactioncapacity = 5000
```

This configuration file configures the source to pull data from an ActiveMQ message queue, which reads from a JMS queue at host *usingflume.oreilly.com:61616*. The queue information is passed in via various parameters. The initial context factory is set as `org.apache.activemq.jndi.ActiveMQInitialContextFactory`, as per ActiveMQ documentation. The `JsonMessageConverter` is used with the ISO-8859-1 character set.

## Converting JMS Messages into Flume Events*

The JMS Source can be configured to use custom code to convert JMS messages into Flume events, much like the HTTP Source's handler. This makes the JMS Source extremely flexible, and allows the user to parse data in proprietary formats in the JMS message. Flume comes packaged with a JMS Message Converter that supports default JMS formats. The JMS Source can pass configuration into the message converter, just like the HTTP Source. This configuration can be used to set up any initial configuration or state required for the converter. All of the JMS transaction handling is done by the source; the converter need not worry about any of that.

The default JMS Message Converter that comes packaged with Flume converts individual JMS messages into Flume events based on their format and content. A JMS `ByteMessage` is simply read, and the bytes read from the message are placed into the body of a Flume event. For a JMS `TextMessage`, the converter encodes the text into a byte array and places it into the body of a Flume event. The encoding to be used is configurable through the source configuration. If an `ObjectMessage` is read off the JMS queue, the converter wraps the object in an `ObjectOutputStream` and writes it out to a `ByteArrayOutputStream`. The bytes are then read from this stream and set as the Flume event's body. In most cases, this is what users need.

Sometimes, though, it might make more sense to parse out any schemas in the message and convert them into a format that can be serialized at the terminal sink more easily. For example, if there are several different applications writing to the JMS queue in different serialization formats like JSON or XML, then a converter can be written to convert these into a unified format that can be parsed more easily at the terminal sink.

Converters must implement the `JMSMessageConverter` interface, which is shown in Example 3-12. The JMS Source instantiates a `JMSMessageConverter$Builder` class, and then passes the configuration via a `Context` instance to the Builder's `build` method, which is expected to return a fully configured converter instance.

*Example 3-12. JMS converter interface*

```
package org.apache.flume.source.jms;
public interface JMSMessageConverter {
  public List<Event> convert(Message message)
          throws JMSException;
  /**
   * Implementors of JMSMessageConverter must either provide
   * a suitable builder or implement the Configurable interface.
   */
  public interface Builder {
    public JMSMessageConverter build(Context context);
  }
}
```

Example 3-13 shows an example of a JMS Message Converter that reads the JMS messages formatted as JSON and converts them into Flume events. Converters can implement Configurable to accept configuration, and the JMS Source passes any parameters specified with the converter. prefix to the converter. This converter accepts a configuration that tells the converter which charset to use to convert the JSON events to Flume events.

*Example 3-13. An example of a JMS Message Converter*

```
package usingflume.ch03;

public class JsonMessageConverter implements JMSMessageConverter,
  Configurable {

  private static final Logger LOGGER =
    LoggerFactory.getLogger(JsonMessageConverter.class);
  private final Type listType
    = new TypeToken<List<JSONEvent>>() {
  }.getType();
  private final Gson gson
    = new GsonBuilder().disableHtmlEscaping().create();
  private String charset = "UTF-8";

  @Override
  public List<Event> convert(javax.jms.Message message)
    throws JMSException {

    Preconditions.checkState(message instanceof TextMessage,
      "Expected a text message, but the message received " +
        "was not Text");
    List<JSONEvent> events =
      gson.fromJson(((TextMessage) message).getText(), listType);
    return convertToNormalEvents(events);
  }
```

```
private List<Event> convertToNormalEvents(List<JSONEvent> events) {
    List<Event> newEvents = new ArrayList<Event>(events.size());
    for(JSONEvent e : events) {
        e.setCharset(charset);
        newEvents.add(EventBuilder.withBody(e.getBody(),
            e.getHeaders()));
    }
    return newEvents;
}

@Override
public void configure(Context context) {
    try {
    charset = context.getString("charset", "UTF-8");
    } catch (Exception ex) {
        LOGGER.warn("Charset not found. Using UTF-8 instead", ex);
        charset = "UTF-8";
    }

  }
}
```

The converter shown in Example 3-13 simply takes a message that it expects to be a JMS `TextMessage`. This message is expected to be in JSON format converted into a list of Flume JSON events. Once the JSON events are created, a list of "simple" Flume events are created to avoid the additional overhead of converting the string to a byte array each time it is read. To configure the JMS Source with this converter, Example 3-11 can be used.

To deploy a custom converter, make sure the JAR file containing the class is deployed in the *plugins.d* directory and the `converter.type` parameter specifies the FQCN of the class that is to be used. While writing your deserializer, include the `flume-jms-source` artifact in your application's *pom.xml* file:

```
<dependency>
    <groupId>org.apache.flume.flume-ng-sinks</groupId>
    <artifactId>flume-hdfs-sink</artifactId>
    <version>1.5.0</version>
</dependency>
```

Custom converters can be installed to the *plugins.d* directory as explained in "Deploying Custom Code" on page 204.

# Writing Your Own Sources*

Sources are the points of entry for data into a Flume agent. It is likely that users will have custom or proprietary communication formats that need to be used to write data into Flume. This is often more efficient and easier than pushing data via the

Flume SDK. To integrate with other systems, users can write their own Flume sources and deploy them, using Flume's *plugins.d* mechanism.

Each source "generates" events and then forwards the events to the channel processor for the source. Each time an event is generated by the source, the source can either write it to the channel processor by calling the channel processor's `processEvent` method or wait for a batch of events to be generated and then send them to the channel processor using the channel processor's `processEventBatch` method. It is almost always better to use the `processEventBatch` method with a list of events. Each `processEventBatch` call starts a transaction with each of the channels and writes the entire batch in one transaction, and then commits it. `processEvent`, on the other hand, creates transactions of just one event, which can cause a severe overhead that affects the channels' performance. This is why it is recommended that sources use `processEventBatch` unless each event is known to be large (on the order of hundreds of kilobytes to a few megabytes). To get access to the channel processor for a source, the source can call the `getChannelProcessor` method defined in the `AbstractSource` class.

If data coming from an external source requires that an acknowledgment be sent, it is important that this be sent only after the `processEventBatch` method returns. If a commit to one of the channels fails, we must inform the original data source that the data needs to be sent again. Sending the ACK after the `processEventBatch` method returns avoids the problem. `ChannelExceptions` thrown by this method can be caught and a failure can be reported to the data source so that the data can be sent again.

The channel processor for each source is created and set up by the Flume framework, so the source does not need to handle the creation or configuration of the channel processor. In this section, we will take a look at how to write custom sources.

All classes described as dependencies in this section are part of the `flume-ng-core` artifact or its dependencies. Example 3-6 describes how to include this artifact in your plug-in's *pom.xml* file. Custom sources can be deployed to Flume just like any other plug-in, as shown in "Deploying Custom Code" on page 204.

## Event-Driven and Pollable Sources

Each source is run in its own thread, called a `SourceRunner`. The source runner runs a single thread that operates on the source. Flume has two types of sources: *event-driven sources* and *pollable sources*. Based on the type of source, the Flume framework creates an `EventDrivenSourceRunner` or a `PollableSourceRunner` to run the source.

## Developing pollable sources

Pollable sources do not run their own threads; instead, they are controlled by the Flume framework, which calls the source's process method in a loop. These sources extend the AbstractPollableSource class and implement the process method. A pollable source can accept a configuration from the user via the Flume configuration system by implementing the Configurable interface in addition to extending the AbstractPollableSource class.

Pollable sources are sources that run a loop to generate data or poll an external system to receive data, rather than running a server. Once the configuration provider instantiates and configures a pollable source, the Flume framework creates a Polla bleSourceRunner to run the source.

The Flume framework runs a thread for each pollable source that repeatedly calls the process method. Each time the process method is called, the source "generates" events and passes them to the channel processor. The source is responsible for informing the framework whether it was successfully able to generate data or not. If the source was successfully able to generate events, then the source returns Pollable Source.Status.READY to the runner thread that called it, which will call the process method again immediately. Otherwise, the source returns PollableSource.Sta tus.BACKOFF. In such a case, the Flume framework will initiate a backoff with the process method being called only after a brief timeout, which increases by one second each time the source returns failure (the maximum timeout is five seconds). A pollable source is expected to generate data on its own, or by polling some other source.

If the processEventBatch method throws an exception, the source can catch the exception to report failure to the system from which data is being retrieved. In the case of a JMS Source, this might result in a JMS transaction being rolled back. Otherwise, success can be reported to the external system, like a JMS transaction commit.

A pollable source is extremely simple to write. An example of a pollable source is shown in Example 3-14. The StockTickerSource periodically polls an external service for the prices of a preconfigured set of stock tickers and creates Flume events from the data received. This source simply converts the stock prices into simple strings and creates the event body from the string's UTF-8 representation.

*Example 3-14. An example of a pollable source*

```
package usingflume.ch03;

public class StockTickerSource extends AbstractPollableSource {

  private static final String CONF_TICKERS = "tickers";
  private static final String CONF_REFRESH_INTERVAL = "refreshInterval";
  private static final int DEFAULT_REFRESH_INTERVAL = 10;

  private int refreshInterval = DEFAULT_REFRESH_INTERVAL;

  private final List<String> tickers = new ArrayList<String>();
  private final QuoteProvider server = new RandomQuoteProvider();

  private volatile long lastPoll = 0;

  @Override
  protected Status doProcess() throws EventDeliveryException {
    Status status = Status.BACKOFF;
    if(TimeUnit.MILLISECONDS.toSeconds(System.currentTimeMillis() - lastPoll) >
      refreshInterval) {
      final List<Event> events = new ArrayList<Event>(tickers.size());
      Map<String, Float> prices = server.getQuote(tickers);
      lastPoll = System.currentTimeMillis();
      // Convert each price into ticker = price form in UTF-8 as event body
      for(Map.Entry<String, Float> e: prices.entrySet()) {
        StringBuilder builder = new StringBuilder(e.getKey());
        builder.append(" = ").append(e.getValue());
        events.add(EventBuilder.withBody(builder.toString().getBytes(Charsets
          .UTF_8)));
      }
      getChannelProcessor().processEventBatch(events);
      status = Status.READY;
    }
    return status;
  }

  @Override
  protected void doConfigure(Context context) throws FlumeException {
    refreshInterval = context.getInteger(CONF_REFRESH_INTERVAL,
      DEFAULT_REFRESH_INTERVAL);
    String tickersString = context.getString(CONF_TICKERS);
    Preconditions.checkArgument(tickersString != null && !tickersString
      .isEmpty(), "A list of tickers must be specified");
    tickers.addAll(Arrays.asList(tickersString.split("\\s+")));
  }

  @Override
  protected void doStart() throws FlumeException {
    server.start();
```

```
  }

  @Override
  protected void doStop() throws FlumeException {
    server.stop();
  }
}
```

This source extends the `AbstractPollableSource` class, whose parent, `BasicSource Semantics`, implements the `start`, `stop`, and `configure` methods. Calls to these methods are delegated to the `doStart`, `doStop`, and `doConfigure` methods of this source.

When the agent starts, the framework configures this source. Any configuration must be set up through the `doConfigure` method that gets called. In this example, the list of tickers for which the quote must be retrieved is fetched from the configuration file. The interval between consecutive event generation is also read from the configuration.

After this, the `doStart` method of this source gets called. This method can be used to set up any network clients. In this case, the service that fetches the stock quotes is started (since this is just an example, the service in this case simply returns random values).

The pollable source runner then calls the `process` method (implemented in `Basic SourceSemantics`), which delegates the calls to the `doProcess` method. The `doProcess` method generates the events from the data fetched from the external service. When the source successfully *translates* the incoming quotes into Flume events and writes events out to the channels via the channel processor's `processEventBatch` method, it returns `Status.READY`; otherwise, it returns `Status.BACKOFF`. In this case, if consecutive calls to `doProcess` occur in less time than the refresh interval, the source simply returns `Status.BACKOFF`, indicating that the source runner should wait for a while before calling the `process` method again.

Eventually, when the agent is stopped, the `doStop` method gets called. This is where any cleanup can be done, like closing network connections. Once the agent is stopped, the instance may be garbage-collected.

This is a simple example of a pollable source. For a more realistic example, please take a look at the JMS Source in Flume [jms_src_code].

### Building event-driven sources

Event-driven sources implement the `EventDrivenSource` interface, which is simply a marker interface for the Flume framework to choose the `SourceRunner` implementation to run the source. Event-driven sources usually run their own threads, which are started when the Flume framework calls the `start` method. Such sources control the rate at which they write data to the channels.

For example, the HTTP Source that comes bundled with Flume is an event-driven source that runs a web server that listens on a particular port. It generates Flume events based on the HTTP requests sent to it, and writes those events out into the channel(s) associated with it. Event-driven sources typically run their own threads or thread pools, which handle event generation and writing those events to the channels. Since these sources respond to some external stimulus, the Flume framework creates a new `EventDrivenSourceRunner` that simply starts these sources by calling the `start` method in a new thread and then allows them to manage themselves. When the agent is stopped or reconfigured, the `stop` method is called to stop the source.

Event-driven sources respond to an external event to produce data. Most sources that receive data from an external entity would fall into this category. Event-driven sources run their own threads that they use to receive data and generate events. Most of the sources that come bundled with Flume, like the Avro Source, HTTP Source, Exec Source, etc., are event driven.

An event-driven source is slightly more complex than a pollable source because this source has to keep track of an external process that produces the data and handle the incoming data without help from the Flume framework. Event-driven sources can also be configured via the configuration file, by implementing the `Configurable` interface.

To write an event-driven source, extend the `AbstractEventDrivenSource` class, which already implements the `Configurable` interface. Alternatively, simply implement the marker interface, `EventDrivenSource`, which extends the `Source` interface. As a result, the only methods that the source needs to implement are the ones defined by the `Source` interface and, if required, the `Configurable` interface.

The `AbstractEventDrivenSource` class extends the `BasicSourceSemantics` class, which implements the `start`, `stop`, and `configure` methods. These calls get delegated to the `doStart`, `doStop`, and `doConfigure` methods of this class.

Once the framework starts the source, it is pretty much on its own, until the framework stops it. It is completely up to the implementor of the source to create threads to handle the external events that generate Flume events.

Example 3-15 shows an example of an event-driven source that accepts data from an external service via Netty-Avro IPC. We will not go into a detailed discussion of the IPC protocol here, but the basic idea is that a handler class, in this case the `Transac tionSource` class, must implement an interface, `FlumeCreditCardAuth`, which is generated by Avro from the protocol definition file and is shown here:

```
@namespace("usingflume.ch03")

protocol FlumeCreditCardAuth {

  record CreditCardTransaction {
    string cardNumber;
    string location;
    float amount;
  }

  enum Status {
    OK,
    FAILED
  }

  Status transactionsCompleted(array<CreditCardTransaction> transactions);
}
```

The Avro compiler generates classes representing the `CreditCardTransaction` and an interface that represents the callback whose `transactionCompleted` method gets called when the client sends data to this host. The `TransactionSource` implements this interface. More information about the Avro IDL can be found in the Avro documentation [avro-idl].

*Example 3-15. An example of an event-driven source*

```
package usingflume.ch03;

public class TransactionSource extends AbstractEventDrivenSource implements
  FlumeCreditCardAuth {

  private static final String CONF_HOST = "host";
  private static final String CONF_PORT = "port";
  private static final String DELIMITER = ";";

  private String host;
  private Integer port;
  private Server srv;

  @Override
  protected void doConfigure(Context context) throws FlumeException {
    host = context.getString(CONF_HOST);
    Preconditions.checkArgument(host != null && !host.isEmpty(),
      "Host must be specified");
    port = Preconditions.checkNotNull(context.getInteger(CONF_PORT),
      "Port must be specified");
  }

  @Override
  protected void doStart() throws FlumeException {
    srv = new NettyServer(
```

```
       new SpecificResponder(FlumeCreditCardAuth.class, this),
       new InetSocketAddress(host, port));
    srv.start();
    super.start();
  }

  @Override
  protected void doStop() throws FlumeException {
    srv.close();
    try {
      srv.join();
    } catch (InterruptedException e) {
      throw new FlumeException("Interrupted while waiting for Netty Server to" +
        " shut down.", e);
    }
  }

  @Override
  public Status transactionsCompleted(List<CreditCardTransaction> transactions)
    throws AvroRemoteException {
    Status status;
    List<Event> events = new ArrayList<Event>(transactions.size());
    for (CreditCardTransaction txn : transactions) {
      StringBuilder builder = new StringBuilder();
      builder.append(txn.getCardNumber()).append(DELIMITER)
        .append(txn.getLocation()).append(DELIMITER)
        .append(txn.getAmount()).append(DELIMITER);
      events.add(EventBuilder.withBody(builder.toString().getBytes(
        Charsets.UTF_8)));
    }
    try {
      getChannelProcessor().processEventBatch(events);
      status = Status.OK;
    } catch (Exception e) {
      status = Status.FAILED;
    }
    return status;
  }
}
```

The source takes a few configuration parameters, like the hostname and port to which the server must bind. The `configure` method is called by the Flume framework once the source is initialized and all configuration specific to this source is passed in via the `Context` instance. All relevant configuration must be validated and saved to relevant fields in this method. For example, the `doConfigure` method of the `TransactionSource` verifies that the hostname and port are supplied by the user in the configuration file, throwing an exception if they are not specified.

Once configured, the framework starts the source by calling `start`, which gets delegated to the `doStart` method of this class. In this method, the source starts the server process. Once started, the framework does not interact with the source until it is to be stopped. Any servers or threads that are to be started to receive data must be started in this method. In the case of the `TransactionSource`, a `NettyServer` is started in this method.

The `NettyServer` manages several threads that receive data over the network. When a complete Avro message is received, it calls the `transactionCompleted` method, to which it passes the data. This method converts the data from the Avro format to Flume events. Being demo code, the translation is simply into a byte representation of a string-formatted version of the data. This conversion can involve any arbitrary logic, though it is a good idea to keep this logic simple as this code will execute for every event received and will have a direct impact on the performance of the source.

Once the incoming data is converted to Flume events, the entire batch of Flume events are passed to the channel processor via the `processEventBatch` method. The channel processor handles the transaction processing with the channel(s) and throws an exception if commits to any channel fail, in which case the source returns `Status.FAILED` to the sender, who may send the same data again to ensure it is persisted to the Flume channels. If the events are successfully written out, the source returns `Status.OK`, indicating that the data has been committed to the channel(s).

When the agent stops or is being reconfigured, the `stop` method gets called. This call gets delegated to the `doStop` method, which must do any cleanup required. In this case, this method stops the `NettyServer` instance, and waits for it to terminate before returning. If event-driven sources start threads or create thread pools, or open sockets or files, they must be shut down or closed, respectively, in the `stop` method.

# Summary

In this chapter, we discussed the two types of Flume sources (pollable and event driven). We also looked at the various sources that come bundled with Flume, their configuration, their plug-ins, etc. We also looked at some of the best practices with respect to the sources, mostly with reference to batching. In the end, we wrote custom event-driven and pollable sources to get a better understanding of how sources are written.

In the next chapter, we will cover the basics of channels, the two channels that come bundled with Flume, and how to configure them.

# References

- [netty] The Netty Project, *http://netty.io*
- [nio] Java New I/O API, *http://bit.ly/1wxlcQC*
- [zlib_ch3] zlib compression library, *http://www.zlib.net*
- [keystore] Java `KeyStore` API, *http://bit.ly/1wxlgQg*
- [keystore-type] Java `KeyStore` types, *http://bit.ly/1wxll6y*
- [java-security] Customizing Java security, *http://bit.ly/1wxlmrj*
- [thrift_ch3] Apache Thrift project, *http://thrift.apache.org*
- [jms_src_code] Apache Flume JMS Source, *http://bit.ly/1wxlreC*
- [line-deserializer] Line deserializer, *http://bit.ly/1wxlyXC*
- [schema-fp] Avro Schema Fingerprints, *http://bit.ly/1wxlF5s*
- [blob] Binary large object, *http://en.wikipedia.org/wiki/Binary_large_object*
- [avro-idl] Avro IDL documentation, *http://avro.apache.org/docs/current/idl.html*

# CHAPTER 4

# Channels

Channels are buffers that sit in between sources and sinks. As such, channels allow sources and sinks to operate at different rates. Channels are key to Flume's guarantees of not losing data (of course, when configured properly). Sources write data to one or more channels, which are read by one or more sinks. A sink can read only from one channel, while multiple sinks can read from the same channel for better performance. Channels have transactional semantics that allow Flume to provide explicit guarantees about the data written in a channel.

Having a channel operating as a buffer between sources and sinks has several advantages. The channel allows sources operating on the same channel to have their own threading models without being worried about the sinks reading from the channel, and vice versa. Having a buffer in between the sources and the sinks also allows them to operate at different rates, since the writes happen at the tail of the buffer and reads happen off the head. This also allows the Flume agents to handle "peak hour" loads from the sources, even if the sinks are unable to drain the channels immediately.

Channels allow multiple sources and sinks to operate on them. Channels are *transactional* in nature. Each write to a channel and each read from a channel happens within the context of a transaction. Only once a write transaction is committed will the events from that transaction be readable by any sinks. Also, if a sink has successfully *taken* an event, the event is not available for other sinks to take until and unless the sink rolls back the transaction.

Temporary load spikes are common in most real-time applications, and Flume is designed to handle these cases. The events will be buffered in the channel until the sinks remove them, allowing the agent to handle changes in incoming load. How much additional data each agent can handle depends on the capacity of the channel. The capacity of the channel should be allocated based on the expected combined maximum peak load of all sources writing to the channel and the combined rate of drain of all sinks. This design also allows the sources and sinks to have retry logic on failure. On failure, sources can reattempt writing to the channel and sinks can reattempt reads.

# Transaction Workflow

As discussed in "Transactions in Flume Channels" on page 23, Flume channels are transactional. *Transactions* are essentially batches of events written into a channel atomically. Either all or none of the events in the batch are present in the channel. Transactions are important to provide guarantees of exactly when an event is written to or removed from the channel. For example, a sink could take an event from the channel and attempt to write it to HDFS and fail. In this case, the event should go back to the channel and be available for this sink or another one to take and write to HDFS.

Making sure that takes cause events to be removed only on transaction commit guarantees that events are not lost even if the write fails once, at which point the sink can just roll back this transaction. Transactions could have one event or many events, but for performance reasons it is always recommended to have a reasonably large number of events per transaction.

It is important to batch writes to channels, especially durable channels. Durable channels guarantee no data loss even in the event of agent or machine restarts, so they have to flush and sync all buffered event data to disk during a transaction commit, which occurs once per batch. Syncing to disk is an expensive and time-consuming operation and should be done only when a reasonably large chunk of data has been written to the page cache. Also, time taken to sync to disk includes the nontrivial cost of making a system call before the actual sync, which adds up over time. Each such batch is also represented by a transaction, making transactions important for performance as well as reliability.

Each channel can have several sources and sinks, respectively writing to and reading from the channel. Sources and sinks operate in slightly different ways with respect to transactions. Sources do not directly work with transactions; instead, a source's *channel processor* handles the transactions on its behalf. The way the channel processor works with transactions is almost identical to the way sinks do (except that sinks take from the channels, while channel processors put data into the channels).

The sink initiates a transaction with the channel by calling the channel's `getTransaction` method, which returns an instance of a `Transaction`. The sink then calls `begin` on the transaction object, which allows the channel to set up any internal state it requires for the transaction. Usually, this includes creation of queues for temporarily holding the events until the transaction is completed.

Once the transaction is started, the sink calls take (put in the case of channel processors) on the channel, until the sink is ready to commit the transaction. Once a sink takes an event, it will not be available for the same or another sink to take unless the transaction is rolled back.

Sinks (and channel processors) usually batch several events into one transaction for performance reasons. Once the sink has completed its batch, the sink calls commit on the transaction. Once a sink-side transaction (a transaction with only takes) is committed, the events in that transaction are marked as deleted by the channel and will not be available to any sink again. Once a source-side transaction (owned by the channel processor) is committed, the events are safely in the channel. This means that the events will be deleted from the channel only when a sink takes the events and commits.

Be aware that if a sink has taken an event, that event is no longer available to any sink unless and until this sink rolls back the transaction, causing the events in it to be available for takes again. This is specifically designed to avoid duplicates when multiple sinks operate on the same channel. Every event in the channel can be taken and committed exactly once, after which the event is removed from the channel.

Depending on the specific channel used, the events may be available in the channel even if the machine or the JVM restarts. It is also likely that the sink may have failed to write all the events to wherever it was supposed to and hence has to retry. In this case, the sink rolls back the entire transaction using the rollback method in the transaction. Once a transaction is rolled back on the sink side, the channel restores the events to the channel and makes them available for sinks to take. In the case of a source-side transaction rollback, it is as if the transaction never happened, and the events written during that transaction are not written into the channel. Rollbacks could potentially cause duplicates when they are caused by timeouts or other failures where the events may have been committed to the next hop's channel.

After the transaction is committed or rolled back, it is closed by calling the close method to clear up any resources to be used by the transaction. Figure 4-1 illustrates the workflow for a transaction.

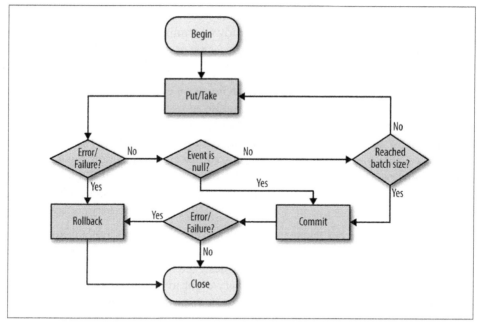

*Figure 4-1. Transaction workflow*

A single transaction cannot put and take events. This ensures that sources can only put events into the channel and sinks can only take events from the channel.

# Channels Bundled with Flume

Flume comes bundled with two channels: the *Memory Channel* and the *File Channel*. Both channels work on the same basic principles explained here. Both channels are fully thread-safe and can operate with multiple sources and sinks. As the names imply, the Memory Channel stores committed events in main memory while the File Channel writes out events to files on disk. In this section, we will discuss both of these channels and the different factors to consider while selecting between the two.

## Memory Channel

The Memory Channel is an in-memory channel that stores events written to it on the heap. For all practical purposes, the Memory Channel is an in-memory queue—the sources write to its tail and sinks read off its head. The Memory Channel supports very high throughput, as it holds all data in memory. As mentioned earlier, the channel is thread-safe and can handle writes from several sources and reads from several sinks at the same time. The Memory Channel should be used when data loss is not a concern, since the channel does not persist the data to disk. If data loss is a concern, then the Memory Channel should not be used, since process death or machine crashes or restarts can cause data to be lost.

The Memory Channel supports Flume's transactional model and maintains separate queues for each transaction in progress. Once a source-side transaction is committed, the events in the queue for that transaction are moved to the channel's main queue atomically. If the commit successfully completes, the events in the transaction will be available for the sinks to take. If it fails, the transaction has to be rolled back by the source and the events will be discarded. For sink-side transactions, the events are moved to the transaction's queue each time the sink does a *take*. This ensures that exactly one sink "takes" an event. When the sink commits the transaction, the transaction queue is discarded and the events are dereferenced, to be garbage-collected. Therefore, the sink implementation must be careful to commit the transaction if and only if the events have been successfully written to the destination.

If the transaction fails, the events are reinserted at the head of the channel in the reverse order, so the events are available to be "taken" again in the same order as they were originally inserted. In this way, although Flume does not guarantee ordering, the Memory Channel does make the events available for takes in the order they were written. However, when certain transactions are rolled back, it is possible that events written after the events in those transactions will get written out to their destination earlier (since another sink may have committed a transaction containing events that are "newer" than the ones in the rolled-back transactions).

The Memory Channel can be configured without much effort and is one of the easiest Flume components to configure. Table 4-1 lists the configuration parameters for the channel.

*Table 4-1. Memory Channel configuration*

| Config parameter | Default value | Description |
| --- | --- | --- |
| **type** | - | The alias for the Memory Channel is memory. The FQCN is org.apache.flume.channel.MemoryChannel (case sensitive). |
| capacity | 100 | The maximum number of committed events the channel can hold. |
| transactionCapacity | 100 | The maximum number of events that can be put or taken in a single transaction. |

| Config parameter | Default value | Description |
| --- | --- | --- |
| byteCapacity | 80% of the total amount of heap space available to the process | The maximum amount of heap space (in bytes) this channel is allowed to use. |
| byteCapacityBufferPercentage | 20 | The percent of byteCapacity to consider keeping as a buffer between the byte capacity of the channel and the total size of the bodies of all events currently in the channel. |
| keep-alive | 3 | The maximum period of time (in seconds) each put or take should wait for completion. |

The Memory Channel holds all events in memory—therefore, the channel's capacity is limited and is defined by the capacity parameter. This parameter defines the total number of committed events that the channel can hold at any given time. The difference between the total number of events committed into the channel and the number of events taken out of the channel (and committed) at any time should be less than or equal to the capacity of the channel. If the channel is at capacity, any more attempts to insert events into the channel will fail with a ChannelException until at least an equivalent number of events are taken from the channel.

The maximum number of events that can be put or taken in a transaction is controlled by the transactionCapacity parameter. This parameter is also a good defense against rogue clients pushing a huge number of events to a source, causing the agent to run out of memory. This parameter forces batches to be of limited size and thus limits the number of events per RPC call, and is a simple defense against denial of service (DoS) attacks.

The total amount of memory that the events in the channel use can be restricted by the byteCapacity parameter. The byteCapacityBufferPercentage parameter represents the percentage of the byte capacity that is reserved for the event headers. When an event is about to be committed to the channel, the event is inserted into the channel if and only if the combined size of the bodies of all events in the channel plus the size of the body of the current event is less than or equal to the amount of memory available that is not reserved for the event headers.

When an event is about to be inserted into the channel, it is possible that the channel is full at that time. In this case, the thread inserting the events will wait for a maximum of keep-alive seconds before failing. The thread taking events from the channel will also wait for keep-alive seconds for an event to be available in the channel. In most cases, there should be no need to set this parameter. It is a safety valve to throttle the write or read rate. Throttling the rate is useful when the take rate is much faster than the put rate, or vice versa.

The following configuration shows a Memory Channel configured to hold up to 100,000 events, with each transaction being able to hold up to 1,000 events. The total memory occupied by all events in the channel can be a maximum of approximately 5 GB of space. Of this 5 GB, the channel considers 10% to be reserved for event headers (as defined by the `byteCapacityBufferPercentage` parameter), making 4.5 GB available for event bodies:

```
agent.channels = mc
agent.sources = sq

agent.channels.mc.type = memory
agent.channels.mc.capacity = 100000
agent.channels.mc.transactionCapacity = 1000
agent.channels.mc.byteCapacity = 5000000000
agent.channels.mc.byteCapacityBufferPercentage = 10

agent.sources.sq.type = seq
agent.sources.sq.channels = mc
```

## File Channel

The File Channel is Flume's persistent channel. It writes out all events to disk and thus does not lose data on process or machine shutdown or crash. The File Channel ensures that any events committed into the channel are removed from the channel only when a sink takes the events and commits the transaction, even if the machine or agent crashed and was restarted. It is designed to be highly concurrent and to handle several sources and sinks at the same time. The File Channel's design is roughly based on the paper about log-structured file systems by Rosenblum and Ousterhout [lfs-paper]. The design is discussed in more detail later in this section.

The File Channel is designed to be used in situations where data durability is required and data loss cannot be tolerated. Since the channel writes data to disk, it does not lose data on crash or failure. An additional bonus due to the fact that it writes data to disk is that the channel can have a very large capacity, especially compared to the Memory Channel.

As long as disk space is available, the File Channel can have an extremely large capacity, up to tens or hundreds of millions of events. This is especially useful when it is expected that the sinks taking from the channel will not be able to keep up with a limited peak period, and a large backlog of events is possible. The File Channel as a result can also handle much longer downstream downtimes, if configured correctly. Since the channel does not keep the events in memory once they've been committed, it requires much less heap space than a Memory Channel of equivalent capacity.

The File Channel guarantees that every event written to it will be available through agent and machine failures or restarts. It does this by writing out every event put to the channel to disk. Once a transaction is committed, the events in that transaction are made available for takes. The events are read from disk and passed to the sink when they are taken from the channel, and are completely dereferenced and eligible for removal once the take transaction is committed. More details on the implementation will be discussed later in this section.

The File Channel allows the user to configure the use of multiple disks by having them mounted at different mountpoints. When configured to use multiple disks, the channel round-robins between the disks, thus allowing the channel to perform better when more disks are available to it. It is recommended (though not required) to use a separate disk for the File Channel checkpoint. The checkpoint reflects the exact state of the channel at the instant the checkpoint was written out. The File Channel uses the checkpoint to restart quickly without having to read all the data files. It writes out the checkpoint to disk periodically while it is in operation. On restart, the channel loads the last checkpoint written out and only replays the puts and takes that happened after this checkpoint, allowing the channel to start up quickly and be ready for normal operation. The interval between two consecutive checkpoints is set to 30 seconds by default, though it is configurable.

The File Channel allows users to pass in several configuration parameters, allowing them to fine-tune the channel's performance based on the hardware. The configuration parameters for the File Channel are described in Table 4-2.

*Table 4-2. File Channel configuration*

| Config parameter | Default value | Description |
| --- | --- | --- |
| type | - | The alias for the File Channel is file. The FQCN is org.apache.flume.channel.file.FileChannel (case sensitive). |
| capacity | 1000000 | The maximum number of committed events the channel can hold. |
| transactionCapacity | 1000 | The maximum number of events that can be put or taken in a single transaction. |
| checkpointDir | ~/flume/ filechannel/ checkpoint | The directory to which the channel should write out the checkpoint. |
| dataDirs | ~/flume/ filechannel/data | A comma-separated list of directories to use to write the events to. Configuring multiple directories, each mounting a different disk, can dramatically improve performance by writing to the disks in parallel. |

| Config parameter | Default value | Description |
|---|---|---|
| useDualCheckpoints | false | Tells the channel whether to back up the checkpoint once it has completely been written out. This must be either true or false. If this is set to true, **backupCheckpointDir** must be set. |
| backupCheckpointDir | - | The directory to back up the checkpoint to. If the primary checkpoint is corrupt or incomplete, the channel can recover from the backup, thus avoiding a full replay of the data files. This parameter should point to a directory different to **checkpointDir**. |
| checkpointInterval | 30 | The time period (in seconds) between consecutive checkpoints. |
| maxFileSize | 1623195647 | The maximum size (in bytes) of each data file. Once the file reaches this size (or will reach it once the next event is written to it), the file is rolled and a new data file is created in that directory. If this value is set to higher than the default value, the channel still uses the default as the maximum value. |
| minimumRequiredSpace | 524288000 | The minimum amount of space (in bytes) required on each volume for the channel to continue operation. If any one of the volumes on which the data directories is mounted has only this much space remaining, the channel will stop operation to prevent corruption and avoid incomplete data being written out. The minimum possible value for this parameter is 1048576 (1 MB). |
| keep-alive | 3 | The maximum period of time (in seconds) each put or take should wait for completion. |

The File Channel, being Flume's main persistent channel, often dictates the performance of the agent as a whole. It is possible to fine-tune several aspects of the channel through configuration. The File Channel has capacity and transactionCapacity parameters, which are exactly the same as those of the Memory Channel, though they default to higher values of 1000000 and 1000, respectively.

As discussed earlier, the File Channel can write data to multiple disks, though the channel is not directly aware of this. Different disks can be mounted at different mountpoints and the channel can be configured to write data in a round-robin fashion to these directories. The channel will always append to exactly one file per data directory, though it will read from all of the files as required. Since multiple sources can write to the channel (and each source can write from multiple threads), the channel will write to different data directories in parallel from different threads (each source and sink runs at least one thread, and in many cases, like the Avro Source, they may run more than one thread), thus parallelizing disk usage, resulting in better performance. Therefore, if you give the File Channel more disks to work with, it is likely that the performance of the channel will improve.

The File Channel takes a comma-separated list of data directories as the value of the dataDirs parameter. The default value should only be used for testing and is not recommended for production use. Even for a single disk or a limited number of disks, multiple data directories can be used per disk for better performance, though the number of directories that can be used such that the performance improves will vary by disk.

The File Channel writes out a checkpoint periodically to make restart or recovery faster. The checkpoint is written to the directory specified as the value of the check pointDir parameter. If the channel is stopped while it is checkpointing, the checkpoint may be incomplete or corrupt. A corrupt or incomplete checkpoint could make the restart of the channel extremely slow, as the channel would need to read and replay all data files.

To avoid this problem, it is recommended that the useDualCheckpoints parameter be set to true and that backupCheckpointDir be set. It is recommended that this directory be on a different disk than the one where the original checkpoint is stored. When these parameters are set, Flume will back up the checkpoint to the backup CheckpointDir as soon as it is completed. This ensures that once the channel has been in operation for a brief period of time (enough time for the first checkpoint to be written out and backed up), it will be able to restart from a checkpoint, even if the newest one is corrupt or incomplete, reducing the restart time drastically. The time period between consecutive checkpoints is controlled by the checkpointInterval parameter.

The remaining parameters are meant to fine-tune the File Channel's performance and disk usage. Flume appends each event to the end of a data file and retains that file as long as the file contains events that have not yet been taken and committed, or is still being written to. The maximum size the file should grow to before Flume rolls it and considers it read-only is controlled by the maxFileSize parameter. This parameter defaults to the equivalent of about 1.6 GB, which is also the maximum value for this parameter. If this is set to higher than the default value, the file will still be rolled once it reaches the default size. It must be noted that each file is deleted if and only if all of the events written to the channel are taken and committed (in fact, the file is deleted only at the time of the checkpoint following the last event being taken and committed). If the files are to be deleted sooner, this parameter should be set to a lower value, so that all events get taken out from individual files faster (since the files are smaller, they will contain fewer events than a larger file). Keeping this value too small can lead to too many files being created on the disks being used, though, so it is better to not reduce this value from the default. The channel is also conservative with regard to deletion of files. It will always retain two files per data directory, even if the files do not have any events to be taken and committed. The channel will also not delete the file currently being written to.

To ensure that the channel does not write to disks with low disk space, the minimumRe quiredSpace parameter can be configured. Once the disk space on a specific disk goes down to the value set by this parameter (or 1 MB, whichever is higher), the channel ceases operation. To conserve system resources and not affect performance, the channel does not check the disk space on every write, but does it periodically, maintaining counters internally to calculate the space available on disk. *This makes the assumption that no other channel or process is writing to this disk, which would make the available disk space decrease faster.*

As discussed earlier, the File Channel writes a checkpoint out to disk periodically. As the checkpoint reflects the state of the channel at the time it was written, normal operations cannot be performed while the checkpoint is being written. The keep-alive parameter works similarly to the one in the Memory Channel, specifying the time to wait for capacity to be available or the checkpoint to complete for an event to be put or an event to be available for taking from the channel.

Typically, the channel performs better when more disks are available to it. If enough disk space is available, the channel should be configured to a capacity high enough to accommodate downstream failures or traffic spikes. Based on the expected through-put per channel and expected maximum downtime of downstream agents or destinations, the channel capacity can be configured to handle big backlogs. The channel is fast enough to be able to clear off tens of millions of events within a few minutes, though performance to a large extent will depend on the underlying hardware.

The following configuration file shows a File Channel named fc configured to be able to hold one million events. This channel stores data to three disks, writing to them in round-robin order. The channel is also configured to back up the checkpoint to a different directory to recover from failure quickly. It is configured to support transactions of up to 10,000 events. To garbage-collect files faster, the channel also sets the maximum file size of the data files to approximately 900 MB:

```
agent.channels = fc
agent.sources = sq

agent.channels.fc.type = file
agent.channels.fc.capacity = 1000000
agent.channels.fc.transactionCapacity = 10000
agent.channels.fc.checkpointDir = /data1/fc/checkpoint
agent.channels.fc.dataDirs = /data1/fc/data,/data2/fc/data,/data3/fc/data
agent.channels.fc.useDualCheckpoints = true
agent.channels.fc.backupCheckpointDir = /data4/fc/backup
agent.channels.fc.maxFileSize = 900000000

agent.sources.sq.type = seq
agent.sources.sq.channels = fc
```

### Best Practices with the File Channel

You can have the File Channel write to multiple disks by specifying several data directories in the configuration. Adding more disks directly improves performance, since the File Channel round-robins writes between disks.

The File Channel can back up the checkpoint and start from the backup if the checkpoint itself is incomplete or corrupt (this might happen if the machine or agent crashes while the channel is check-pointing). Enabling checkpoint backup allows the channel to restart fast even if the checkpoint itself is corrupt.

The File Channel can lose data if the disk it is writing to fails. Even if just one of the many disks the channel is writing data to fails, the channel may not be able to recover any of the data—even events that are on disks that have not failed. To avoid such a situation, it is a good idea to used RAID-ed disks with the File Channel.

Using NFS-mounted disks with the File Channel is not a good idea, since NFS does not provide the same guarantees as local disks. Specifically, the fsync system call does not guarantee that data is persisted onto a physical disk, so it is possible that the File Channel data might be lost if the machine or agent crashes.

### Design and implementation of the File Channel*

As discussed previously, the File Channel persists every event to disk and ensures that the events are available even in the event of agent or machine crashes and restarts. The File Channel also persists every operation that is performed to disk. This means the channel can replay each record in the same order as it happened to get itself back to the same state it was in when the channel shut down. When the channel has com-pleted replaying the records, it is ready for normal operation. In this section, we will take a more detailed look at the internals of the File Channel.

The File Channel maintains two separate data structures: the Flume event queue (which will be referred to as the *queue*) and the *write-ahead log* (WAL). Every put, take, commit, and rollback is represented by a transaction event record (referred to from here on as a *record*), with the type of the record representing the operation—put, take, commit, or rollback. Each File Channel operation is recorded in the WAL as a record. Each time an event is put into the channel, a put record is written to the WAL, even if the transaction does not actually get committed.

Similarly, for a take, a take record is written out. Each record has a unique, monoton-ically increasing ID, the write ID, which is recorded when the record is written to the WAL. Each record also contains the unique ID of the transaction that the record is a part of. Since each put (or take) record contains the transaction ID, it is possible to figure out which events were committed and which ones rolled back by mapping this transaction to the corresponding commit or rollback record.

By reading the WAL and performing each operation in the order it actually happened (which can be inferred from the write IDs of the operations), we can reconstruct the file state of the channel at any point. When the channel is reconstructed by reading all data files fully, it is called a *full replay*. Full replays are often time-consuming and disruptive, as all data files have to be read and every operation in the WAL has to be processed. This is especially true when the WAL contains millions of put records and take records—even if the final state contains very few events, each record has to be read and stored in memory until we read the corresponding commit or rollback record.

Each time a put happens, a put record is written to disk. Using the file ID and offset of the record in the file, the channel constructs a unique Flume event pointer for that record. Each time an event is put into the channel, the pointer representing the record is stored in an in-memory queue local to the transaction. When the transaction is committed, the pointers from the local queue are copied to the tail of the File Channel's main queue: the Flume event queue. That queue, therefore, represents the current state of the channel at any point in time.

When a sink takes an event from the channel, the head of the queue is removed and the pointer is dereferenced. The event is then stored in a queue local to the transaction. On commit, the local queue is discarded since the events are completely removed. On rollback, the events are pushed back into the queue. The queue is actually a memory-mapped file—the mapped buffer is updated and pushed to disk during a checkpoint.

At startup, Flume begins a process called *replay* to get the channel back to the exact state it was in when it was previously stopped. The queue is loaded back into memory at the time of startup by simply memory-mapping the checkpoint file. The data files are then read from the offset at the time of the checkpoint (this offset is recorded in the data files' metadata at the time of the checkpoint), and the puts and takes are applied to the queue in order.

All pointers representing the current incomplete transactions (called *inflights*) are also written to disk so that any events taken out but not yet committed at the time of the checkpoint can be reinserted into the queue after loading the checkpoint. Put transactions that were still in progress at the time of the checkpoint are also recovered using the inflight files. (There may be events in data files that were written before the checkpoint but committed after. They are not inserted into the queue at the time of the checkpoint and thus are not replayed from the data files, as the data files are replayed only from their offset at the time of the checkpoint.)

Once the replay is completed, the channel is ready for normal operation. When no queue is present or when it is incomplete, the channel does a full replay. As discussed earlier, the channel can back up each checkpoint immediately after it is completed, so that if the current checkpoint is corrupted, or the agent is killed before it is complete, the previous one can be loaded to avoid a full replay.

## Summary

In this chapter we discussed *channels*, which are buffers that sit between sources and sinks and hold the data brought into a Flume agent by a source, until it is removed by a sink. Channels can be in memory or on disk, with the in-memory *Memory Channel* giving better performance while the on-disk *File Channel* guarantees durability through agent and machine restarts by persisting all operations and data to disk.

In the next chapter, we will discuss how sinks are designed and the various sinks that come packaged with Flume. We will also look at how to write custom sinks.

## References

- [lfs-paper] "The design and implementation of a log-structured file system," *http://bit.ly/1wxCsoM*

# CHAPTER 5

# Sinks

Flume is designed with the ability to plug in practically every component, including the ones that write the data out to the eventual destination—in most cases, some data store.

The component that removes data from a Flume agent and writes it to another agent or a data store or some other system is called a *sink*. To facilitate this process, Flume allows the user to configure the sink, which could be one of the sinks that comes bundled with Flume or one that was written by the user (for custom sinks not built into Flume, the JARs should be dropped into Flume's *plugins.d* directory).

Sinks are the components in a Flume agent that keep draining the channel, so that the sources can continue receiving events and writing to the channel. Sinks continuously poll the channel for events and remove them in batches. These batches of events are either written out to a storage or indexing system, or sent to another Flume agent.

Sinks are fully transactional. Each sink starts a transaction with the channel before removing events in batches from it. Once the batch of events is successfully written out to storage or to the next Flume agent, the sink commits the transaction with the channel. Once the transaction is committed, the channel removes the events from its own internal buffers.

Flume comes packaged with a number of sinks that can write to storage and indexing systems such as HDFS, HBase, Solr, Elastic Search, etc. These sinks are what are generally referred to as *terminal* sinks, because they usually appear at the terminus of a Flume pipeline. Flume pipelines are built by Flume agents that send data to one another. This communication happens via the RPC sink–source pairs. Flume comes packaged with Avro- and Thrift-based RPC sinks that can be used to send data to the respective RPC sources on remote Flume agents.

In this chapter, we will discuss the various sinks, their configuration and management, how to serialize data for each of them so the data can be written in a format of the user's choice, and how to write custom sinks.

# Lifecycle of a Sink

Sinks are configured using the standard Flume configuration system. Each agent can have zero or more sinks. Each sink can read events from exactly one channel. If no channel is configured for a sink, the sink is removed from the agent. The configuration system ensures that:

- Each sink reads from exactly one properly configured "connected" channel.
- Each sink has a defined type parameter.
- The sink is in the active list of sinks for the agent.

Like sources, each sink (if properly configured) is instantiated by the Configuration Provider and then configured. Misconfigured sinks and sinks whose configure method throws an exception are removed from the agent. Once sinks are configured, they are started by the configuration system. Flume can group threads together into *sink groups*, which we will discuss in a later section. Each sink group can contain one or more sinks. If no sink group is defined for a sink, then the sink can be thought of as being in a group with that sink as its only member.

Each sink group is run by a *sink runner*, which is a single thread that calls the process method in a loop on the sink group, which in turn forwards the call to the process method of one of the sinks in the group. The process method returns Status.READY if the sink can immediately process more events, usually when the current call processed at least one event. If the sink failed to process any events, the sink returns Status.BACKOFF, indicating that the runner thread should back off for some time before trying again. *It is not mandatory to define sink groups for sinks.* If a sink is active, but not in a sink group, it gets a sink runner for itself, which calls the sink's process method. The backoff semantics for this sink are the same as those for a sink group. We will discuss when to use sink groups and sink processors in "Sink Groups and Sink Processors" on page 157.

Sinks can be specified in the configuration using either their FQCNs or, for built-in sinks, their aliases. Each sink must have exactly one channel configured. The sink is started only if the channel was configured correctly and started successfully. Table 5-1 lists the required parameters.

*Table 5-1. Mandatory configuration parameters for all sinks*

| Parameter | Description |
|---|---|
| type | The type of the sink. This can be the fully qualified class name or the alias of the sink (only for sinks that are part of Flume itself). The class must be in Flume's classpath. The alias for each of Flume's built-in sinks is mentioned in the relevant section. |
| channel | The channel to read events from. |

Like all other components (other than the Memory Channel), instances of sinks are not reused when Flume is reconfigured. Therefore, the sinks *should not buffer* any events that have been taken and committed. This is because committing the transaction indicates that the channel can delete the events that were taken in the context of that transaction. Buffering these events in the sinks could lead to data loss when the agent restarts, since the data is not in a persistent store or buffer, but in internal data structures owned by the sink that may not get reused. Once committed, the sinks must guarantee that the events have been committed to the next agent's channel (in the case of RPC sinks) or were persisted to the final destination.

# Optimizing the Performance of Sinks

Each sink is, in general, run by one thread: the sink runner. Since each sink is run by one thread, and most sinks tend to be I/O-bound, there may be instances when the sink is waiting on I/O to complete and no events are being removed from the channel. Therefore, in most cases, when an individual sink is notably slower than the write rate to a particular channel, it is worthwhile to add multiple sinks that write to the same destination and read from the same channel. This is especially useful for the HDFS and HBase Sinks, for improving the write rate to HDFS or HBase.

The number of sinks required for optimal performance depends on various factors, including the sink being used, the destination (Avro Source/HDFS/HBase), the network throughput, the channel, and the I/O performance of the disks the channel is using. Therefore, it is usually a good idea to try various configurations with varying numbers of sinks before settling on one. While increasing the number of sinks to improve performance, one must also ensure that resources don't end up being over-utilized, creating situations where there is too much context switching or networks are being clogged. When this point is reached, it indicates that the hardware on that machine is being utilized to the maximum; if the HDFS or HBase cluster still has capacity, more Flume agents can be added on other machines.

# Writing to HDFS: The HDFS Sink

Flume was primarily designed to write data in a scalable way to HDFS. Often users have hundreds or even thousands of data sources writing data to HDFS. If all these sources wrote data directly to HDFS, it would create a lot of stress on the name node and the HDFS cluster in general. It is therefore recommended to fan in the data using multiple tiers of Flume agents, with the last and smallest tier writing data to HDFS. This is explained in "Complex Flows" on page 17. The agents that eventually write data into HDFS will use the HDFS Sink to do so. The HDFS Sink is very flexible and can be configured to write to different directories based on event headers, the time-stamp of the event (or current time at the sink), etc. We will look into the details of how the sink works with respect to the bucketing of events into different directories on HDFS later in this section.

The HDFS Sink allows the user to customize the format in which events are written to HDFS using *serializers* that the user can write and deploy. The HDFS Sink supports both Hadoop 1 and Hadoop 2, though the code has to be specifically compiled against the relevant version of Hadoop. For example, Flume compiled against Hadoop 2 will not be able to write data to a Hadoop 1 HDFS cluster. This is due to binary incompatible changes between Hadoop 1 and 2. Therefore, the binaries compiled against the specific version of HDFS in use must be used. Apache Flume currently ships only binaries compiled against Hadoop 1, but there are several vendors who ship binaries compatible with their own distributions based on Hadoop 2 (they may not work against the binaries shipped by the Apache Hadoop project, though).

The HDFS Sink writes data to *buckets* on HDFS. A bucket, for all practical purposes, is a directory (though multiple sinks can write to the same directory, the user needs to carefully configure it in such a way that exactly one sink writes to a given file). We can therefore think of a bucket as a directory to which the HDFS Sink writes data, based on the criteria specified by the configuration.

An HDFS Sink can write data to multiple buckets at the same time, though each event will go to exactly one bucket. Each bucket will have at most one file open at any point in time, though each sink could have several files open in different buckets. Flume allows the user to dynamically create buckets based on various parameters specified in the configuration file, like the timestamp in the event headers, a specific header's value, etc. Each event is then evaluated based on these parameters and written to exactly one bucket. The HDFS Sink processes events in batches and flushes all events in a batch to HDFS.

If the version of HDFS Flume is writing to supports it, Flume flushes the entire batch to data node memory, and the data will then be available for reads by other processes. Data visibility is an important aspect of working with HDFS, and it is important to understand when the data written by Flume will be visible to other processes. By default, Flume *does not* write to hidden files on HDFS, but to files that end with a *.tmp* extension. This can be changed in the configuration. Since Flume writes each batch of events out and flushes the data out to HDFS, other processes running on HDFS will be able to see data written by Flume immediately after the batch is successfully flushed to HDFS. If Flume fails to write an event to HDFS or the write times out, the sink rolls back the transaction with the channel and closes the file that was being written to. Only if the write was successful will the sink commit the transaction with the channel, thus ensuring that the data is removed from the channel if and only if the data was successfully written to HDFS. If an event gets written to the same bucket again, then a new file is created by the sink.

## Understanding Buckets

As discussed previously, sinks can decide which directory on HDFS an event gets written to. The HDFS Sink builds the bucket path using several parameters. To build these paths dynamically, the configuration file must specify a path as the parameter of hdfs.path. This path can specify one or more escape sequences that the sink will replace to construct the real path to which to write the event.

To generate the filenames dynamically, the value of the hdfs.filePrefix parameter also can be escaped. In simple words, *escaping* is done by replacing a sequence of characters specified in the configuration with another sequence. In the HDFS Sink, all escape sequences begin with a % character. The HDFS Sink recognizes several escape sequences, replacing each of them with another value. We'll illustrate this with an example, showing how Flume can insert the value of a specific event header into the path.

Consider adding the following configuration parameter to an HDFS Sink:

```
agent.sinks.hdfsSink.hdfs.path = /Data/Flume/%{topic}
```

When the HDFS Sink reads an event off of the channel, it reads the value of the topic header and replaces the escape sequence in the path from the configuration parameter with the value of the header named topic. For example, an event whose topic header has the value inputData would get written out to a file in the directory on HDFS with the path */Data/Flume/inputData*. Another event whose topic header has the value logData would get written out to a file in the directory on HDFS with the path */Data/Flume/logData*. This configuration parameter is often used to replace host information that was inserted by the host interceptor, or, more often, the timestamps inserted by the timestamp interceptor or by the system that generated the event.

The HDFS Sink provides extremely powerful escaping of timestamps. It supports several escape sequences that use the value of the timestamp event header. To use the timestamp for escaping, the sink expects a numerical value for the header with the key `timestamp` (or the `hdfs.useLocalTimestamp` parameter in the configuration must be set to `true`). The HDFS Sink considers the value of the timestamp to be in epoch time, defined as the total number of seconds since 00:00:00 UTC on January 1, 1970, not counting leap seconds. Based on the value of this header, the sink can replace multiple escape sequences with a corresponding value. The escape sequences based on timestamps are listed in Table 5-2.

*Table 5-2. HDFS Sink timestamp escape sequences*

| Escape sequences | Replacement value |
| --- | --- |
| %t | Epoch time in milliseconds |
| %s | Epoch time in seconds |
| %H | Hour of the day specified in 24-hour clock (00..23) |
| %I | Hour specified in 12-hour clock (01..12) |
| %M | Minute of the hour (00..59) |
| %S | Second of the minute (00..59) |
| %k | Same as %H, except that the leading 0 is removed (0..23) |
| %p | AM or PM (or their equivalent in the current locale) |
| %z | Time zone specified as offset from UTC in +hhmm format (e.g., +0530 would represent Indian Standard Time, 5 hours 30 minutes ahead of GMT) |
| %a | Short name for the day of the week in the current locale (e.g., Mon, Tue, etc.) |
| %A | Long name for the day of the week in the current locale (e.g., Monday, Tuesday, etc.) |
| %b | Short name for the month in the current locale (e.g., Jan, Feb, etc.) |
| %B | Long name for the month in the current locale (e.g., January, February, etc.) |
| %d | Day of the month (e.g., 01, 02, etc.) |
| %c | Day, date, and time specified in the current locale (e.g., Sun Feb 9 14:05:45 2014) |

| Escape sequences | Replacement value |
| --- | --- |
| %m | Numerical representation for month (e.g., January would be 01) |
| %D | Date represented as mm/dd/yy |
| %y | Years since the beginning of the century (00..99) |
| %Y | The current year (e.g., 2013, 2014, etc.) |

Multiple escape sequences can be used in the same path. This essentially means that users can bucket their messages according to the date, hour, minute, etc., as shown here:

```
agent.sinks.hdfsSink.hdfs.path = /Data/Flume/%{topic}/%Y/%m/%d/%H
```

This example would write all events with timestamps within the same hour in the same directory for each topic. If an event with topic UsingFlume came in with a time-stamp of 2:35 PM on September 1, 2014, it would get written to the */Data/Flume/UsingFlume/2014/09/01/14* directory.

Most often time-based bucketing is used to load data into systems like Hive or Impala by running a query to load the data into the system a few minutes after the hour, usu-ally using Oozie or a cron job (to account for the delay in the Flume pipeline). One important aspect of such bucketing is that it is possible for data to be written to a bucket with an older timestamp, since the timestamp used by the sink is based on the header in the event—if the timestamp is inserted on event creation or by an intercep-tor in a Flume agent, agent downtime or network delays can cause the event to arrive at the HDFS Sink much later than that time. If a Hive query is loading data based on time-based buckets, such delayed writes must be accounted for. If only the latest directories are scanned, then the new data in directories with much older timestamps may never get loaded.

The HDFS Sink has a configuration parameter, hdfs.useLocalTimestamp, that if set to true forces the sink to use the system timestamp of the machine that is running the agent; it can be used to ensure that the data gets written based on the local time-stamp. This parameter should be used with caution, since the HDFS cluster and the Flume agent may not be synchronized and may not have exactly the same time.

One issue with the time-based bucketing configuration described here is that bucket-ing can be done per year, day, hour, minute, or second, but it is not possible to create a new bucket once every few minutes; for example, a new bucket every 10 minutes. If the user wants buckets for every 10 minutes, he will need to have buckets for each minute—which means he could end up with a large number of small files on HDFS. The HDFS Sink does provide a way to achieve this, though, through a combination of configuration parameters. The three configuration parameters required are shown in Table 5-3.

*Table 5-3. HDFS Sink round-down parameters*

| Parameter | Default value | Description |
|---|---|---|
| hdfs.round | false | Indicates whether the timestamp on the event should be rounded down. |
| hdfs.roundValue | 1 | The timestamp will be rounded to the largest multiple of this parameter in the units specified by the hdfs.roundUnit parameter. |
| hdfs.roundUnit | second | The unit of the hdfs.roundValue configuration parameter (can be second, minute, or hour). |

If the hdfs.round parameter is true, the HDFS Sink reads the timestamp from the event headers and rounds it down to the highest multiple of the value specified by hdfs.roundValue in the unit specified by hdfs.roundUnit. Rounded-down values are not used when the %t escape sequence is used. Let's consider a sink with the configuration parameters shown here:

```
agent.sinks.hdfsSink.hdfs.path = /Data/Flume/%{topic}/%Y/%m/%d/%H/%M
agent.sinks.hdfsSink.hdfs.round = true
agent.sinks.hdfsSink.hdfs.roundUnit = minute
agent.sinks.hdfsSink.hdfs.roundValue = 10
```

If an event with the timestamp equivalent of *2:35* PM on September 1, 2014 comes in, the HDFS Sink rounds the timestamp down to *2:30* PM on September 1, 2014 and writes the event out to the */Data/Flume/UsingFlume/2014/09/01/14/30* directory. In fact, every event between 2:30:00:00:000 PM and 2:39:59:59:999 will get written out to the same directory. Using a similar configuration mechanism (as shown next), the user can have buckets of two hours each:

```
agent.sinks.hdfsSink.hdfs.path = /Data/Flume/%{topic}/%Y/%m/%d/%H/%M
agent.sinks.hdfsSink.hdfs.round = true
agent.sinks.hdfsSink.hdfs.roundUnit = hour
agent.sinks.hdfsSink.hdfs.roundValue = 2
```

## Configuring the HDFS Sink

The HDFS Sink has quite a large number of configuration parameters, allowing the user to control the behavior of the sink at a pretty granular level. Table 5-4 lists the parameters that are used to configure the HDFS Sink.

*Table 5-4. HDFS Sink configuration*

| Parameter | Default value | Description |
|---|---|---|
| **type** | - | The alias for the HDFS Sink is `hdfs`. The FQCN, which is `org.apache.flume.sink.hdfs.HDFSEventSink`, can also be used. |
| **hdfs.path** | | The directory path this sink should write to. Escape sequences are allowed. |
| hdfs.filePrefix | FlumeData | The prefix of the filename. The filename will consist of this prefix followed by a number and then the name. |
| hdfs.fileSuffix | - | The suffix to use for the filenames. If extensions are required, the "." should be explicitly specified. |
| hdfs.inUsePrefix | - | The prefix to use for the filename while the HDFS Sink is writing to it. |
| hdfs.inUseSuffix | .tmp | The suffix to use for the filename while the HDFS Sink is writing to it. |
| hdfs.timeZone | - | The time zone to use for creating the bucket path. |
| hdfs.rollInterval | 30 | The time in seconds before a file is rolled. Set this to 0 to disable time-based file rolling. |
| hdfs.rollSize | 1024 | The number of events to be written into a file before it is rolled. Set this to 0 to disable event count–based file rolling. |
| hdfs.batchSize | 100 | The maximum number of events to write per batch. |
| hdfs.idleTimeout | 0 | The maximum time period in seconds to wait between consecutive events to a file before closing it. Setting this to 0 disables this. |
| hdfs.fileType | SequenceFile | The file format to use. This can be one of `SequenceFile`, `Data Stream`, or `CompressedStream`. |
| hdfs.codeC | - | The compression codec to be used to compress the file. This can be one of `gzip`, `bzip2`, `lzo`, `lzop`, or `snappy`. |
| hdfs.maxOpenFiles | 5000 | The maximum number of files the HDFS Sink can keep open at a time. |
| hdfs.callTimeout | 10000 | The delay, in milliseconds, to wait before timing out each HDFS operation. |
| hdfs.threadsPoolSize | 10 | The number of threads in the pool that performs HDFS operations. |

| Parameter | Default value | Description |
| --- | --- | --- |
| hdfs.rollTimerPoolSize | 1 | The number of threads in the pool that rolls HDFS files based on the hdfs.rollInterval and hdfs.idleTimeout parameters. |
| hdfs.kerberosPrincipal | - | The Kerberos principal to use to log in to the Kerberos key distribution center (KDC) (to be used with secure HDFS). |
| hdfs.kerberosKeytab | - | The path to the keytab file to use with hdfs.kerberosPrincipal to log in to the KDC (to be used with secure HDFS). |
| hdfs.proxyUser | - | The user Flume should impersonate, if required. If set to none, Flume writes data as the current user. |
| hdfs.useLocalTimeStamp | false | If set to true, the HDFS Sink will use the timestamp on the current agent to do time-based bucketing. |
| hdfs.round | false | Indicates whether the timestamp on the event should be rounded down. |
| hdfs.roundUnit | second | The unit of the hdfs.roundValue configuration parameter (can be second, minute, or hour). |
| hdfs.roundValue | 1 | The timestamp will be rounded to the largest multiple of this parameter in the units specified by the hdfs.roundUnit parameter. |
| serializer | TEXT | The serializer to use. Other built-in serializers can be used by setting this to AVRO_EVENT or HEADER_AND_TEXT. To use a custom class, this should be the FQCN of the Builder class of the serializer, which implements EventSerializer$Builder. The serializer itself must implement EventSerializer. See "Controlling the Data Format Using Serializers*" on page 108. |
| serializer.* | - | Configuration parameters to be passed to the serializer. See "Controlling the Data Format Using Serializers*" on page 108. |

To use the HDFS Sink, set the sink's type parameter to hdfs or use the FQCN org.apache.flume.sink.hdfs.HDFSEventSink.

The HDFS Sink requires the user to supply a directory path to which the files are written. This directory path should be passed in as the value of the hdfs.path parameter. This parameter supports bucketing, as explained in "Understanding Buckets" on page 97. Therefore, this path need not actually specify exactly one directory, but rather a set of directories based on the bucketing specified. The name of each file created by the HDFS Sink follows a specific pattern specified by a set of parameters in the HDFS configuration.

The `hdfs.filePrefix` parameter specifies the prefix of the filename to be used. Bucketing is allowed in this parameter, but time-based bucketing will be done only when the first file is created and will remain the same for all files in the bucket, so it is best to avoid time-based bucketing and use only header-based bucketing in the file prefixes.

The `hdfs.fileSuffix` parameter can be used to specify a suffix for a filename. Usually, the extension for the file is specified using this parameter. Flume will not automatically add a period (.) before the extension, so if an extension like "txt" is required, the value of this parameter should be specified as `.txt`. Eventually, the filename will be composed of the file prefix, the file suffix, and a counter in between. Consider the following configuration:

```
agent.sinks.hdfsSink.hdfs.filePrefix = UsingFlume
agent.sinks.hdfsSink.hdfs.fileSuffix = .oreilly
```

This configuration would eventually yield files that would be named something like *UsingFlume.33434321.oreilly*, *UsingFlume.33434322.oreilly*, etc.

When the file is still being written to, it is recommended that systems like Hive or MapReduce ignore the file until Flume closes it. This ensures that the content of the file does not get updated while MapReduce or Hive is reading from it. Unfortunately, it is not easy to find out if a file is being written to and if the content will get updated. To work around this problem, the HDFS Sink allows the user to add a suffix and prefix to the filename that get removed once the file is closed by Flume.

By using these parameters, the MapReduce job or Hive query can filter out such files. While the file is being written to, the filename will have the in-use prefix at the beginning, the in-use suffix at the end, and the eventual filename in between (based on the file prefix and file suffix parameters explained earlier). Once again, let's look at a configuration example:

```
agent.sinks.hdfsSink.hdfs.filePrefix = UsingFlume
agent.sinks.hdfsSink.hdfs.fileSuffix = .oreilly
agent.sinks.hdfsSink.hdfs.inUsePrefix = .
agent.sinks.hdfsSink.hdfs.inUseSuffix = .temp
```

This would create files that are named *.UsingFlume.33434321.oreilly.temp*, *.UsingFlume.33434322.oreilly.temp*, etc., which once closed would get renamed to *UsingFlume.33434321.oreilly*, *UsingFlume.33434322.oreilly*, etc. The previous configuration ensures that the files are hidden until they are eventually closed, when they get renamed to the filenames defined by the `hdfs.filePrefix` and `hdfs.fileSuffix` parameters described earlier.

The HDFS Sink can do bucketing based on time, as described in "Understanding Buckets" on page 97. The sink translates the epoch timestamp to dates and times for bucketing, based on the `hdfs.timeZone` parameter. If no time zone is specified, the local time zone of the machine running the agent is used. Time zones are specified in the standard format specified by the Internet Assigned Numbers Authority (IANA) [tz-list].

To make sure the files are closed and the data is available to systems that process the data, the HDFS Sink can be configured to roll the files based on time, event counts, or the precompressed size of events written to the file. The hdfs.rollInterval parameter controls the rolling of files based on time. Each file is flushed, closed, and renamed after the time (in seconds) specified by this parameter. Setting this to 0 disables time-based rolling.

The HDFS Sink can also roll the files based on the number of events written to them. The hdfs.rollCount parameter controls this. Setting this to 0 disables count-based rolling. Finally, it is possible to roll the files based on the total size of the event bodies in them using the hdfs.rollSize parameter (this is the precompressed size even if the data is being written in a compressed format). The value of this parameter is specified in bytes. As soon as one of the rolling parameters is reached, the file is rolled (e.g., even if the number of events reaches the roll count before the roll interval is reached, then the file is rolled). So, more than one of these can be enabled at the same time.

When time-based bucketing is used, it is possible that after a certain point in time, no more events get written to a bucket. It will take at least as long as the roll interval, if enabled, for the file to be closed. If the roll interval is not enabled, such a file might never get closed. So, it is always recommended to set hdfs.idleTimeout, which is the time in seconds to wait before closing a file after the last event was written to the file. In most cases, it makes sense to set this value much smaller than the roll interval, so the data becomes available sooner than the roll interval when data is no longer being written to a bucket. It should, though, be set to be slightly more than the average time between events being written to a bucket, so that the files don't get closed more often than required—otherwise, there would be many small files on HDFS, which can stress the HDFS name node.

When there are multiple HDFS Sinks writing to HDFS, in the same agent or different agents, it is important that each agent writes to a different directory or uses different file prefixes. This is important because exactly one HDFS Sink can write to each file; other HDFS Sinks attempting to write to the same files might face exceptions and will not be able to write the data. To avoid this, it is advisable to bucket the data in such a way that each HDFS Sink "owns" the directory it is writing to and no other sink or process is writing to it. This can be done by using the hostname and sink name as part of the bucket name (the hostname can be inserted by the host interceptor that comes bundled with Flume), or by using the multiplexing channel selector to make sure exactly one HDFS Sink writes data belonging to a certain topic, etc.

The HDFS Sink allows users to write data as sequence files or compressed files, or in any binary or text format. The hdfs.fileType parameter controls the file format. To write the data as sequence files, set this parameter to SequenceFile. For sequence files, Flume writes the event body as the value corresponding to a numerical key, written as a LongWritable. If there is a timestamp in the event headers, that is used as the key; otherwise, the current time in milliseconds is used. The event body is itself written out as a ByteWritable or a TextWritable, based on the hdfs.writeFormat parameter. To use TextWritable, this parameter should be set to text; it should be set to writable for ByteWritable. When using sequence files, the serializer and serializer.* parameters are ignored. The hdfs.writeFormat parameter is ignored when using a data stream or compressed stream.

The HDFS Sink allows the user to specify a *serializer* to convert the events into a data format suitable to the user. The serializer is enabled and used only if the file type is set to DataStream or CompressedStream. The serializer can then write the data to disk in the format of its choice. The serializer can do any compression internally, but Flume itself does not compress the data being written using a data stream. To compress the data, the file type must be set to CompressedStream, and the hdfs.codeC parameter should be set to one of gzip, bzip2, lzo, lzop, or snappy, indicating which codec to use to write to HDFS. The codec should not be set when a data stream is used. When a compressed stream is used, files are written using the correct extension for the compression codec configured if the file suffix is not specified (file suffix will override the default extension for the codec).

If required, HDFS can be secured using Kerberos [kerberos]. The HDFS Sink can write to a secure HDFS cluster using credentials that are specified in the configuration file. The hdfs.kerberosPrincipal parameter specifies the principal to be used to log in to a key distribution center (KDC). The hdfs.kerberosKeytab parameter should specify the full path to the Kerberos keytab file. This file should be readable by the user running the Flume agent and must contain the keytab corresponding to the principal being used. HDFS allows users to impersonate other users. Flume supports this feature through the hdfs.proxyUser parameter. To impersonate another user, specify that the user's username as the value to this parameter, and Flume will write data to HDFS as that user. See the HDFS documentation [impersonation] for details on configuring this. To use this functionality, the user running the Flume agent must be authorized to impersonate the user Flume is writing as in the HDFS configuration.

### Kerberos, HDFS, and HBase Sinks

All HDFS Sinks within the same agent must use the same Kerberos credentials to log in. In addition, all HBase Sinks must use the same credentials. Using different credentials for different HDFS and HBase Sinks will cause one or more of them to not be able to write to HDFS or HBase. If multiple HDFS or HBase clusters need the same data but have different credentials, the data must be routed from the originating Flume agent (the one that received/generated the data) to different Flume agents, each writing using one of the multiple credentials. This can easily be done by having multiple channels attached to the source that receives the data, having an Avro Sink pulling out from each of these channels, and sending them to different Flume agents that write to HDFS.

The HDFS Sink can time out each HDFS operation after a configured time period. This ensures that the sink does not stop processing events in case a data node hangs. The timeout is configured in milliseconds as the value of the `hdfs.callTimeout` parameter. The optimum value of this parameter depends on the user's specific deployment and should be configured carefully to avoid too many timeouts occuring or the sink waiting for too long, as this might affect throughput. These operations are performed using a separate thread pool whose size can be configured using the `hdfs.threadsPoolSize` parameter, though this rarely needs to be changed.

To trigger rolling and idle timeouts, Flume uses a separate thread pool whose size can be configured too, though this is rarely required. This can be tweaked using the `hdfs.rollTimerPoolSize` parameter.

The HDFS client API keeps internal buffers for open files, especially for compressed files. To limit the number of files open and thus conserve the resources used, the sink automatically closes files that were written to earliest, once the number of open files reaches an upper limit. This upper limit is specified by the `hdfs.maxOpenFiles` parameter.

The `hdfs.useLocalTimestamp` parameter, if set to `true`, would use the local time on the machine hosting the agent for time-based bucketing.

The maximum number of events written out per transaction is controlled by `hdfs.batchSize` (provided there are enough events available in the channel—if there are fewer events in the channel, the batch is considered complete immediately). Each transaction with the channel is committed per batch.

Let's take a look at some real examples of HDFS configuration. The following configuration writes events out in 10-minute buckets, using time-based bucketing and rounding, in Snappy format. The files will automatically get suffixed with *.snappy* if no file suffix is configured. The sink rolls files every 2 minutes or when 100,000 events have been written to a file, whichever comes first, and closes a file if it's been open for 30 seconds with no writes, using idle timeout. The sink also rolls the file if 128 MB of uncompressed data has been written to the file.

This sink writes events as text using the built-in TEXT serializer. The sink also closes the files that were written to earliest when 100 files are open at any point in time. It uses Kerberos credentials to log in using the flume principal, and writes data as the UsingFlume user. The flume user must be authorized to impersonate the UsingFlume user in the HDFS configuration. When a file is being written to this sink keeps it hidden by using the . prefix, and suffixes the filename with *.temporary*. Once the file is rolled, it is renamed to the eventual filename:

```
agent.sinks = hdfsSink
agent.channels = memoryChannel

agent.channels.memoryChannel.type = memory
agent.channels.memoryChannel.capacity = 10000

agent.sinks.hdfsSink.type = hdfs
agent.sinks.hdfsSink.channel = memory
agent.sinks.hdfsSink.hdfs.path = /Data/UsingFlume/%{topic}/%Y/%m/%d/%H/%M
agent.sinks.hdfsSink.hdfs.filePrefix = UsingFlumeData
agent.sinks.hdfsSink.hdfs.inUsePrefix = .
agent.sinks.hdfsSink.hdfs.inUseSuffix = .temporary
agent.sinks.hdfsSink.hdfs.fileType = CompressedStream
agent.sinks.hdfsSink.hdfs.codeC = snappy
agent.sinks.hdfsSink.hdfs.rollSize = 128000000
agent.sinks.hdfsSink.hdfs.rollCount = 100000
agent.sinks.hdfsSink.hdfs.rollInterval = 120
agent.sinks.hdfsSink.hdfs.idleTimeout = 30
agent.sinks.hdfsSink.hdfs.maxOpenFiles = 100
agent.sinks.hdfsSink.hdfs.round = true
agent.sinks.hdfsSink.hdfs.roundUnit = minute
agent.sinks.hdfsSink.hdfs.roundValue = 10
agent.sinks.hdfsSink.hdfs.kerberosPrincipal = flume/_HOST@OREILLY.COM
agent.sinks.hdfsSink.hdfs.kerberosKeytab = /etc/flume/conf/UsingFlume.keytab
agent.sinks.hdfsSink.hdfs.proxyUser = UsingFlume
```

**Writing to Hadoop 1 and Hadoop 2***

Flume can write to HDFS from Hadoop 1 or Hadoop 2. The binary artifacts released by the Apache Software Foundation are built against Hadoop 1. If data is being written to a Hadoop 2.x cluster, then the user must recompile Flume using the command `mvn clean install -Dhadoop.profile=2` (this command requires that HBase 0.94.2 compiled against Hadoop 2.x be available in the Maven cache), or `mvn clean install -Dhadoop.profile=hbase-98` to compile against Hadoop 2.4.0 and HBase 0.98. Flume does not package Hadoop or its dependencies with Flume's binaries. If Hadoop is installed on the machine, Flume will automatically pick up the dependencies; otherwise, the user must add the directories that contain HDFS client libraries and their dependencies to Flume's classpath. Hadoop vendors usually ship the versions of HDFS client libraries that the Flume binaries they ship use.

# Controlling the Data Format Using Serializers*

The data written out to HDFS will eventually be consumed by various other systems. Therefore, it is important that the HDFS Sink be flexible enough to support data formats that can be understood by these systems. The HDFS Sink allows users to write data to HDFS in a format that is suitable for them by allowing the users to plug in serializers that convert the Flume events into a format that can be understood by the systems that process them and writes them out to a stream that eventually gets flushed out to HDFS. Flume comes packaged with a few serializers that support common formats such as text and Avro. Remember that serializers are used only when events the HDFS sink is configured to use data stream or compressed stream. This section will illustrate how to write a serializer and how to tell the HDFS Sink to use that serializer.

## File Formats

When writing data to HDFS, or any other system where the data is likely to be processed by applications and not meant for humans to read, it makes much more sense to use binary formats like Avro, Protobuf, etc. Binary formats are often more efficient when it comes to the amount of space taken on disk, and hence the amount of time taken to write the data out. This is because binary formats can more efficiently encode the data—an integer is four bytes in Avro, while if text is used, it will be more than four bytes if the number has more than four digits (in plain old ASCII). Several binary formats are also able to compress the data before writing it.

With Flume, there is another significant advantage to binary formats. Flume writes out transactions in batches to HDFS, which allocates blocks as and when required. If a block allocation fails or if the write fails for any other reason, a partial event might get written. Flume will retry the event in a new file when such a failure occurs, but the partial event will still be there in the HDFS file. If this partial event represents a row of data that Hive is to consume, it might fail the Hive query since the data might not make sense or might be incomplete. Even worse, there is no way to know whether the data was valid if the parsing did not fail, since the write may have failed in the middle of the last column in a row. Such failures can cause *bad* data to be processed. On the other hand, binary formats will fail to read an incomplete write, usually by means of an exception—thus letting the application reading the data know that the data is bad and can be skipped. In such a case, the reading application can just move on to the next file. Being better at error detection, binary formats should generally be used to write data out from Flume.

What about binary columnar formats like RCFile, ORCFile, Parquet, etc.? Most columnar formats are optimized for bulk writes, i.e., writing large batches of data in a single write. Flume, on the other hand, writes data as it comes in. This may not be very suitable for such formats. A good way to use formats like Parquet with Flume is to write data as Avro and then convert it into Parquet using the tools that come with Parquet or using Impala.

An HDFS serializer is usually a pretty simple class that can be configured using the Flume configuration system. The serializer class itself must implement the `org.apache.flume.serialization.EventSerializer` interface. Flume requires that the class be built using a builder class that inherits from the `org.apache.flume.seri alization.EventSerializer.Builder` class. All builder classes must have a public no-argument constructor, which is used by the sink while instantiating the builder.

The `EventSerializer` interface is shown in Example 5-1.

*Example 5-1. EventSerializer interface*

```
package org.apache.flume.serialization;
public interface EventSerializer {
  public static String CTX_PREFIX = "serializer.";
  public void afterCreate() throws IOException;
  public void afterReopen() throws IOException;
  public void write(Event event) throws IOException;
  public void flush() throws IOException;
  public void beforeClose() throws IOException;
  public boolean supportsReopen();
  public interface Builder {
    public EventSerializer build(Context context, OutputStream out);
  }
}
```

The HDFS Sink passes an `OutputStream` instance and a `Context` instance to the builder, which in turn builds and configures the `Serializer` instance that is returned to the sink. The serializer is expected to convert the events passed in to its write method into the required format and then write the data out to the output stream provided. Serializers can be configured using the Context instance passed in.

The afterOpen method is called immediately after the file is opened. This method can be used to write file-level header information, like the top-level tag in a serializer that may be writing data in XML.

Every time the sink reads an event, the write method is called. This method is responsible for converting the Flume event into the required format and then writing it to the output stream. Once the sink completes an entire batch, it calls the flush method. This method must flush the data in any internal buffers of the serializer into the stream itself. If the stream is wrapped in a BufferedOutputStream by the serializer, the serializer must flush the buffered stream so that all data is flushed to the output stream passed in to the serializer. The serializer need not flush the stream that is passed in, since that is done by the HDFS Sink itself.

Just before the HDFS Sink closes the file, the beforeClose method is called. This method can be used to write any trailers to the file (like the closing top-level header). If the supportsReopen method returns true, the HDFS Sink may append to the file. So, this method must return true only if the file can be closed and then reopened for writes.

The serializer shown in Example 5-2 serializes Flume events into a file that contains serialized Protobufs using the Protobuf definition shown in Example 3-8. Each event is represented as an integer representing the length of the event followed by the Protobuf serialized event.

*Example 5-2. Protobuf event serializer*

```
package usingflume.ch05;

public class ProtobufSerializer implements EventSerializer {
  private final boolean writeHeaderAndFooter;
  private final BufferedOutputStream stream;
  private static final byte[] footer = ("End Using Flume protobuf " +
    "file").getBytes();
  private static final byte[] header = ("Begin Using Flume protobuf" +
    " file").getBytes();


  private ProtobufSerializer(Context ctx, OutputStream stream) {
    writeHeaderAndFooter = ctx.getBoolean("writeHeaderAndFooter",
      false);
    this.stream = new BufferedOutputStream(stream);
  }

  @Override
```

```java
public void afterCreate() throws IOException {
  if(writeHeaderAndFooter) {
    stream.write(header);
  }
}

@Override
public void afterReopen() throws IOException {

}

@Override
public void write(Event event) throws IOException {
  UsingFlumeEvent.Event.Builder
    builder = UsingFlumeEvent.Event.newBuilder();
  for (Map.Entry<String, String> entry : event.getHeaders()
    .entrySet()) {
    builder.addHeader(UsingFlumeEvent.Header.newBuilder()
      .setKey(entry.getKey())
      .setVal(entry.getValue()).build());
  }
  builder.setBody(ByteString.copyFrom(event.getBody()));
  UsingFlumeEvent.Event e = builder.build();
  stream.write(ByteBuffer.allocate(Integer.SIZE / 8).putInt(e
    .getSerializedSize()).array());
  e.writeTo(stream);
}

@Override
public void flush() throws IOException {
  stream.flush();
}

@Override
public void beforeClose() throws IOException {
  if (writeHeaderAndFooter) {
    stream.write(footer);
  }
}

@Override
public boolean supportsReopen() {
  return false;
}

public static class Builder implements EventSerializer.Builder {

  @Override
  public EventSerializer build(Context context,
    OutputStream outputStream) {
    return new ProtobufSerializer(context, outputStream);
  }
```

```
    }
  }
```

Any configuration parameters passed to the HDFS Sink with the suffix `serializer.` get passed to the serializer. For example, a serializer that requires a character set could be configured like the following:

```
agent.sinks.hdfsSink.serializer.bufferSize = 4096
agent.sinks.hdfsSink.serializer.charset = UTF-8
```

These parameters get passed through the Context instance (only the parameters and values are passed—everything before that is not) and are used for configuring the serializer. The serializer, for simplicity, assumes that the body of the event is already encoded in the correct format; it does not change it and writes it out as is.

There are three serializers that come built into Flume: the TEXT serializer, the HEADER_AND_TEXT serializer, and the AVRO_EVENT serializer. The TEXT serializer writes out the event body to the file as is, and optionally inserts a new line between events. The HEADER_AND_TEXT serializer does exactly the same thing, but also includes the event headers in a "key=value" format, followed by the event body. A new line is inserted between events by default. This can be disabled by setting the value of `appendNewline` to `false`, as shown here:

```
agent.sinks.hdfsSink.fileType = DataStream
agent.sinks.hdfsSink.serializer = HEADER_AND_TEXT
agent.sinks.hdfsSink.serializer.appendNewline = false
```

The AVRO_EVENT serializer writes the events out as Avro container files [container-files] with the schema shown here:

```
{
  "type": "record",
  "name": "Event",
  "fields": [
    {
      "name": "headers",
      "type": {
        "type": "map",
        "values": "string"
      }
    },
    {
      "name": "body",
      "type": "bytes"
    }
  ]
}
```

MapReduce jobs can read Avro container files directly using the Avro MapReduce module. The Avro container format is supported in other systems by Hive, Pig,

Cloudera Impala, etc. To compress Avro container files, Avro's native compression should be used rather than using Flume's compressed stream. To use Avro's native compression, pass the `compressionCodec` parameter to the serializer with the value set to either `deflate` or `snappy` for the corresponding compression codec. The Avro container format allows the user to specify the amount of data between sync markers, which can be set using `syncIntervalBytes`, which is specified in bytes. It defaults to `2048000` (2 MB). An example of Avro serializer configuration is shown here:

```
agent.sinks.hdfsSink.fileType = DataStream
agent.sinks.hdfsSink.serializer = AVRO
agent.sinks.hdfsSink.serializer.syncIntervalBytes = 4096000
agent.sinks.hdfsSink.serializer.compressionCodec = snappy
```

The `EventSerializer` interface is a part of the `flume-ng-core` artifact and can be added to your serializer's *pom.xml* file, as shown in Example 3-6.

## The Difference Between Ingest Format and Output Format*

A major source of confusion when using Flume is the relation between the format in which data gets written to its eventual destination and the format in which it was ingested. The *ingest format* could be anything—depending on which source is used, the way the input data is converted into Flume events will vary. For example, if the data is ingested via an RPC client and RPC source, the application will convert the data into Flume events. For other sources, like the spooling directory, a pluggable component does the conversion from the original data format to Flume events.

Once the events are in Flume, the event data is like a black box for Flume until it reaches the destination sink. The one exception to this rule is when *interceptors*, which are components that can actually modify events, are used. We will discuss interceptors in Chapter 6. When writing the data to the storage system, the Flume event itself needs to be converted into the format that is used by the processing systems that read the data from the storage system. This is the *output format*. Most sinks that behave as terminal sinks, like the HDFS, HBase, and Morphline Solr Sinks, accept a plug-in that can convert the Flume events to the eventual destination format.

As you can see, there is an initial conversion from the original format to a Flume event at the source, and a second conversion to the eventual destination format at the destination sink. If the original and eventual formats are the same, it might make sense to simply convert the original format into a byte array and then write that byte array in as pre-encoded data.

A good example of writing pre-encoded data is the way it is done in the `AvroEvent Serializer` that comes bundled with Flume. If an event comes in as Avro, it can simply be encoded into a byte array using the Avro API and set as the event's body. It can be written to HDFS using this serializer, which simply writes the data as is, thus making the data available in the original Avro format in an Avro container file on HDFS.

# HBase Sinks

HBase has become increasingly popular for accumulating real-time data, and Flume supports writing to HBase. Flume has two HBase sinks, the *HBase Sink* and the *Async HBase Sink*, with slightly different implementations but very similar configurations. The HBase Sink uses the HBase client API to write data to HBase. The HBase Sink, therefore, is more likely to be in sync with HBase wire protocol changes.

The HBase client API is blocking, so the HBase Sink sends events to the HBase cluster one by one. On the other hand, the Async HBase Sink uses the AsyncHBase API [asynchbase], which is nonblocking and uses multiple threads to write data to HBase. So, in most cases, the Async HBase Sink is likely to give better performance. The HBase Sink, though, supports *secure HBase*, which the Async HBase Sink does not. Both sinks support serializers, which allows the user to use custom logic to translate Flume events into HBase-friendly objects. The serializers are configurable through the Flume configuration file. In this section, we will discuss the two types of HBase sink and how to implement serializers for both sinks.

Both HBase sinks connect to one or more HBase clusters, whose quorums are specified either via the Flume configuration file or from the first *hbase-site.xml* file in the classpath. The HBase sinks have fewer configuration parameters than the HDFS Sink. All parameters shown in Table 5-5 are common to both sinks.

*Table 5-5. Configuration for both HBase sinks*

| Parameter | Default value | Description |
| --- | --- | --- |
| `type` | - | The alias for the HBase Sink is `hbase`. The FQCN, which is `org.apache.flume.sink.hbase.HBase Sink`, can also be used. The alias for the Async HBase Sink is `asynchbase`. The FQCN, which is `org.apache.flume.sink.hbase.AsyncHBa seSink`, can also be used. |
| `table` | - | The table the sink writes events to. This table *must exist* in HBase—Flume *will not* create it. |
| `columnFamily` | _ | The column family to create the columns in. Flume *will not* create the column family either. This *must exist* in HBase. |
| `batchSize` | 100 | The number of events written per batch. |

| Parameter | Default value | Description |
|-----------|---------------|-------------|
| zookeeperQuorum | - | A list of Zookeeper servers in the quorum that the HBase cluster uses. |
| znodeParent | /hbase | The parent znode used by the HBase cluster on the Zookeeper quorum. |
| serializer | SimpleHbaseEventSerializer for HBase Sink, SimpleAsyncHbaseEventSerializer for Async HBase Sink | The FQCN on the serializer to use. More details on how to write serializers are discussed in "Translating Flume Events to HBase Puts and Increments Using Serializers*" on page 117. |
| serializer.* | - | A list of configuration parameters to pass the serializer. |

These parameters are accepted by both sinks, and both sinks have the same behavior with respect to these parameters. As with all the other components we have seen until now, the sink's type parameter can be the alias or the actual FQCN of the sink: hbase or org.apache.flume.sink.hbase.HBaseSink for the HBase Sink and asynchbase or org.apache.flume.sink.hbase.AsyncHBaseSink for the Async HBase Sink. Both HBase sinks can write to only one table and one column family, specified by the table and columnFamily parameters.

Both sinks write events out in batches. The maximum number of events written out per transaction is controlled by the batchSize parameter (provided there are enough events available in the channel—if there are fewer events in the channel, the batch is considered complete immediately). Each transaction with the channel is committed per batch. The transaction is committed if and only if all events from a batch are successfully written out to HBase. It is important to try different values for the batch size before settling on one number, as the most appropriate value depends on the exact data coming in, the HBase cluster topology, the schema design, how the table is split across various region servers, and the network architecture. Design details for HBase clusters and HBase schema can be found in the HBase documentation or *HBase: The Definitive Guide* [hbase-book].

By default, both sinks will look for the client configuration file, *hbase-site.xml*, in the classpath and use the information from that to connect to HBase. This brings up an interesting issue—every sink in an agent sees the same classpath, which means it becomes impossible to write data to more than one HBase cluster. Flume does allow the user to override this through configuration.

The sinks accept a parameter, zookeeperQuorum, that accepts a comma-separated list of hostnames and ports. The hostnames and posts are specified in the following format: hostname1:port1, hostname2:port1 (all servers must use the same port, which is an HBase requirement). The sinks also accept another parameter, znodeParent, which is the parent znode that the HBase cluster uses (this most often does not need to be changed).

Each type of HBase sink also takes some parameters that are specific to only that sink. As discussed earlier, the HBase Sink has the ability to write to a secure HBase cluster. Therefore, it takes in security-related parameters in the configuration. The parameters in Table 5-6 are accepted by the HBase Sink and are not used by the Async HBase Sink (as with other components, adding them in the configuration for the Async HBase Sink causes no harm—they are simply ignored) [hbase-security].

*Table 5-6. HBase Sink security configuration*

| Parameter | Default value | Description |
|---|---|---|
| kerberosPrincipal | - | The Kerberos principal to use to log in to the KDC. |
| kerberosKeytab | - | The path to the keytab file to use with kerberosPrincipal to log in to the KDC. |

These parameters have exactly the same meaning as the hdfs.kerberosPrincipal and hdfs.kerberosKeytab parameters.

The Async HBase Sink accepts one parameter in addition to the parameters common to both sinks: timeout, which is the time period (in milliseconds) for an entire batch to be successfully written out to HBase. If the entire batch is not successfully written out within this timeout period, the sink rolls back the entire transaction with the channel and makes the events available to this and other sinks. The default value for this parameter is 60000.

An example of an Async HBase Sink that is configured with a custom serializer and specifies the zookeeper quorum in the configuration is shown in Example 5-3.

*Example 5-3. Example of an Async HBase Sink configuration*

```
agent.sinks = asynchbase
agent.channels = memory

agent.sinks.asynchbase.type = asynchbase
agent.sinks.asynchbase.channel = memory
agent.sinks.asynchbase.zookeeperQuorum = zk1.usingflume.com:2181,
zk2.usingflume.com:2181,zk3.usingflume.com:2181
agent.sinks.asynchbase.znodeParent = /hbase
agent.sinks.asynchbase.table = usingFlumeTable
agent.sinks.asynchbase.columnFamily = usingFlumeFamily
agent.sinks.asynchbase.batchSize = 1000
agent.sinks.asynchbase.timeout = 60000
agent.sinks.asynchbase.serializer = usingflume.ch05.AsyncHBaseDirectSerializer
```

```
agent.channels.memory.type = memory
agent.channels.memory.size = 100000
```

## Translating Flume Events to HBase Puts and Increments Using Serializers*

HBase sinks can write data or increment counters in HBase. Just like the HDFS Sink, the HBase sinks allow users to convert Flume events into the format required by the destination system: in this case, HBase *Puts* and *Increments*. This can be done with the help of serializers. Each sink has its own serializer interface; they are slightly different from each other, mainly in the API used to represent the writes to HBase. We will discuss the serializer interface that plugs into the Async HBase Sink first. The Async HBase Sink interface is shown in Example 5-4, followed by an explanation of each of the methods. The serializer for the HBase Sink is very similar.

*Example 5-4. Async HBase Sink serializer interface*

```
package org.apache.flume.sink.hbase;
public interface AsyncHbaseEventSerializer extends Configurable,
ConfigurableComponent {
  public void initialize(byte[] table, byte[] cf);
  public void setEvent(Event event);
  public List<PutRequest> getActions();
  public List<AtomicIncrementRequest> getIncrements();
  public void cleanUp();
}
```

Though not evident in the interface, the `AsyncHbaseEventSerializer` (and the `HbaseEventSerializer`) does have the ability to accept configurations from the Flume configuration system. Any configuration parameters passed in through the configuration file get passed in to the serializer's `configure` method (inherited from the `Configurable` interface). When the sink starts up, the sink creates an instance of the serializer and then calls the `initialize` method, to which it passes the `table` and `columnFamily` set in the configuration.

Once the sink reads an event from the channel, it calls the serializer's `setEvent` method and passes in the event. Immediately after that, the sink calls `getActions`, which returns a list of `PutRequest` objects [put-request] (Async HBase's equivalent of HBase Puts), followed by `getIncrements`, which returns a list of `AtomicIncrementRequest` objects [increment-request] (Async HBase's equivalent of HBase Increments).

As is evident, each Flume event can generate zero or more HBase Puts and zero or more HBase Increments. This allows users to be extremely flexible in how they parse the events, with data based on each event written to several rows or columns and multiple counters incremented. The `AsyncHBaseDirectSerializer` shown in

Example 5-5 does exactly that. This serializer looks for three headers: rowKey, incre mentColumns, and payloadColumn. If the rowKey header is not present, the event is simply ignored. If the incrementColumn header is present, it is treated as a list of comma-separated strings and each of these columns is incremented for the row specified by the rowKey header. If the payloadColumn header is present, the event body is written out to that column in the row specified by the rowKey header. This serializer does not accept any configuration, but it is possible to pass configurations to the serializers via the configuration file. This configuration is passed in to the serializer's configure method.

*Example 5-5. Example of a serializer for the Async HBase Sink*

```
package usingflume.ch05;

public class AsyncHBaseDirectSerializer
  implements AsyncHbaseEventSerializer {
  private byte[] table;
  private byte[] columnFamily;
  private Event currentEvent;
  private static final String ROWKEY_HEADER = "rowKey";
  private static final String INCREMENTCOLUMNS_HEADER
    = "incrementColumns";
  private static final String PAYLOADCOLUMN_HEADER = "payloadColumn";
  private final ArrayList<PutRequest> putRequests
    = Lists.newArrayList();
  private final ArrayList<AtomicIncrementRequest> incrementRequests
    = Lists
    .newArrayList();
  private byte[] currentRow;
  private String incrementColumns;
  private String payloadColumn;
  private boolean shouldProcess = false;

  @Override
  public void initialize(byte[] table, byte[] cf) {
    this.table = table;
    this.columnFamily = cf;
  }

  @Override
  public void setEvent(Event event) {
    this.currentEvent = event;
    Map<String, String> headers = currentEvent.getHeaders();
    String rowKey = headers.get(ROWKEY_HEADER);
    if (rowKey == null) {
      shouldProcess = false;
      return;
    }
    currentRow = rowKey.getBytes();
```

```java
    incrementColumns = headers.get(INCREMENTCOLUMNS_HEADER);
    payloadColumn = headers.get(PAYLOADCOLUMN_HEADER);
    if (incrementColumns == null && payloadColumn == null) {
      shouldProcess = false;
      return;
    }
    shouldProcess = true;
  }

  @Override
  public List<PutRequest> getActions() {
    putRequests.clear();
    if (shouldProcess && payloadColumn != null) {
      putRequests.add(new PutRequest(table, currentRow, columnFamily,
        payloadColumn.getBytes(), currentEvent.getBody()));
    }
    return putRequests;
  }

  @Override
  public List<AtomicIncrementRequest> getIncrements() {
    incrementRequests.clear();
    if (shouldProcess && incrementColumns != null) {
      String[] incrementColumnNames = incrementColumns.split(",");
      for (String column : incrementColumnNames) {
        incrementRequests.add(
          new AtomicIncrementRequest(table, currentRow,
            columnFamily, column.getBytes()));
      }
    }
    return incrementRequests;
  }

  @Override
  public void cleanUp() {
    // Help garbage collection
    putRequests.clear();
    incrementColumns = null;
    payloadColumn = null;
    currentEvent = null;
    currentRow = null;
    table = null;
    columnFamily = null;
  }

  @Override
  public void configure(Context context) {
    // No configuration required
  }

  @Override
  public void configure(ComponentConfiguration conf) {
```

```
  // No configuration required
  }
}
```

It is possible to write a serializer for the HBase Sink that has the exact same behavior. The interface that needs to be implemented is shown in Example 5-6.

*Example 5-6. Serializer interface for the HBase Sink*

```
package org.apache.flume.sink.hbase;
public interface HbaseEventSerializer extends Configurable,
    ConfigurableComponent {
  public void initialize(Event event, byte[] columnFamily);
  public List<Row> getActions();
  public List<Increment> getIncrements();
  public void close();
}
```

The serializer for the HBase Sink does not have a global initialization method; HBase Puts and Increments do not need information about the table, so this is handled by the sink directly. Instead, the `initialize` method in the `HbaseEventSerializer` does the same thing as the `setEvent` method in the `AsyncHbaseEventSerializer`, passing the next event to be serialized along with the column family it needs to go to. The `getActions` and `getIncrements` methods do the exact same thing as the `AsyncHbaseE ventSerializer`'s methods of the same name, the only difference being the API used. The sink calls these methods immediately after the `initialize` method is called to pass in the event. The `close` method does any cleanup required. The sink calls this method only when it is being stopped.

The serializers of both sinks are part of the `flume-ng-hbase-sink` package. You can add it to your *pom.xml*'s dependency section as follows:

```
<dependency>
    <groupId>org.apache.flume.flume-ng-sinks</groupId>
    <artifactId>flume-ng-hbase-sink</artifactId>
    <version>1.5.0</version>
</dependency>
```

**HBase Versions**

Prior to HBase 0.96, Apache did not ship HBase JARs that were compiled against Hadoop 2. The `hadoop-2` profile in Apache Flume compiles against HBase 0.94.2 by default. Unfortunately, this version of HBase built against Hadoop 2 is not available on Maven Central. So, the user must build HBase using the Hadoop 2 profile to ensure that Flume is built against the correct version of HBase. The default profile builds against HBase 0.92.1. Flume can also be built against HBase 0.98.x and Hadoop 2.4.0 using the `hbase-98` profile. If any other version of HBase is being used, make sure the correct versions of HBase are in the classpath and the Flume *pom.xml* file is modified to point to the correct version of HBase.

# RPC Sinks

As explained in earlier chapters, cluster topology can require Flume agents to send data to other Flume agents. To send data from one Flume agent to another, RPC sinks are used. RPC sinks use the same RPC protocol as the corresponding Flume RPC sources. Refer to "Sink-to-Source Communication" on page 36 for more details on RPC sources. Due to this, RPC sinks can send data to RPC sources. This is the method that can be used to send data from one Flume agent to another. Since RPC sources act as servers listening on a specified port, it is possible for several Flume agents to send data to one or a number of Flume agents using the corresponding RPC sink(s).

Flume supports two RPC systems, as explained in "Sink-to-Source Communication" on page 36: Avro and Thrift [thrift_ch5]. Avro is considered to be the primary RPC format for Flume, so we will spend more time discussing the Avro Sink in this section. We will also briefly go over the Thrift Sink, but since the Avro Sink is more mature, it is still the recommended method for communication between Flume agents. Both RPC sinks share some of the basic configuration parameters, though the Avro Sink has a lot more features and hence has more configuration options. Note that an Avro Sink can *only* send data to a Flume Avro Source (or a Java server that is built on Avro's Netty RPC format), while the Thrift Sink can send data to the Flume Thrift Source and a server process written in any language that has a Thrift server listening on the port the sink is sending data to.

## Avro Sink

The Avro Sink uses Avro's Netty-based RPC protocol to send data to an Avro Source. It is implemented as a transaction-aware wrapper around Flume's `NettyAvroRpc Client`. As a result, they share several configuration parameters. The Avro Sink can send batches of events to the Avro Source. This is important since the Avro Source does not control the number of events written out per transaction—it will write out an entire batch as is. For the File Channel, it is important to write out reasonably large batches since the channel will `fsync` the data file to disk for each transaction. To avoid too many `fsyncs`, which can be expensive, the batch sizes must be reasonably large.

Another reason for large batch sizes is that each batch is sent out as one RPC call. Having small batches could mean that the RPC overhead is a large percentage of the size of the payload, which should be avoided. The best batch size will be different for every deployment. As with the HDFS Sink, it will depend on the hardware being used, the network, and even the configuration (the File Channel will perform better if the batches are large on both agents—the one hosting the sink and the one hosting the source it is writing to.

The configuration parameters of the Avro Sink are listed in Table 5-7.

*Table 5-7. Avro Sink configuration*

| Parameter | Default value | Description |
| --- | --- | --- |
| **type** | - | The alias for the Avro Sink is `avro`. The FQCN, which is `org.apache.flume.sink.AvroSink`, can also be used. |
| **hostname** | - | The hostname of the machine on which the agent is hosting the source that this sink should connect to. |
| **port** | - | The port that the source that this sink is connecting to is listening on. |
| batch-size | 100 | The number of events to be sent per RPC call. This is also the number of events that the sink takes from the channel in a single transaction. |
| compression-type | - | The compression format used to decompress the incoming data. As of Flume 1.5.0, the only compression format supported is zlib [zlib_ch5]. To accept zlib-compressed data, set this parameter to `deflate`. |
| compression-level | 6 | The compression level to be used if compression is enabled using the `compression-type` parameter. Valid values are 1–9. The higher the number, the better the compression. |
| connect-timeout | 20000 | The timeout, in milliseconds, for the initial connection and handshake to complete. |
| request-timeout | 20000 | The timeout, in milliseconds, for the entire RPC call to complete succesfully. |
| ssl | false | To encrypt the data sent to the server, this should be set to `true`. |

| Parameter | Default value | Description |
|---|---|---|
| trust-all-certs | false | If set to true, all SSL certificates are accepted by this sink. |
| truststore | - | The path to the trust store to use. If this is not set, the default Java trust store is used. |
| truststore-password | - | The password to use to open the trust store. |
| truststore-type | JKS | The Java trust store type. |
| reset-connection-interval | - | The interval after which the sink must disconnect from and reconnect to the source. |

The alias for the Avro Sink is avro, and the FQCN is org.apache.flume.sink.Avro Sink; either of these can be used.

The hostname parameter specifies the hostname of the host that the sink should connect to. The source that accepts the data from this sink should be running on this machine. The port parameter specifies the port that the source is listening to. The sink connects to this port on the host specified by the hostname parameter.

The maximum number of events to be sent per RPC call (provided there are enough events available in the channel—if there are fewer events in the channel, the batch is considered complete immediately) is specified by the batch-size parameter, which defaults to 100. Each transaction with the channel is committed per batch.

The Avro Sink can compress data before sending it over the wire. To enable compression, set the compression-type to deflate. The level of compression can be controlled using the compression-level parameter. The value of this parameter can be any whole number between 1 and 9, with 1 being the worst compression and 9 being the best. Note that the time taken to compress at the sink and decompress at the source is higher for higher compression levels. The default value of this parameter is 6. When compression is enabled, the Avro Source to which an Avro Sink is sending compressed data should be configured to accept compressed data by setting the compression-type parameter of the Avro Source to deflate as well. Compression happens at the batch level, so an entire batch of events is compressed at once, before it is sent.

The Avro Sink supports encrypted communication using SSL. The source accepting the data must also be configured to accept encrypted data from the Avro Sink. To enable encryption, set the ssl parameter to true. This parameter, by default, is set to false. Unless directed otherwise, Flume will use Java's default JSSE certificate authority files, *jssecacerts/cacerts*, to determine if the Avro Source's SSL certificate should be trusted.

If a custom trust store is to be used, set the value of the truststore parameter to the path to the respective trust store file. The user running the agent should have read access to the file. The truststore-password parameter's value is used as the password to open this file. The trust store type is set by the truststore-type parameter. By default it is set to JKS, but this can be any supported Java trust store type. If the sink should send data without checking the source's SSL certificates, set trust-all-certs to true. This should *not* be set to true, except for testing purposes. Trusting the source's SSL certificates blindly means that any source will be able to read the data sent—this undermines the security provided by SSL. More details about SSL in Java and how to create trust stores can be found in the Oracle Java CAPS documentation [truststores].

In many cases, agents communicate with each other with a load balancer in the middle. Since the connections between the agents are sticky, adding new agents hosting Avro Sources behind the load balancer would require the agents hosting the Avro Sinks to be restarted to make sure that the new agents actually receive connections. To avoid having to do this, the user can force the Avro Sinks to periodically terminate their connections to the agents and reconnect, by setting the reset-connection-interval parameter.

An example of an Avro Sink configuration is shown in "Avro Source" on page 36.

## Thrift Sink

The Thrift Sink can be used for communication between Flume agents using Thrift RPC. In general, the Thrift Sink works exactly like the Avro Sink, but it lacks compression and SSL capabilities. It is recommended to use Avro RPC for communication between Flume agents. Thrift Sinks should be used to write data to Thrift Sources that are already running, and perhaps to receive data from RPC clients written in other languages that use the Thrift RPC client.

The Thrift Sink configuration parameters are shown in Table 5-8.

*Table 5-8. Thrift Sink configuration*

| Parameter | Default value | Description |
| --- | --- | --- |
| type | - | The alias for the Thrift Sink is thrift. The FQCN, which is org.apache.flume.sink.ThriftSink, can also be used. |
| hostname | - | The hostname of the machine on which the agent is hosting the source that this sink should connect to. |

| Parameter | Default value | Description |
|---|---|---|
| port | - | The port that the source that this sink is connecting to is listening on. |
| batch-size | 100 | The number of events to be sent per RPC call. This is also the number of events that the sink takes from the channel in a single transaction. |
| request-timeout | 20000 | The timeout, in milliseconds, for the entire RPC call to complete succesfully. |
| reset-connection-interval | - | The interval after which the sink must disconnect from and reconnect to the source. |
| maxConnections | 5 | The maximum number of connections that the sink opens to the source. |

All of these configuration parameters except for maxConnections have the same meaning as the parameters with the same names for the Avro Sink. The maxConnections parameter controls the maximum number of connections that each sink should open to the source, if required. This parameter can be used to fine-tune the resources that are used by this sink.

An example of a Thrift Sink configuration is shown in "Thrift Source" on page 40.

# Morphline Solr Sink

Morphlines is a highly extensible ETL (extract, transform, and load) framework released as part of the Kite SDK [morphlines_ch5]. *Commands* operate on individual *records*. A command does a specific transformation on the input record to generate zero or more output records. Several commands can be chained together, with the output of one command being the input of the next, to perform heavyweight transformation of data. Such a chain of commands is referred to as a *Morphline*. The Morphline Solr Sink integrates the Morphline framework with Flume by providing a sink that can transfer data from a Flume pipeline into such a morphline (chain of commands). The most important use of the Morphline Solr Sink is with respect to the integration of morphlines with Apache Solr [solr] search.

The Morphline Solr Sink converts each Flume event into a record by moving the event body to the *_attachment_body* field of the record. The headers are populated into fields named the same as the header keys, with the values set to the corresponding values from the Flume headers. Each batch of events read from the channel is processed as part of a single morphline transaction, so if one event fails anywhere in the morphline, the entire transaction gets rolled back.

As mentioned earlier, the most important use of the Morphline Solr Sink is to actually load Flume events into Solr for indexing. The Morphline library provides a command called loadSolr that can load records into Solr. To load Flume events into Solr using this sink, the morphline configuration file to be used must list loadSolr as the last command. Each Flume event undergoes transformations by each command configured and eventually gets loaded into Solr by the loadSolr command. The transformations can be used to parse text out of data represented in complex formats such as PDF, XML, etc., before loading the searchable text into Solr. Before we go into details of the Solr use case, let's take a look at the configuration parameters for the Morphline Solr Sink in Table 5-9.

*Table 5-9. Morphline Solr Sink configuration*

| Parameter | Default value | Description |
| --- | --- | --- |
| type | - | The alias for the Morphline Solr Sink is morphlinesolr. The FQCN, which is org.apache.flume.sink.solr.morphline.MorphlineSolr Sink, can also be used. |
| morphlineFile | - | The full path of the file to read the morphline from. |
| morphlineId | - | The ID of the morphline that the sink should use to process events, if there are multiple morphlines in the same file. |
| batchSize | 1000 | The number of events to be written per batch. |
| batchDurationMillis | 1000 | The time in milliseconds after which a batch is considered complete (and gets loaded to Solr, if the loadSolr command is present). |

The alias for the Morphline Solr Sink is morphlinesolr and the FQCN is org.apache.flume.sink.solr.morphline.MorphlineSolrSink. Either can be used. The morphline to be used by the sink is read from the file whose path is specified by the morphlineFile parameter.

The Morphlines framework allows morphline files to contain multiple morphlines, each represented by an ID. If there is more than one morphline in the file, the ID of the morphline to be used from the file should be specified by the morphlineId parameter.

The batchSize parameter specifies the maximum number of events that the sink reads from the channel in one transaction (if there are fewer events than this available in the channel, the batch is considered complete immediately after reading the last event from the channel). This is also the total number of events in one morphline session. It is also possible to close a morphline session after a fixed duration. This is specified in milliseconds as the value of batchDurationMillis.

For indexing data on Solr, each record inserted into Solr requires a unique key that identifies the record. The field to use as the key is specified using the <uniqueKey> tag in the *schema.xml* file for the Solr collection [solr-unique-key]. In this example, let's assume that the field specified to be the unique key is id. Let's first take a look at the morphline file (shown in Example 5-7) that could be used to load this data into Solr.

*Example 5-7. A morphline configuration file*

```
SOLR_LOCATOR: {
  collection : usingFlumeCollection
  zkHost : "com.usingflume.solrZk:2181/solr"
}

morphlines : [
  {
              id : usingFlumeMorphline

    importCommands : ["org.kitesdk.**", "org.apache.solr.**"]
    # Convert the event into a UTF-8 encoded string
commands : [
        {
              readClob {
                charset : UTF-8
              }
        }

    # Generate a UUID that can be used for the Solr unique key field
    {
      generateUUID {
          field : id
      }
    }

    # Load the record into Solr
    {
      loadSolr: {
          solrLocator : ${SOLR_LOCATOR}
      }
    }
        ]
  }
]
```

The Morphline Solr Sink starts a morphline session, reads events from the channel, and converts them into records with the event body set to the _attachment_body field. The sink then passes the events to the morphline one by one. Each record is passed to the readClob command, which reads the body, converts it into a UTF-8 string, and sets the string as the value of the message field.

The generateUUID command generates a UUID and sets it as the value of the id field, which (as discussed earlier) is the unique key that Solr is using. The event is then loaded into Solr for indexing by the loadSolr command. The loadSolr command also allows loading data into a SolrCloud cluster for scaling.

Adding more morphline sinks can increase the number of events being loaded into Solr, until the available capacity in Solr is used up. Once the total number of events read reaches the batch size or the time since the batch was started exceeds the value of batchDurationMillis (or, like for all other sinks, the channel does not have any more events), the sink commits the morphline transaction followed by the sink transaction. Any failure will lead to both the morphline transaction and the transaction with the channel being rolled back.

This sink can be configured using a configuration file similar to the one shown in Example 5-8.

*Example 5-8. Example of a Morphline Solr Sink configuration*

```
agent.sinks = morphline
agent.channels = solrChannel

agent.sinks.morphline.type = morphlinesolr
agent.sinks.morphline.morphlineFile = /etc/morphline/conf/morphline.conf
agent.sinks.morphline.morphlineId = usingFlumeMorphline
agent.sinks.morphline.batchSize = 1000
agent.sinks.morphline.batchDurationMillis = 2500
agent.sinks.morphline.channel = solrChannel

agent.channels.solrChannel.type = memory
agent.channels.solrChannel.capacity = 100000
```

This configuration file represents an agent that receives data from other Flume agents or applications via the Avro Source and then replicates this data via two Memory Channels to HDFS and Solr. This is an example of a typical setup that can be used to ensure near real-time search indexing using Flume.

It is common for events to be replicated to HDFS as well by having the source write the same events to the channel feeding this sink and an HDFS Sink. To merge Solr shards and reconcile the data on HDFS with Solr, the data on HDFS can be used as input to a MapReduce job [solr-on-hdfs].

In this agent, the morphline sink uses the morphline configuration file */etc/morphline/conf/morphline.conf* and reads the morphline with ID usingFlumeMorphline. The sink uses a batch size of 1,000 but commits the batch if it takes more than 2.5 seconds to reach this number.

The morphline JARs and the morphline configuration files should be added to the Flume classpath using the plug-in deployment system shown in "Deploying Custom Code" on page 204.

# Elastic Search Sink

Flume can also load data in real time to Elastic Search for indexing using the Elastic Search Sink. The Elastic Search Sink requires that the user install the correct version of the Elastic Search client JAR and its dependencies in the classpath, since Elastic Search requires the client JAR version to match the server version. The sink dynamically creates new indices on the Elastic Search cluster at midnight UTC every day. By default, this sink is compatible with the Kibana UI [kibana].

The configuration parameters of the Elastic Search Sink are shown in Table 5-10.

*Table 5-10. Elastic Search Sink configuration*

| Parameter | Default value | Description |
|---|---|---|
| **type** | - | The alias for the Elastic Search Sink is elasticsearch. The FQCN, which is org.apache.flume.sink.elastic search.ElasticSearchSink, can also be used. |
| **hostNames** | - | A comma-separated list of hostnames and ports of Elastic Search hosts. |
| batchSize | 100 | The maximum number of events per transaction. |
| ttl | - | The time period, in days, after which expired documents are deleted. |
| indexName | flume | The prefix of the index name. |
| indexType | logs | The type of index on Elastic Search. |
| clusterName | elasticsearch | The name of the Elastic Search cluster to write to. |
| serializer | ElasticSearchLogStash EventSerializer | The FQCN of a class that implements ElasticSearchEvent Serializer or ElasticSearchIndexRequestBuilder Factory. "Customizing the Data Format*" on page 131 discusses how to write data in custom formats using this sink. |
| serializer.* | - | Parameters to pass to the serializer. |

The Elastic Search Sink can be initialized using the elasticsearch alias or the FQCN org.apache.flume.sink.elasticsearch.ElasticSearchSink. The list of Elastic Search servers to which the sink writes data can be specified as the value of the host Names configuration parameter. The hostnames are specified as a comma-separated list in the hostname:port format. The port can be omitted if the cluster uses the default port, 9300. The maximum size of each transaction with the channel can be controlled by the batchSize parameter, which specifies the maximum number of events the sink will remove per transaction, if events are available in the channel.

Elastic Search allows users to set an expiry date on indexed documents. To automatically delete such documents, the user can configure the ttl (time to live in days) of documents.

The indexName parameter specifies the prefix of the name of the index. The serializer is responsible for deciding which index each event goes to, but it is expected to use this parameter to create the indexes. When using the default serializer (or if the custom serializer extends from AbstractElasticSearchIndexRequestBuilderFactory), the sink creates a new index every day, with the value of the indexName parameter as the prefix and the current date as the suffix. The index name is of the form <indexName>-DAY, MONTH DD, YYYY. The default value of the parameter is flume, so an example index name would be flume-Monday, September 22, 2014. The user can also specify the type of data in the index as a value of the indexType parameter. This type is indexed by Elastic Search, and can be used to search specific types of documents. The name of the Elastic Search cluster to write the indices to is specified by the value of the clusterName parameter.

Just like the Morphline Solr Sink, the Elastic Search Sink can be configured to index data (in this case, in Elastic Search) while an HDFS Sink writes data in parallel to HDFS. The configuration file in Example 5-9 shows an Elastic Search Sink configured to write to indices that start with usingFlume, of index type books.

*Example 5-9. Elastic Search configuration example*

```
agent.sinks = elasticsearch
agent.channels = esChannel

agent.sinks.elasticsearch.type = elasticsearch
agent.sinks.elasticsearch.hostNames = es1.usingflume.com:5400,es2.usingflume.com,
es3.usingflume.com
agent.sinks.elasticsearch.batchSize = 1000
agent.sinks.elasticsearch.ttl = 2
agent.sinks.elasticsearch.indexName = usingFlume
agent.sinks.elasticsearch.indexType = books
agent.sinks.elasticsearch.clusterName = usingFlumeCluster
agent.sinks.elasticsearch.serializer =
usingflume.ch05.HeaderAndBodyIndexRequestBuilderFactory
```

```
agent.sinks.elasticsearch.serializer.writeHeaders = true
agent.sinks.elasticsearch.channel = esChannel

agent.channels.esChannel.type = memory
agent.channels.esChannel.capacity = 100000
```

## Customizing the Data Format*

It is possible to customize the format in which the data is written out to Elastic Search using a pluggable class that implements ElasticSearchIndexRequestBuilderFac tory to build an IndexRequest for Elastic Search. This is the preferred way of adding events to Elastic Search. There is a deprecated method to do this as well, which is to implement ElasticSearchEventSerializer; this is still supported, though it might be removed in the future.

To use a custom class to serialize data when writing to Elastic Search, specify the FQCN of the class as the value of the serializer parameter. This class must implement either ElasticSearchIndexRequestBuilderFactory or ElasticSearchEvent Serializer. If this parameter is not specified, the events are serialized in a Kibana-friendly format. Any parameters to be passed to the serializer can be passed using the serializer. prefix. The ElasticSearchIndexRequestBuilderFactory interface is shown in Example 5-10.

*Example 5-10. ElasticSearchIndexRequestBuilderFactory interface*

```
package org.apache.flume.sink.elasticsearch;
public interface ElasticSearchIndexRequestBuilderFactory extends Configurable,
    ConfigurableComponent {
  IndexRequestBuilder createIndexRequest(Client client,
      String indexPrefix, String indexType, Event event) throws IOException;
}
```

To make it easier to implement this interface, Flume provides an abstract class that provides a basic implementation, AbstractElasticSearchIndexRequestBuilderFac tory, that creates a new index daily, as explained in the previous section. A serializer that inherits from this class would automatically create a new index per day (if, of course, the class does not override the createIndexRequest method to change this behavior).

To use the automatic index creation functionality, and also insert the data in some custom format, the FQCN of a class that inherits this class should be the value of the serializer parameter. To customize the data inserted into the index, the prepareIn dexRequest method should be implemented. Example 5-11 can be used to insert events into an Elastic Search index. If configured to write the headers, the headers are inserted with their respective keys and the body is inserted with the body key (this

serializer makes the assumption that there is no header with the body key). If the
headers are not configured to be written, the body is simply written as is.

*Example 5-11. Example of an IndexRequestBuilderFactory implementation*

```
package usingflume.ch05;

public class HeaderAndBodyIndexRequestBuilderFactory extends
  AbstractElasticSearchIndexRequestBuilderFactory {

  private String CONFIG_WRITE_HEADERS = "writeHeaders";
  // By default, don't write the headers.
  private boolean DEFAULT_WRITE_HEADERS = false;
  private boolean writeHeaders = false;
  private static final String BODY_HEADER = "body";

  public HeaderAndBodyIndexRequestBuilderFactory() {
    this(FastDateFormat.getDateInstance(FastDateFormat.FULL));
  }

  protected HeaderAndBodyIndexRequestBuilderFactory(
    FastDateFormat dateFormat) {
    super(dateFormat);
  }

  @Override
  public void configure(Context context) {
    writeHeaders = context.getBoolean(CONFIG_WRITE_HEADERS,
      DEFAULT_WRITE_HEADERS);
  }

  @Override
  public void configure(
    ComponentConfiguration componentConfiguration) {
  }

  @SuppressWarnings("unchecked")
  @Override
  protected void prepareIndexRequest(
    IndexRequestBuilder indexRequestBuilder,
    String indexName, String indexType, Event event)
    throws IOException {
    indexRequestBuilder.setIndex(indexName).setType(indexType);
    if (writeHeaders) {
      Map source = (Map) event.getHeaders();
      source.put(BODY_HEADER,
        new String(event.getBody(), Charsets.UTF_8));
      indexRequestBuilder.setSource((Map<String, Object>) source);
    } else {
      indexRequestBuilder.setSource(event.getBody());
    }
```

```
    }
}
```

An example of this serializer being configured is shown in Example 5-9.

Both of the serializer base classes shown here are part of the `flume-ng-elasticsearch-sink` artifact. To include it while building your serializer, add the following to the *pom.xml* file's dependency section:

```
<dependency>
    <groupId>org.apache.flume.flume-ng-sinks</groupId>
    <artifactId>flume-ng-elasticsearch-sink</artifactId>
    <version>1.5.0</version>
</dependency>
```

### Elastic Search Client API

Since Elastic Search requires that Flume use the exact same version of Elastic Search as the cluster, Flume does not package the Elastic Search client libraries with it. The user must deploy the libraries and all their dependencies in the agent's classpath for the sink to be able to write data.

# Other Sinks: Null Sink, Rolling File Sink, Logger Sink

Flume comes packaged with several sinks that can be used for testing purposes. Though we will not go into each one of these in detail, we will take a look at their functionality and configuration. The Null Sink is a very simple sink that takes events off the channel and discards them. The purpose of this sink is to test the functionality and performance of the rest of the agent. The Null Sink removes events from the channel in batches. The size of each batch is controlled by the `batchSize` parameter. The sink can also update the log file every time it discards a certain number of events. The number of events after which the sink logs to the log file is controlled by the `logEveryNEvents` parameter. The Null Sink takes only a few parameters, listed in Table 5-11.

*Table 5-11. Null Sink configuration*

| Parameter | Default value | Description |
|---|---|---|
| **type** | - | The alias for the Null Sink is `null`. The FQCN, which is `org.apache.flume.sink.NullSink`, can also be used. |
| batchSize | 100 | The number of events the sink removes from the channel before the transaction is committed. |

| Parameter | Default value | Description |
|---|---|---|
| logEveryNEvents | 10000 | The number of events after which the sink logs to the log file. |

The Rolling File Sink writes events to files on the local file system. The directory to which the events should be written is specified by the sink.directory parameter. This sink supports the same serializers as the HDFS Sink. The serializer is specified by the sink.serializer configuration parameter. Just like with the HDFS Sink, configuration can be passed to the serializer using the sink.serializer. prefix. The sink can roll the files based on a time interval. This interval is specified by the sink.roll Interval (in seconds). The sink also supports batching of events into one transaction. The batch size is specified in the sink.batchSize parameter. The parameters for Rolling File Sink configuration are shown in Table 5-12.

*Table 5-12. Rolling File Sink configuration*

| Parameter | Default value | Description |
|---|---|---|
| **type** | - | The alias for the Rolling File Sink is file_roll. The FQCN, which is org.apache.flume.sink.RollingFileSink, can also be used. |
| sink.batchSize | 100 | The number of events the sink removes from the channel before the transaction is committed. |
| sink.directory | - | The directory that the sink should write events to. |
| sink.rollInterval | 30 | The time interval, in seconds, after which the file should be rolled. |
| sink.serializer | TEXT | The serializer to use to write events. This can be an alias for built-in serializers, or the FQCN for custom classes. |
| sink.serializer.* | - | The configuration parameters to be passed to the serializer. |

The Logger Sink logs to the log4j log file configured for the Flume agent in the *log4j.properties* file. All of the configuration for the sink is picked up from the *log4j.properties* file, and it does not require any other configuration (except the type and channel parameters). The parameter for Logger Sink configuration is shown in Table 5-13.

*Table 5-13. Logger Sink configuration*

| Parameter | Default value | Description |
|-----------|---------------|-------------|
| **type** | - | The alias for the Logger Sink is `logger`. The FQCN, which is `org.apache.flume.sink.LoggerSink`, can also be used. |

# Writing Your Own Sink*

In many cases, it is likely that users will have to write custom sinks. An example of such a case would be if the user needs to write the data to a proprietary data store or in a custom format. In this section we will cover the basic workflow of a sink and write an example of a custom sink.

A custom sink must implement the `Sink` interface, and optionally the `Configurable` interface if the sink needs to accept configuration from the configuration system. To better understand how to write a sink, it is important to understand how the Flume framework interacts with a sink itself.

When the agent starts up, the framework checks to make sure each sink has a `type` specified and has a `channel` parameter with a value representing a channel that exists in the agent that has been properly configured. Then the sink is instantiated and the configuration is passed to its `configure` method. If the `configure` method fails and throws an exception, the sink is removed from the agent and the instance is discarded. Once the sink is successfully configured, it is *connected* to the channel it is supposed to read events from.

From then on, the sink is managed by a *sink runner*. The sink runner is simply a thread that is responsible for running a sink. The framework starts the sink by calling the `start` method. If the `start` method fails, the framework will repeatedly retry starting the sink.

Once the sink is started, the sink runner thread calls the `process` method in a loop. This method is responsible for reading data from the channel and writing it out to the next hop or to the final destination. Each `process` call must process an entire transaction—start a transaction, read events from the channel, commit or roll back the transaction, and eventually close the transaction. If the channel does not contain any events for the sink to remove, the `process` method must return `Status.BACKOFF`, which causes the sink runner to retry only after an interval that increases each consecutive time the sink returns `Status.BACKOFF`. This mechanism slows down the sink when there is not enough data coming in. If the sink is successful, it must return `Status.READY` and the runner will call the `process` method again immediately.

The sink must either return `Status.BACKOFF` or throw an exception to report failure if it hits some exception while reading from the channel or writing to the destination. This slows down the sink runner and is a regulating mechanism to avoid sending data to the next hop if it is unable to clear data to downstream agents or the final destination. The `process` method must be thread-safe for proper execution within the Flume framework. An example of a custom sink is illustrated in Example 5-12.

*Example 5-12. Example of a custom sink*

```
package usingflume.ch05;

public class S3Sink extends AbstractSink implements Configurable {
  private String objPrefix;
  private final AtomicLong suffix = new AtomicLong(System
    .currentTimeMillis());
  private String awsAccessKeyId;
  private String awsSecretKey;
  private String bucket;
  private int batchSize;
  private String endPoint;
  private int bufferSize;
  private AmazonS3 connection;

  // 64K buffer
  public static final int DEFAULT_BUFFER_SIZE = 64 * 1024;
  public static final int DEFAULT_BATCH_SIZE = 1000;
  public static final String DEFAULT_OBJECT_PREFIX = "flumeData-";

  @Override
  public void start() {
    // Set up Amazon S3 client
    AWSCredentials credentials = new BasicAWSCredentials(
      awsAccessKeyId, awsSecretKey);
    ClientConfiguration config = new ClientConfiguration();
    config.setProtocol(Protocol.HTTP);
    connection = new AmazonS3Client(credentials, config);
    connection.setEndpoint(endPoint);
    if (!connection.doesBucketExist(bucket)) {
      connection.createBucket(bucket);
    }
    super.start();
  }

  @Override
  public synchronized void stop() {
    super.stop();
  }

  @Override
  public Status process() throws EventDeliveryException {
```

```java
    Status status = Status.BACKOFF;
    Transaction tx = null;
    final ByteArrayOutputStream data
      = new ByteArrayOutputStream(bufferSize);
    try {
      tx = getChannel().getTransaction();
      tx.begin();
      int i = 0;
      for (; i < batchSize; i++) {
        Event e = getChannel().take();
        if (e == null) {
          break;
        }
        byte[] body = e.getBody();
        data.write(
          ByteBuffer.allocate(Integer.SIZE / 8).putInt(body.length).array());
        data.write(body);
      }
      if (i != 0) {
        connection.putObject(bucket,
          objPrefix + suffix.incrementAndGet(),
          new ByteArrayInputStream(data.toByteArray()),
          new ObjectMetadata());
        status = Status.READY;
      }
      tx.commit();
    } catch (Exception e) {
      if (tx != null) {
        tx.rollback();
      }
      throw new EventDeliveryException("Error while processing " +
        "data", e);
    } finally {
      if (tx != null) {
        tx.close();
      }
    }
    return status;
  }

  @Override
  public void configure(Context context) {
    awsAccessKeyId = context.getString("awsAccessKeyId");
    Preconditions.checkArgument(!Strings.isNullOrEmpty(awsAccessKeyId),
                                "AWS Key Id is required");

    awsSecretKey = context.getString("awsSecretKey");
    Preconditions.checkArgument(!Strings.isNullOrEmpty(awsSecretKey),
                                "AWS Secret Key must be specified");

    bucket = context.getString("bucket");
    Preconditions.checkArgument(!Strings.isNullOrEmpty(bucket),
```

```
                        "Bucket name must be specified");

    endPoint = context.getString("endPoint");
    Preconditions.checkArgument(!Strings.isNullOrEmpty(endPoint),
                        "Endpoint cannot be null");

    batchSize = context.getInteger("batchSize", DEFAULT_BATCH_SIZE);
    objPrefix = context.getString("objectPrefix", DEFAULT_OBJECT_PREFIX);
    bufferSize = context.getInteger("bufferSize", DEFAULT_BUFFER_SIZE);
  }
}
```

This example shows a sink that writes data to Amazon S3 buckets [s3]. This sink is an example of a terminal sink that writes data to a storage system. It reads data from channels and writes them out in batches to text files on Amazon S3.

The S3 Sink inherits from the `AbstractSink` class and implements the `Configurable` interface. When the agent starts up, the framework configures the sink by calling the `configure` method. The sink sets up the credentials that are required to log in to the S3 service. The bucket name and endpoint to which to connect are also read from the configuration file. Since these parameters are *required*, the method validates that these values are passed in by the configuration file and are not empty. Parameters like `batchSize` and an object name prefix can be optionally passed in. If they are not, defaults are used.

The Flume framework then starts the sink by calling the `start` method. In this method, the sink sets up the required connections and bucket information.

Once the sink is started, the sink runner calls the `process` method in a loop. In the `process` method, the sink creates a transaction by calling the channel's `getTransaction` method. The transaction is started using the `Transaction.begin` method, then the sink reads as many events as the batch size by calling the `take` method on the channel (or until no more events are available from the channel—the `take` method returns `null` at this point), and writes them out to S3. The sink also prepends the length of each event to every event to ensure that we can read multiple events from the same file. Once the data is successfully written, the transaction is committed; otherwise, it is rolled back. Eventually, the transaction must be closed (this should always be done in a `finally` block). If no events were read, the sink runner is asked to slow down by returning `Status.BACKOFF` from the `process` method; otherwise, the method returns `Status.READY`. If any exception is thrown, the sink runner catches the exception and backs off automatically.

Eventually, when the agent is stopped, the `stop` method is called. The `stop` method must close any network connections and shut down any threads or thread pools that may have been created.

Custom sinks can be deployed to a Flume agent using the plug-in deployment framework shown in "Deploying Custom Code" on page 204.

# Summary

In this chapter, we discussed the basic sink concepts and the various sinks that come bundled with Flume, including the RPC sinks and sinks that push data to storage and indexing systems. We also discussed how to write custom sinks to move data to systems that Flume does not support out of the box.

In the next chapter, we will cover other components in the Flume architecture: interceptors, channel selectors, sink groups, and sink processors, which allow Flume to be even more flexible and extensible.

# References

- [tz-list] IANA Time Zone Data, *http://www.iana.org/time-zones*
- [kerberos] MIT Kerberos, *http://web.mit.edu/~kerberos/*
- [impersonation] Hadoop impersonation configuration, *http://bit.ly/1ARZHsp*
- [container-files] Avro container file specification, *http://bit.ly/1ARZKoe*
- [asynchbase] AsyncHBase, *https://github.com/OpenTSDB/asynchbase*
- [hbase-book] *HBase: The Definitive Guide*, O'Reilly Media
- [hbase-security] HBase client-side security configuration, *http://bit.ly/1AS0qKj*
- [put-request] AsyncHBase `PutRequest`, *http://bit.ly/1ARZVjm*
- [increment-request] AsyncHBase `AtomicIncrementRequest`, *http://bit.ly/1ARZYLX*
- [thrift_ch5] Apache Thrift, *http://thrift.apache.org/docs/concepts*
- [zlib_ch5] zlib compression library, *http://www.zlib.net*
- [truststores] Oracle Java trust store, *http://bit.ly/1AS0bPj*
- [morphlines_ch5] Morphlines: Kite SDK, *http://bit.ly/1AS0g5I*
- [solr] Apache Solr, *https://lucene.apache.org/solr/*
- [solr-unique-key] Apache Solr unique key, *http://bit.ly/1AS0fi8*
- [solr-on-hdfs] Apache Solr on HDFS, *http://bit.ly/1AS0jhN*
- [kibana] Kibana Elastic Search UI, *http://www.elasticsearch.org/overview/kibana/*
- [s3] Amazon S3, *http://aws.amazon.com/s3/*

# CHAPTER 6

# Interceptors, Channel Selectors, Sink Groups, and Sink Processors

As we discussed in previous chapters, the most important Flume agent components are sources, channels, and sinks. In addition to these, a Flume agent has a few more components that make Flume even more flexible. In this chapter, we will discuss interceptors, channel selectors, sink groups, and sink processors.

## Interceptors

Interceptors are simple pluggable components that sit between a source and the channel(s) it writes to. Events received by sources can be transformed or dropped by interceptors before they are written to the corresponding channels. Each interceptor instance processes events received by only one source. Interceptors can remove events or transform them based on any arbitrary criteria, but an interceptor must return only as many (or as few) events as originally passed to it.

Any number of interceptors can be added to transform events coming from a single source, in a chain. The source passes all events in one transaction to the channel processor, which in turn passes it to the interceptor chain, which passes the events to the first interceptor in the chain. The list of events resulting from the transformation of events by this interceptor gets passed to the next interceptor in the chain, and so on. The final list of events returned by the last interceptor in the chain gets written out to the channel.

Since the interceptors must complete their transformations before the events get written to the channel, RPC sources (and any other sources that may have timeouts) will respond to the client or the sinks that sent the events only after the interceptors have successfully transformed the events. Therefore, it is a not a good idea to do a lot of heavyweight processing in interceptors. If the processing being done in the interceptors is heavy and time-consuming, timeouts should be adjusted accordingly.

The only configuration parameter common to all interceptors is the `type` parameter, which must be the alias of the interceptor or the FQCN of a `Builder` class that can build the interceptor. As mentioned previously, there can be an arbitrary number of interceptors connected to a single source.

Interceptors are named components, and an interceptor instance is identified by a name. To add interceptors to a source, list the names of the interceptors that the source should be connected to as the value of the `interceptors` parameter in the configuration of the source. Any values prefixed in the source configuration with `interceptors.` followed by the name of the interceptor and the parameter are passed to the interceptor. The following configuration shows an example of how to configure interceptors:

```
agent.sources.avroSrc.interceptors = hostInterceptor timestampInterceptor
agent.sources.avroSrc.interceptors.hostInterceptor.type = host
agent.sources.avroSrc.interceptors.hostInterceptor.preserveExisting = true
agent.sources.avroSrc.interceptors.timestampInterceptor.type = timestamp
agent.sources.avroSrc.interceptors.timestampInterceptor.preserveExisting = false
```

There are several interceptors that come bundled with Flume, with more being added regularly. In this section, we will discuss a few of the most commonly used interceptors that are built into Flume.

## Timestamp Interceptor

One of the most commonly used interceptors, the *timestamp interceptor* inserts the timestamp into the Flume event headers, with the `timestamp` key, which is the header that the HDFS Sink uses for bucketing. If the timestamp header is already present, this interceptor will replace it unless the `preserveExisting` parameter is set to `false`. To add a timestamp interceptor, use the alias `timestamp`. This interceptor is commonly used on the first-tier agent that receives the data from a client, so that the HDFS Sink can use the timestamp for bucketing. The configuration parameters for the timestamp interceptor are shown in Table 6-1.

*Table 6-1. Timestamp interceptor configuration*

| Parameter | Default | Description |
|---|---|---|
| **type** | - | The type name is `timestamp`. The FQCN of the `Builder` class, `org.apache.flume.interceptor.TimestampInterceptor$Builder`, can also be used. |
| `preserveExisting` | `false` | If set to `true`, the value of the timestamp header is not replaced if the header is already present in the event. |

An example of an agent with a source connected to a timestamp interceptor is shown here:

```
agent.sources.avro.interceptors = timestampInterceptor
agent.sources.avro.interceptors.timestampInterceptor.type = timestamp
agent.sources.avro.interceptors.timestampInterceptor.preserveExisting = false
```

## Host Interceptor

The *host interceptor* inserts the IP address or hostname of the server on which the agent is running into the Flume event headers. The key to be used in the headers is configurable using the `hostHeader` parameter, but defaults to `host`.If the header that this interceptor is configured to use exists in the event, it will be replaced if `preser veExisting` is `false` (or is not specified). To insert the hostname instead of the IP address, set `useIP` to `false`. The configuration parameters for the host interceptor are outlined in Table 6-2.

*Table 6-2. Host interceptor configuration*

| Parameter | Default | Description |
|---|---|---|
| **type** | - | The type name is host. The FQCN of the Builder class, org.apache.flume.interceptor.HostInterceptor$Builder, can also be used |
| hostHeader | host | The key for the header in which to insert the IP address/hostname. |
| useIP | true | If set to true, the value inserted for the host key is the IP address. |
| preserveExisting | false | If set to true, the value of the host header is not replaced if the header is already present in the event. |

The following example shows the configuration of a host interceptor configured to write the hostname in the event headers, and not replace the value of the header if it already exists in the event:

```
agent.sources.avro.interceptors = hostInterceptor
agent.sources.avro.interceptors.hostInterceptor.type = host
agent.sources.avro.interceptors.hostInterceptor.useIP = false
agent.sources.avro.interceptors.hostInterceptor.preserveExisting = true
```

## Static Interceptor

The static interceptor simply inserts a fixed header key and value into every event that it intercepts. The header key and value are configurable, though they default to `key` and `value`, respectively. The interceptor also has the `preserveExisting` parameter, which preserves the existing key-value pair in the headers if the key already exists in the headers. This parameter has a default value of `true` (unlike in the timestamp and host interceptors). The configuration parameters for the static interceptor are shown in Table 6-3.

*Table 6-3. Static interceptor configuration*

| Parameter | Default | Description |
|---|---|---|
| **type** | - | The type name is `static`. The FQCN of the `Builder` class, `org.apache.flume.interceptor.HostInterceptor$Builder`, can also be used. |
| key | `key` | The key to use for the header. |
| value | `value` | The value to insert for the specific key. |
| preserveExisting | true | If set to `false`, the value for the specified key is replaced by the value specified in the `value` parameter, if the key already exists in the event headers. |

The following configuration causes every event processed by the interceptor to have a header with the key `book` with the value `usingFlume`:

```
agent.sources.avro.interceptors = staticInterceptor
agent.sources.avro.interceptors.hostInterceptor.type = static
agent.sources.avro.interceptors.staticInterceptor.key = book
agent.sources.avro.interceptors.staticInterceptor.value = usingFlume
agent.sources.avro.interceptors.staticInterceptor.preserveExisting = false
```

## Regex Filtering Interceptor

The regex filtering interceptor can be used to filter events passing through it. The filtering is based on a regular expression (regex) supplied in the configuration. Each regex filtering interceptor converts the event's body into a UTF-8 string and matches that string against the regex provided. Once matched, it can either allow the event to pass through or drop the event. The interceptor can be configured to drop events matching the regex or allow events matching the regex to pass through.

Several such interceptors can be added to a single source to perform more complex filtering, with only events matching certain patterns being written to the channel, while if they also match another pattern, they can be dropped. Regex filtering interceptors can be used to make sure only important events are passed through Flume agents to reduce the volume of data being pushed into HDFS or HBase. Table 6-4 lists the regex filtering interceptor configuration parameters.

*Table 6-4. Regex filtering interceptor configuration*

| Parameter | Default | Description |
|---|---|---|
| **type** | - | The type name is `regex_filter`. The FQCN of the `Builder` class, `org.apache.flume.interceptor.RegexFilteringInterceptor $Builder`, can also be used. |
| `regex` | `.*` | The regex to match the event body against. |
| `excludeEvents` | `false` | If set to `true`, events that match the regex are dropped; otherwise, only events that match the regex are allowed to pass through. |

The `excludeEvents` parameter decides what is to be done when the event body matches the regex. If this parameter is set to `true`, all events that match the regex are dropped and all the remaining events are let through. If this is set to `false`, events matching this regex are the only ones that are let through, and all others are dropped.

The following configuration shows a set of two regex filtering interceptors that allow through any events with the word "flume" in them, but not if the word "DEBUG" appears anywhere in the messages. Such combinations can be used to ensure that only messages that come from a particular source and that match some other criteria are let through:

```
agent.sources.avroSrc.interceptors = include exclude
agent.sources.avroSrc.interceptors.include.type = regex_filter
agent.sources.avroSrc.interceptors.include.regex = .*flume.*
agent.sources.avroSrc.interceptors.include.excludeEvents = false
agent.sources.avroSrc.interceptors.exclude.type = regex_filter
agent.sources.avroSrc.interceptors.exclude.regex = .*DEBUG.*
agent.sources.avroSrc.interceptors.exclude.excludeEvents = true
```

## Morphline Interceptor

We discussed the Morphline Solr Sink in "Morphline Solr Sink" on page 125, in which we also described how morphlines can be used for processing events and then loading them into Solr. It is also possible to use the same morphline commands to make event transformations. This interceptor simply takes information about which morphline file to use and which morphline from that file to use for processing the events.

If heavyweight processing is required, it is better to use the Morphline Solr Sink, as time taken in processing in the interceptor should not cause timeouts for the source or the Avro Sink writing to the source. Complex morphlines like `loadSolr` should not be used from the interceptor. For more details on how to use morphlines, refer to the Kite SDK documentation [morphlines_ch6]. Table 6-5 outlines the configuration parameters for the morphline interceptor.

*Table 6-5. Morphline interceptor configuration*

| Parameter | Default | Description |
|---|---|---|
| **type** | - | The FQCN of the Builder class, `org.apache.flume.sink.solr.morph line.MorphlineInterceptor$Builder`, must be used. |
| **morphlineFile** | - | The file containing the morphline to use. |
| morphlineId | - | The ID of the morphline to use if there are multiple morphlines in the file. |

The `morphlineFile` parameter specifies the full path to the file containing the morphline that is to transform the event. The `morphlineId` parameter specifies the ID of the morphline in that file that should be used to transform the event.

An example of a morphline interceptor configuration that loads the morphline with ID `usingFlume` from the file */etc/flume/conf/morphline.conf* to process events passed to it is shown here:

```
agent.sources.avroSrc.interceptors = morphlineInterceptor
agent.sources.avroSrc.interceptors.morphlineInterceptor.type = \
org.apache.flume.sink.solr.morphline.MorphlineInterceptor$Builder
agent.sources.avroSrc.interceptors.morphlineInterceptor.morphlineFile = \
/etc/flume/conf/morphline.conf
agent.sources.avroSrc.interceptors.morphlineInterceptor.morphlineId = usingFlume
```

As with the Morphline Solr Sink, the morphline configuration file and the JARs containing the morphlines used must be deployed using the plug-in deployment framework described in "Deploying Custom Code" on page 204.

## UUID Interceptor

Systems like Solr require each document written to them to have a unique ID. The UUID (universally unique identifier) interceptor can be used to generate such unique identifiers for every event. The UUID generated can be set as the value of a configurable parameter. It can be optionally prefixed with a preconfigured prefix string as well. Table 6-6 lists the configuration parameters for the UUID interceptor.

*Table 6-6. UUID interceptor configuration*

| Parameter | Default | Description |
|---|---|---|
| **type** | - | The FQCN of the Builder class, `org.apache.flume.sink.solr.morph line.UUIDInterceptor$Builder`, must be used. |
| headerName | id | The key for the header whose value the UUID should be inserted as. |
| prefix | - | The prefix to be added before the UUID. |

| Parameter | Default | Description |
| --- | --- | --- |
| preserveExisting | true | If set to `false`, the value of the header specified by `headerName` is overwritten with the prefix+UUID generated. |

An example of a UUID interceptor that adds UUIDs (prefixed with `usingFlume-`) as the value of the header `eventId` and replaces any existing `eventId` is shown here:

```
agent.sources.avroSrc.interceptors = uuidInterceptor
agent.sources.avroSrc.interceptors.uuidInterceptor.type = \
org.apache.flume.sink.solr.morphline.UUIDInterceptor$Builder
agent.sources.avroSrc.interceptors.uuidInterceptor.headerName = eventId
agent.sources.avroSrc.interceptors.uuidInterceptor.prefix = usingFlume-
agent.sources.avroSrc.interceptors.uuidInterceptor.preserveExising = false
```

### UUID Generated by the UUID Interceptor

This interceptor generates version 4 UUIDs, which are pseudo-random in nature. For applications that require very strong guarantees of UUID uniqueness, it might be better to write a custom interceptor that gives these guarantees.

## Writing Interceptors*

Interceptors are among the easiest Flume components to write. To write interceptors, the implementor needs to simply write a class that implements the `Interceptor` interface. The interface itself is fairly simple, though Flume mandates that all interceptors must have a `Builder` class that implements the `Interceptor$Builder` interface. All Builders must also have a public no-argument constructor that Flume uses to instantiate them. Interceptors can be configured using the `Context` instance that is passed to the builder. Any required parameters should be passed through this `Context` instance.

Interceptors are commonly used to analyze events and drop events if needed. Often, interceptors are used to insert headers into the events, which are later used by the HDFS Sink (for timestamps or for header-based bucketing), HBase Sink (for row keys), etc. These headers are often also used with the multiplexing channel processor to bifurcate the flow into multiple flows or to send events to different sinks based on priority—which is analyzed by the interceptor. This way string processing to do regex matching and detect the priority (based on things like log levels) can be offloaded from the application that is creating the data.

Example 6-1 shows the `Interceptor` interface that all interceptors *must* implement.

*Example 6-1. Interceptor interface*

```
package org.apache.flume.interceptor;
public interface Interceptor {
  public void initialize();
  public Event intercept(Event event);
  public List<Event> intercept(List<Event> events);
  public void close();
  /** Builder implementations MUST have a no-arg constructor */
  public interface Builder extends Configurable {
    public Interceptor build();
  }
}
```

When implementing an interceptor, there are two methods that process events, both called `intercept`, that take different arguments and also vary in return value. The first variant of this method takes just one event and returns one event (or `null`), and the second variant takes in a list of events and returns a list of events. In both cases, this is what comprises one transaction with the channel. Both these methods must be thread-safe, since these methods can be called from multiple threads if the source runs several threads.

If the variant that takes in one event is called, then the transaction will have exactly one event and is called by the channel processor's `processEvent` method, which is called by the source for processing the event. When the second variant is called, the channel processor's `processEventBatch` method is called by the source, and all events in the list returned by the interceptor are written in a single transaction. See "Writing Your Own Sources*" on page 69 to understand the difference between `processEvent` and `processEventBatch`.

Example 6-2 shows a simple interceptor that illustrates how an interceptor works. The channel processor instantiates the builder and then calls the builder object's con figure method, which it passes the `Context` instance that contains the configuration parameters to be used to configure the interceptor. The channel processor then calls the `build` method, which returns the interceptor. The channel processor initializes the interceptor by calling the `initialize` method of the interceptor instance. It is usually a good idea to pass the configuration to the interceptor via the constructor, so the interceptor can make all state based on configuration `final`, as is done in the `CounterInterceptor` class.

*Example 6-2. A simple interceptor*

```
package usingflume.ch06;

public class CounterInterceptor implements Interceptor {
  private final String headerKey;
  private static final String CONF_HEADER_KEY = "header";
```

```
    private static final String DEFAULT_HEADER = "count";
    private final AtomicLong currentCount;

    private CounterInterceptor(Context ctx) {
      headerKey = ctx.getString(CONF_HEADER_KEY, DEFAULT_HEADER);
      currentCount = new AtomicLong(0);
    }

    @Override
    public void initialize() {
      // No op
    }

    @Override
    public Event intercept(final Event event) {
      long count = currentCount.incrementAndGet();
      event.getHeaders().put(headerKey, String.valueOf(count));
      return event;
    }

    @Override
    public List<Event> intercept(final List<Event> events) {
      for (Event e : events) {
        intercept(
          e); // Ignore the return value; the event is modified in place
      }
      return events;
    }

    @Override
    public void close() {
      // No op
    }

    public static class CounterInterceptorBuilder
      implements Interceptor.Builder {

      private Context ctx;

      @Override
      public Interceptor build() {
        return new CounterInterceptor(ctx);
      }

      @Override
      public void configure(Context context) {
        this.ctx = context;
      }
    }
  }
```

`CounterInterceptor`'s `intercept` methods are thread-safe, because the only variable that is accessed by the instance is either `final` (all variables initialized on the basis of configuration) or uses thread-safe classes (the `AtomicLong` instance used as a counter). The `intercept` method that processes a list of events simply calls the variant of the `intercept` method that processes one event in a loop. It is advised that all custom interceptors follow this pattern. In this case, since the events are just *transformed* in place, a new list is not created and the original list is simply returned with the modified events. It is also possible to create a new list and add new events to that one, if required. Events can be dropped by either removing them from the original list if that is being returned, or by not adding the event to the new list being returned.

### How Many Events Can an Interceptor Return?

An interceptor is not allowed to return more events than originally passed to it, though it may return fewer events. The logic behind this is that interceptors adding more events can cause more events to be written to the channel than its transaction capacity, even if the Avro Sink sending data to the Avro Source is sending fewer events per batch than the transaction capacity. If an interceptor drops all events passed to it, the interceptor must still return a list, which may be empty if all events are dropped.

Custom interceptors can be deployed in the *plugins.d* directory, as explained in "Deploying Custom Code" on page 204.

# Channel Selectors

Channel selectors are the components that decide which channels a specific event received by the source is to be written to. They inform the channel processor, which then writes the events to each channel.

Since Flume does not have two-phase commits, events are written to a channel, then committed before events are written to the next channel. If writes to one of the channels fail, writes of the same events that may have happened to other channels cannot be rolled back. When such a failure happens, the channel processor throws a `Channe lException` and fails the transaction. If the source tries to write the same events again (in most cases it will; only sources like Syslog, Exec, etc. cannot retry since there is no way of producing the same data again), duplicate events will get written to the channels where the previous commit was actually successful. This is one of the ways in which duplicates can occur in a Flume pipeline.

Channel selector configuration is done via the channel processor, though the configuration looks like configuration for a subcomponent of a source. All parameters to be passed to the channel selector are passed as parameters in the source context, with the `selector` suffix. For each source, the selector is specified by using a configuration parameter, `type`. Channel selectors can specify a set of channels as `required` and another set as `optional`, as described in Chapter 2. The one parameter common to all channel selectors is shown in Table 6-7.

*Table 6-7. Channel selector configuration*

| Configuration parameter | Default | Description |
|---|---|---|
| type | replicating | The alias or FQCN of the channel selector to use for the source. |

Flume comes packaged with two channel selectors: `replicating` and `multiplexing`. If a source does not specify a selector in the configuration, then the replicating channel selector is automatically used. An example of a channel selector configuration is shown here:

```
agent.sources.avroSrc.selector.type = multiplexing
agent.sources.avroSrc.selector.header = priority
agent.sources.avroSrc.selector.mapping.1 = channel1
agent.sources.avroSrc.selector.mapping.2 = channel2
agent.sources.avroSrc.selector.default = channel2
```

## Replicating Channel Selector

If no selector is specified for a source, the *replicating channel selector* is used for that source. The replicating channel selector replicates every event to all channels specified by the `channels` parameter for that source.

In addition to the parameter specified in Table 6-7, the replicating selector takes only one configuration parameter, `optional`, which takes a list of space-separated channel names. This parameter is optional. All channels specified in this parameter are considered optional, so if event writes to any of these channels fail, the failure is simply ignored. Any failure to write to any other channel will cause an exception to be thrown to the source, indicating failure and asking the source to retry.

The following source configuration shows the use of a replicating channel selector with no optional channels:

```
agent.sources.avroSrc.type = avro
agent.sources.avroSrc.channels = c1 c2 c3
```

This configuration causes every event received by the Avro Source to get written to all three channels, c1, c2, and c3. If any one of them is full, or cannot be written to for any other reason, the Avro Source gets a `ChannelException`, which causes the source to inform the previous hop (the Avro Sink or RPC client that sent the message) of the failure, causing it to retry (a retry is guaranteed in the case of the Avro Sink, though how the application using the RPC client behaves is application-dependent).

If this configuration is changed to make c3 optional, as shown next, a failure to write to c3 will not cause a ChannelException to be thrown to the source, and the source will inform the previous hop that the write was successful:

```
agent.sources.avroSrc.type = avro
agent.sources.avroSrc.channels = c1 c2 c3
agent.sources.avroSrc.selector.optional = c3
```

Optional channels also must be listed in the source's channels parameter, but they must be *marked* optional using the optional parameter passed to the selector. Note that even though we did not have to specify the selector's type here (since it is the default), the configuration parameters are still passed in. The replicating channel selector does not do any other processing or bifurcation of the flow; it simply *replicates* the data. This allows events to be written to more than one destination, by having sinks going to different destinations read from each of the channels.

## Multiplexing Channel Selector

The multiplexing channel selector is a more specialized channel selector that can be used to dynamically route events by selecting the channels an event should be written to, based on the value of a specific header. Combined with interceptors, it is possible to do some sort of analysis on the event and then decide which channels it should get written to.

The multiplexing channel selector looks for a specific header, specified by the configuration for the selector. Based on the value of this header, the selector returns a subset of channels the event is to be written to. The list of channels to be written to is specified in the configuration for each of the header values. If the value of the header in a specific event is not specified in the configuration, the event is written to the default channels for the channel selector.

Figure 6-1 shows the flow of an event to one or more channels based on the value of a header. In this case, the selector checks the value of the priority header. Events with either priority 1 or 2 are written to HDFS, while events with priority 1 are also written to HBase. Such routing can be done even on tiers where the data is received, to send higher-priority events via a faster, unreliable flow (using Memory Channels) for lower latencies while sending all events (including the high-priority ones) over slightly slower but reliable flows (using File Channels) and later de-deduping, if necessary.

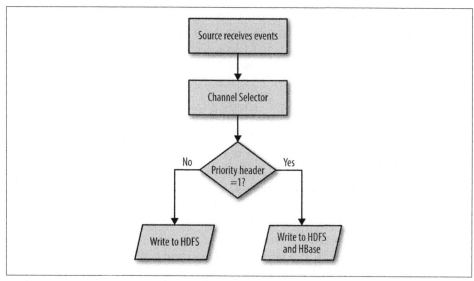

*Figure 6-1. Multiplexing channel selector*

Table 6-8 shows the configuration parameters for multiplexing channel selectors. Note that all configuration parameters shown here must be prefixed with `selector.` in the source context.

*Table 6-8. Multiplexing channel selector configuration*

| Configuration parameter | Default | Description |
|---|---|---|
| **type** | - | `multiplexing` |
| header | `flume.selector.header` | The header whose value must be checked for routing the event. |
| mapping.<hdr-value> | - | The list of mappings for the header. Each mapping is a list of channels the event must be written to, if the value of the header matches the value (<hdr-value>) in this parameter. |
| optional.<hdr-value> | - | Same as `mapping`, but channels specified in this list are considered optional, and write failures are ignored. |
| **default** | - | The list of channels the event must be written to if the header is not present or its value does not have a specified mapping. |

Configuring a multiplexing channel selector is quite a bit different from configuring a replicating selector. As usual, all channels the source writes to must be specified in the source's `channels` parameter. To enable the multiplexing channel selector for a source, the source's `selector.type` parameter must be set to `multiplexing`. All parameters to be passed to the channel selector are passed with the source prefix for that source followed by `selector.`, as shown here:

```
agent.sources.avroSrc.type = avro
agent.sources.avroSrc.channels = c1 c2 c3
agent.sources.avroSrc.selector.type = multiplexing
agent.sources.avroSrc.selector.default = c3
```

For each event, the selector looks for the header with the key specified by the `header` parameter in the configuration. Next, it checks if the value of the header is any one of the values specified in the configuration with the `mapping.` prefix. If one of the *mappings* matches, then it writes the event out to the channels specified by the mapping. Optional mappings can also be specified using the `optional.` prefix instead of the `mapping.` prefix. Any write failures to the list of channels specified as optional for a value are simply ignored. If the selector does not find a match or the header itself does not exist, then it writes the event to the channels specified in the `default` parameter. If an event doesn't map to any required channel, but does map to one or more optional channels, the event is written out to the optional channels and the default channel(s). Any failure to write to the default channel will cause a `ChannelEx ception` to be thrown.

The following shows an example of configuration of a source configured with a multiplexing channel selector:

```
agent.sources.avroSrc.type = avro
agent.sources.avroSrc.channels = c1 c2 c3 c4 c5
agent.sources.avroSrc.selector.type = multiplexing
agent.sources.avroSrc.selector.header = priority
agent.sources.avroSrc.selector.mapping.1 = c1 c2
agent.sources.avroSrc.selector.mapping.2 = c2
agent.sources.avroSrc.selector.optional.1 = c3
agent.sources.avroSrc.selector.optional.2 = c4
agent.sources.avroSrc.selector.optional.3 = c4
agent.sources.avroSrc.selector.default = c5
```

In this example, the Avro Source writes events to four channels. Unlike with the replicating channel selector, though, not all events get written to all the four channels. For each event, the channel selector looks for the header with the `priority` key.

For each event with priority 1, the events are written to three channels, c1, c2, and c3, of which c3 is marked as optional. So, if writes to c1 or c2 fail, the source gets an exception from the channel processor's `processEvent` or `processEventBatch` method and the source has to retry. But since c3 is marked optional, if a write to c3 fails, the source does not get an exception and is unaware of the failure, as this failure is ignored by the channel processor.

Similarly, any event with priority 2 gets written to c2 and optionally c4. As is clear, channels can appear in multiple mappings, like c2 in this example. Channels with priority 1 or 2 are written to c2—this is how the example shown in Figure 6-1 is achieved.

Events where the priority header is missing or has a value other than 1 or 2 get written to the default channel(s)—in this case, c5. If there are no required channels found for an event, the event will get written to the optional channels for that event *and* the default channel. In this example, an event with priority 3 would get written to channels c4 and c5. If the write to c4 fails, it is simply ignored, but if the write to c5 fails, the source gets an exception and the event has to be rewritten.

## Custom Channel Selectors*

It is possible to write and deploy a custom channel selector, allowing you to use deployment-specific logic to control the flow of events. To implement a custom channel selector, the selector needs to implement the ChannelSelector interface or inherit from the AbstractChannelSelector class. The AbstractChannelSelector class is shown in Example 6-3.

For every event, the channel processor calls the getRequiredChannels and getOptio nalChannels methods of the channel selector, which return the list of required and optional channels the event is to be written to. If writes to any of the required channels fail, the channel processor throws a ChannelException, causing the source to retry. Any failure to write to any of the optional channels is ignored.

*Example 6-3. AbstractChannelSelector class that can be inherited by custom selectors*

```
package org.apache.flume.channel;

public abstract class AbstractChannelSelector implements ChannelSelector {

  private List<Channel> channels;
  private String name;

  @Override
  public List<Channel> getAllChannels() {
    return channels;
  }

  @Override
  public void setChannels(List<Channel> channels) {
    this.channels = channels;
  }

  @Override
  public synchronized void setName(String name) {
```

```
    this.name = name;
  }

  @Override
  public synchronized String getName() {
    return name;
  }

  protected Map<String, Channel> getChannelNameMap() {
    Map<String, Channel> channelNameMap = new HashMap<String, Channel>();
    for (Channel ch : getAllChannels()) {
      channelNameMap.put(ch.getName(), ch);
    }
    return channelNameMap;
  }

  protected List<Channel> getChannelListFromNames(String channels,
          Map<String, Channel> channelNameMap) {
    List<Channel> configuredChannels = new ArrayList<Channel>();
    if(channels == null || channels.isEmpty()) {
      return configuredChannels;
    }
    String[] chNames = channels.split(" ");
    for (String name : chNames) {
      Channel ch = channelNameMap.get(name);
      if (ch != null) {
        configuredChannels.add(ch);
      } else {
        throw new FlumeException("Selector channel not found: "
                + name);
      }
    }
    return configuredChannels;
  }

}
```

The channel processor calls the `setChannels` method, to which it passes all the channels from which the selector must select the channels for each event. This class implements the `Configurable` interface, so the `configure` method is called when the selector is initialized. The `getRequiredChannels` and `getOptionalChannels` methods are called by the processor when each event is being processed. The `getAllChannels` method *must* return all the channels that were set by the channel processor during setup.

This class also provides a couple of convenience methods—one that returns a map of channel names to the actual channel instances and another that returns a list of channel instances given a list of channel names represented as a space-delimited string. A custom channel selector can be deployed using the FQCN:

```
agent.sources.avroSrc.type = avro
agent.sources.avroSrc.channels = c1 c2 c3 c4 c5
agent.sources.avroSrc.selector.type = com.usingflume.selector.RandomSelector
agent.sources.avroSrc.selector.default = c5
agent.sources.avroSrc.selector.random.seed = 4532
```

Custom selectors get all configuration parameters that are passed in with the `agent.sources.avro.selector.` in this case, just like any other component. In this example, the selector will get a `Context` instance in the `configure` method with keys `default` and `random.seed` with values `c5` and `4532`, respectively.

Custom channel selectors should be dropped into the *plugins.d* directory as described in "Deploying Custom Code" on page 204.

# Sink Groups and Sink Processors

In Chapter 5, we discussed how sinks work and the various sinks that come bundled with Flume. We also briefly discussed sink groups and sink processors. As we discussed before, the Flume configuration framework instantiates one sink runner per sink group to *run* a sink group. Each sink group can contain an arbitrary number of sinks. The sink runner continuously asks the sink group to ask one of its sinks to read events from its own channel. Sink groups are typically used for RPC sinks to send data between tiers in either a load-balancing or failover fashion.

Since RPC sinks are designed to connect to exactly one RPC source, sending data from one Flume agent to a set of agents in the next tier requires at least as many sinks as the agent is sending events to. To make sure each agent sends events to several destination agents in the next tier, and each tier on one tier sends data to all next-tier agents without overwhelming the network or those agents, each agent can load balance between all the machines in the next tier.

 It is important to understand that all sinks within a sink group are not active at the same time; only one of them is sending data at any point in time. Therefore, sink groups should not be used to clear off the channel faster—in this case, multiple sinks should simply be set to operate by themselves with no sink group, and they should be configured to read from the same channel.

Each sink group is declared as a component in the active list, just like sources, sinks, and channels, using the `sinkgroups` keyword. Each sink group is a named component, since each agent can have multiple sink groups. Sink groups are defined in the following way:

```
agent.sinkgroups = sg1 sg2
```

This configuration shows two sink groups being defined: sg1 and sg2. Each sink group is then configured with a set of sinks that are part of the group. The list of sinks in the active set of sinks takes precedence over the lists of sinks specified as part of sink groups. Therefore, all sinks that are part of a sink group must also be separately defined in the active set of sinks for them to be active. The following shows sg1 and sg2 being configured with a set of sinks:

```
agent.sinks = s1 s2 s3 s4
agent.sinkgroups.sg1.sinks = s1 s2
agent.sinkgroups.sg2.sinks = s3 s4
```

Each sink in a sink group has to be configured separately. This includes configuration with regard to which channel the sink reads from, which hosts or clusters it writes data to, etc. If the sink group represents a set of RPC sinks meant to communicate to the next tier, each host to connect to must have one sink configured to send data to it. Presumably, they all read from the same channel, since this is tier-to-tier communication. Ideally, if several sinks are set up in a sink group, all the sinks will read from the same channel—this helps clear data in the current tier at a reasonable pace, yet ensure the data is being sent to multiple machines in a way that supports load balancing and failover.

For cases where it is important to clear the channel faster than a single sink group is able to do, but it is also required that the agent be set up to send data to multiple hosts, multiple sink groups can be added, each with sinks that have similar configuration. For example, sg1 and sg2 in the previous example have sinks s1, s2 and s3, s4, respectively. s1 and s3 could have the same configuration (pushing data from the same channel to the same host and port), while s2 and s4 could have a similar configuration. This ensures that more connections are open per agent to a destination agent, while also allowing data to be pushed to more than one agent if required. This allows the channel to be cleared faster, while making sure load balancing and failovers happen automatically.

Thus far, we've discussed how sink groups can be used to set up flows to load balance and fail over, but we have not discussed how to actually tell the sink groups that they should load balance or fail over. This is done using the sink processor. Sink processors are the components that decide which sink is *active* at any point in time.

Note that sink processors are *different* from sink runners. The sink runner actually runs the sink, while the sink processor decides which sink should pull events from its channel. When the sink runner asks the sink group to tell one of its sinks to pull events out of its channel and write them to the next hop (or to storage), the sink processor is the component that actually selects the sink that does this processing. Flume comes bundled with two sink processors: the *load-balancing sink processor* and the *failover sink processor*.

A sink processor is configured using the processor.type suffix for the specific sink group it is part of. Configurations can be passed to sink processors using the pro cessor. prefix. Here is an example of how this configuration looks:

```
agent.sinks = s1 s2
agent.sinkgroups = sg1
agent.sinkgroups.sg1.sinks = s1 s2
agent.sinkgroups.sg1.processor.type = load_balance
agent.sinkgroups.sg1.processor.backoff = false
```

## Load-Balancing Sink Processor

Suppose you have a topology in which the first tier receives data from thousands of application servers and the second tier receives data from the first via Avro RPC, before pushing the data into HDFS. For simplicity, let's assume that the first tier has 100 agents and the second tier has 4. In the simplest possible topology, each first-tier agent would have four Avro Sinks pushing data to each of the second-tier agents. This works fine until one of the second-tier agents fails. At this point, the sink configured to send data will not send any data until the second-tier agent that failed comes back online.

Apart from the fact that this sink uses up a few threads on the agent (one for the sink runner and another for the thread pool used by Netty to send the data), thus wasting CPU cycles until the second-tier agent is up and running, the sink also causes additional stress on the channel by creating transactions removing the events and then rolling them back. For the File Channel, even though the transaction does not get committed, a number of *takes* get written to the file (takes are written to the file even if the transaction is not committed), which carries an I/O cost and a disk space cost. This is shown in Figure 6-2.

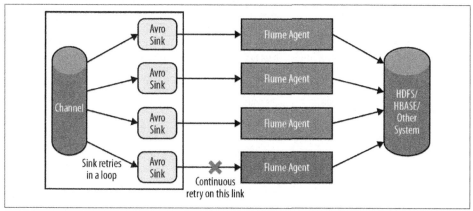

*Figure 6-2. Why we need a load-balancing sink processor*

As you can see, having such a topology can lead not only to an underutilized network, but also unnecessary wastage of CPU cycles and a higher I/O cost. To avoid such a problem, it is a good idea to use a sink group with a load-balancing sink processor, which will select one among all the sinks in the sink group to process events from the channel.

The order of selection of sinks can be configured to be *random* or *round-robin*. If the order is set to random, one among the sinks in the sink group is selected at random to remove events from its own channel and write them out. The round-robin option causes the sinks to be selected in a round-robin fashion: each process loop calls the process method of the next sink in the order in which they are specified in the sink group definition. If that sink is writing to a failed agent or to an agent that is too slow, causing timeouts, the sink processor will select another sink to write data.

The sink processor can be configured to blacklist a failed sink, with the backoff period increasing exponentially until an upper limit is reached. This ensures that the same sink is not retried in a loop and resources are not wasted, until the backoff period has expired.

The configuration parameters for the load-balancing sink processor are shown in Table 6-9. All parameters must be prefixed with the sink group prefix followed by processor. to ensure that the sink processor gets the correct parameters.

*Table 6-9. Load-balancing sink processor configuration*

| Configuration parameter | Default | Description |
|---|---|---|
| type | - | Has to be set to load_balance. |
| selector | round_robin | Can be set to round_robin or random, or the FQCN of a class that implements the LoadBalancingSinkProcessor$SinkSelec tor interface. |
| backoff | false | If set to true, a failed sink will be blacklisted for exponentially increasing periods of time. |
| selector.maxTimeOut | 30000 | The time, in milliseconds, after which the blacklist time period is not increased. |

The load-balancing sink processor is configured in the following way:

```
agent.sinks = s1 s2 s3 s4
agent.sinkgroups = sg1
agent.sinkgroups.sg1.sinks = s1 s2 s3 s4
agent.sinkgroups.sg1.processor.type = load_balance
agent.sinkgroups.sg1.processor.selector = random
```

```
agent.sinkgroups.sg1.processor.backoff = true
agent.sinkgroups.sg1.processor.selector.maxTimeOut = 10000
```

This configuration sets the sink group to use a load-balancing sink processor that selects one of s1, s2, s3, or s4 at random. If one of the sinks (or more accurately, the agent that the sink is sending data to) fails, the sink will be blacklisted with the back-off period starting at 250 milliseconds and then increasing exponentially until it reaches 10 seconds. After this point, the sink backs off for 10 seconds each time a write fails, until it is able to write data successfully, at which point the backoff is reset to 0. If the value of the selector parameter is set to round_robin, s1 is asked to process data first, followed by s2, then s3, then s4, and s1 again.

This configuration means that only one sink is writing data from each agent at any point in time. This can be fixed by adding multiple sink groups with load-balancing sink processors with similar configuration. Note that there may be several agents attempting to write data to each second-tier agent.

### Risks of Having Too Many Sinks Sending Data to the Same Agent

Since each Avro Sink keeps persistent connections open to the Avro Source, having multiple sinks writing to the same agent does add more socket connections and takes up more resources on the second-tier agents. This must be carefully considered before adding too many sinks connecting to the same agent.

## Writing sink selectors*

It is possible to have the load-balancing sink processor use custom logic to select which sink to activate each time the sink runner calls the process method. Custom selectors must implement the LoadBalancingSinkProcessor$SinkSelector interface that is shown here:

```
public interface SinkSelector extends Configurable, LifecycleAware {
    void setSinks(List<Sink> sinks);
    Iterator<Sink> createSinkIterator();
    void informSinkFailed(Sink failedSink);
}
```

When the sink processor starts up, the sink selector is instantiated and the setSinks method is called, to which the list of sinks is passed in. This list is in the same order specified by the configuration file. Each time a sink processes events, the createSinkIterator method is called. This method must return an iterator that returns sinks in the order the sinks must be asked to pull data in.

Once a sink is successfully able to process events and return success, the current iterator is discarded and this method is called again to get a new iterator, which could potentially return sinks in a different order. When a sink fails to send events (indicated by an exception being thrown), the `informSinkFailed` method is called. This can be used to blacklist the sink temporarily, if needed.

To build a custom sink selector, include the `flume-ng-core` artifact in your *pom.xml* file's dependency section as shown in Example 3-6.

## Failover Sink Processor

The same problem shown in Figure 6-2 can be solved in a slightly different way. The problem with the load-balancing sink processor is that since each sink group decides which sink is active on a large number of agents, it is possible that the second-tier agents won't all receive the same amount of data, though on average they should when `round-robin` is used. However, it is possible to configure the sink groups to use hard-wired writes, as described earlier, until a failure actually occurs. By allowing the sink groups to write data consistently to the same sinks most of the time, it is possible to predict how much data is being written to each agent. This can be achieved using the *failover sink processor*.

The failover sink processor selects a sink from the sink group based on priority. The sink with the highest priority writes data until it fails (failure of the sink could even be because the downstream agent died in the case of RPC sinks), and then the sink with the highest priority among the other sinks in the group is picked. A different sink is selected to write the data only when the current sink writing the data fails. This ensures that all agents on the second tier have one sink from each machine writing to them when there is no failure, and only on failure will certain machines see more incoming data.

The failover mechanism, though, does not choose a new sink until and unless the current sink fails. This means even though it is possible that the agent with highst priority may have failed and come back online, the failover sink processor does not make the sink writing to that agent active until the currently active sink hits an error. Figure 6-3 shows the workflow of the failover sink processor.

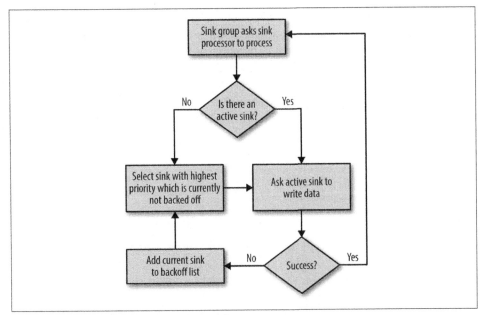

*Figure 6-3. Failover sink processor workflow*

Table 6-10 shows a list of configuration parameters that can be used to configure the failover sink processor. All parameters must be prefixed with the sink group prefix processor. to make sure the parameters are passed in to the sink processor.

*Table 6-10. Failover sink processor configuration*

| Configuration parameter | Default | Description |
| --- | --- | --- |
| type | – | Has to be set to failover. |
| priority.<sink_name> | – | A list of priorities for each sink in the sink group. |
| maxpenalty | 30000 | The maximum backoff period for failed sinks. |

As shown in Table 6-10, the type parameter for the failover sink processor is fail over. Since each sink processor activates sinks in priority order, the sinks' priorities must be set in the configuration using the priority. prefix followed by the sink name, with the value set to the desired priority. Note that *the priorities are considered in increasing order, which means higher the absolute value of the priority is, the earlier the sink is activated.*

For example, a sink with priority 100 is activated before a sink with priority 90. If no priority is set for a specific sink, the priority of the sink is determined based on the order of the sinks specified in the sink group configuration. Each time a sink fails to write data, the sink is considered to have failed and is blacklisted for a brief period of time. This blacklist time interval (similar to the backoff period in the load-balancing sink processor) increases with each consecutive attempt that results in failure, until the value specified by maxpenalty is reached (in milliseconds). Once the blacklist interval reaches this value, further failures will result in the sink being tried after that many milliseconds. Once the sink successfully writes data after this, the backoff period is reset to 0. Take a look at the following example:

```
agent.sinks = s1 s2 s3 s4
agent.sinkgroups.sg1.sinks = s1 s2 s3 s4
agent.sinkgroups.sg1.processor.type = failover
agent.sinkgroups.sg1.processor.priority.s2 = 100
agent.sinkgroups.sg1.processor.priority.s1 = 90
agent.sinkgroups.sg1.processor.priority.s4 = 110
agent.sinkgroups.sg1.processor.maxpenalty = 10000
```

In this configuration, four sinks are used in a failover configuration, with sink s4 having the highest priority, followed by s2 and s1. No priority is set for sink s3. For sinks whose priority is not specified, the first sink with no priority set is given priority 0, the next is given priority –1, the next is given –2, and so on. These priorities are only assigned to sinks with no priority set. Therefore, the sample configuration shown here implicitly assigns sink s3 priority 0, so the sinks are tried in the order s4, s2, s1, s3. Note that if two sinks have the same priority (implicitly or explicitly assigned), the sink specified first in the sink group is the only one activated. Also note that if explicit and implicit priorities are set in the same range, then their values are used as is. For example:

```
agent.sinks = s1 s2 s3 s4
agent.sinkgroups.sg1.sinks = s1 s2 s3 s4 s5 s6
agent.sinkgroups.sg1.processor.type = failover
agent.sinkgroups.sg1.processor.priority.s2 = 0
agent.sinkgroups.sg1.processor.priority.s4 = 110
agent.sinkgroups.sg1.processor.priority.s5 = -5
agent.sinkgroups.sg1.processor.priority.s6 = -2
agent.sinkgroups.sg1.processor.maxpenalty = 10000
```

In this configuration, sink s4 has the highest priority, so s4 is activated first. Sink s1 will be assigned a priority of 0—the same as s2—which means s2 is not activated. s3 gets priority –1, so the order of activation will be s4, s1, s3, s6, s5. Even though s3's priority is not specified in the configuration, its implicitly specified priority is higher than s5's and s6's, so s3 is activated before either of them.

## Summary

In this chapter, we covered interceptors, channel selectors, sink groups, and sink processors. They can be deployed using the *plugins.d* framework, which we will discuss in Chapter 8.

## References

- [morphlines_ch6] Morphlines: Kite SDK, *http://bit.ly/1AS0g5I*

# CHAPTER 7

# Getting Data into Flume*

So far, we've discussed the internals of Flume agents and how to configure the various components that make up an agent. In this chapter, we will look at the various methods by which data can be sent to one or more Flume agents from a client application. Flume has two programmatic ways through which data can be sent to Flume agents: the Flume SDK and the Embedded Agent API. Flume also comes bundled with log4j appenders that can be used to send data from applications to Flume agents.

## Building Flume Events

Before we discuss the API that is used to send data to Flume agents, let's look at how Flume *events* are created. As we discussed in Chapter 2, events are the basic form of representation of data in Flume. *Each Flume event contains a map of headers and a body, which is the payload represented as a byte array.* The Event interface is shown in Example 7-1.

*Example 7-1. Event interface*

```
package org.apache.flume;
public interface Event {
  public Map<String, String> getHeaders();
  public void setHeaders(Map<String, String> headers);
  public byte[] getBody();
  public void setBody(byte[] body);
}
```

As is evident, the internal representation of data within different implementations of the Event interface might differ as long as it exposes the headers and body in the format specified by the interface. In general, most applications build events using Flume's EventBuilder API. The EventBuilder API provides a few static methods to build events. In all cases, the API itself makes no modifications to the actual event data submitted—either the headers or the body. There are four methods that the Even tBuilder API provides that are commonly used to create Flume events. They are shown here:

```java
public class EventBuilder {
    public static Event withBody(byte[] body, Map<String, String> headers);
    public static Event withBody(byte[] body);
    public static Event withBody(String body, Charset charset,
                                 Map<String, String> headers);
    public static Event withBody(String body, Charset charset);
}
```

The first method simply takes the body as a byte array and the headers as a map, while the second takes the body as a byte array, but does not set event headers. The third and fourth methods can be used to create events from Java String instances, which are converted into a byte array encoded using the supplied character set and then used as the body of the Flume event. The third method also takes in the event headers as an argument.

Now that we know how to create Flume events, we can send these events to Flume agents using the Flume SDK or the Embedded Agent API.

### Flume NG SDK Artifact

To use any of the RPC clients or the Event and EventBuilder APIs, make sure you include the Flume Client SDK in your application. The artifacts are available from the Maven central repository. You can include the flume-ng-sdk artifact in your *pom.xml* file by adding the following to the dependencies section:

```xml
<dependency>
  <groupId>org.apache.flume</groupId>
  <artifactId>flume-ng-sdk</artifactId>
  <version>1.5.0</version>
</dependency>
```

# Flume Client SDK

Once an application knows what data is to be sent to HDFS via Flume, the application somehow needs to send the data to a Flume agent. We already discussed the HTTP Source and its pluggable handler in "HTTP Source" on page 43. We also covered the JSON-formatted events the HTTP Source accepts. This is one way of getting data to Flume—use an HTTP Source as the receiving source and have the application use HTTP-friendly formatted data (or JSON-ified data if the default handler is used). The issue with this is that it's more inefficient than it needs to be, with the additional HTTP and the encoding/decoding overhead.

Since the format of Flume events is fixed, the best way to send data to Flume is via RPC calls in one of Flume's supported RPC formats: Avro or Thrift. In general, Avro RPC should be preferred, as this is more mature and better tested by use in production in Flume's case. The downside of using Avro RPC is that the version of Avro RPC used by Flume supports only Java and other JVM languages. Non-JVM languages are supported via Thrift RPC, though in Flume's case, Thrift RPC may lack some features that are available in Avro RPC. In this section, we will discuss the Flume SDK and how to write programs that use this SDK to send data to Flume.

## Building Flume RPC Clients

We'll begin by looking at how to create RPC clients in Java. RPC client instances are created via the `RpcClientFactory` class. This class provides methods to create the various RPC client instances. All classes that are used to create RPC clients accept a `Properties` instance. This `Properties` instance contains configuration information that is used to configure the RPC client. All RPC clients can be created using the following methods:

```
public static RpcClient getInstance(Properties properties);
public static RpcClient getInstance(File properties);
```

The `Properties` instance is basically a map that contains the configuration parameters. The second method takes a `File` instance that represents the configuration in the properties file format, as explained in "Configuring Flume Agents" on page 13. There is only one mandatory parameter required by the factory class—the `client.type` parameter, which specifies the type of RPC client to create. This parameter must be set to one of `default`, `default_failover`, `default_loadbalance`, or `thrift`. Once the RPC client is created, the `Properties` instance is passed to it. Before we look at the various RPC clients available, let's take a look at the RPC client interface that the application developer must program against.

## RPC Client Interface

The RPC client interface is extremely simple and minimalistic. Since RPC clients are themselves configured during creation, the application writer does not need to worry about configuring the RPC clients explicitly. The RPC client interface is shown in Example 7-2.

*Example 7-2. Flume RPC client interface*

```
package org.apache.flume.api;
public interface RpcClient {
  public int getBatchSize();
  public void append(Event event) throws EventDeliveryException;
  public void appendBatch(List<Event> events) throws EventDeliveryException;
```

```
    public boolean isActive();
    public void close() throws FlumeException;
}
```

To send events to a Flume agent using an RPC client instance, the application program must call the appendBatch or append method. These methods accept the event(s) that have to be sent to the Flume agent and send them over the wire before returning. If the method returns successfully, it means that the events were successfully written to the destination agent's channel(s). If the destination agent could not write the events out to one or more of the source's required channels, or if there was a network issue or any other problem that caused the events to not be successfully written out, these methods throw an EventDeliveryException. If an EventDeliveryException is thrown, it is up to the application that is using the RPC clients to decide how to proceed. Applications could back off and retry, or even drop the events based on their own internal logic.

If the number of events passed in the list to appendBatch is greater than the batch size, the RPC client will split the list into multiple batches and write them out one after another, and will return only if all events were successfully written out. The method throws an exception as soon as one batch fails. If some batches succeed and another fails, this could cause duplicates in the final destination if the application retries. Therefore, it is usually a good idea to pass as many events as the batch size, or fewer. The getBatchSize method returns the maximum size of a batch that this RPC client uses.

Before each RPC call, it is a good idea to check if the RPC client is still active and ready for action, by calling the isActive method. Once the RPC client is no longer required, or if isActive returns false, the RPC client must be closed by calling the close method to clean up resources and avoid any resource leaks. This is described by the following snippet:

```
if (client == null) {
    client = RpcClientFactory.getDefaultInstance(host, port);
} else if (!client.isActive()) {
    client.close();
    client = RpcClientFactory.getDefaultInstance(host, port);
}
```

## Configuration Parameters Common to All RPC Clients

There are several configuration parameters that are common to all RPC clients. We will discuss how these are passed to the RPC clients in the following sections. Table 7-1 lists the common RPC client configuration parameters.

*Table 7-1. Common RPC client configuration parameters*

| Parameter | Default | Description |
| --- | --- | --- |
| `client.type` | - | This must be set to `default`, `default_loadbalance`, `default_failover`, or `thrift`. |
| `batch-size` | 100 | The maximum number of events to be sent per batch. |
| `hosts` | - | A list of names that can be used to specify the host parameters. |
| `hosts.<hostalis>` | - | The configuration of the hosts in hostname:port format. |

The `client.type` parameter specifies the RPC client type to use. This can be one of `default`, `default_loadbalance`, `default_failover`, or `thrift`. We will discuss each of these clients in the following sections.

The maximum number of events to be sent per batch can be set using the `batch-size` parameter. If more than this number of events are passed in to a single `appendBatch` method call, multiple batches, each of the specified batch size or below, are sent.

The `hosts` parameter lists the aliases that will be used to identify hosts to which the client must connect (in the case of the default RPC client, all except the first host in the list are ignored). The hostname information must be passed using the `hosts.<hostname>` parameter for the first host in the list, in the hostname:port format. An example of such a configuration is shown here:

```
hosts = h1 h2 h3
hosts.h1 = usingflume1.oreilly.com:5545
hosts.h2 = usingflume2.oreilly.com:5545
hosts.h3 = usingflume3.oreilly.com:5545
```

RPC clients are created using the `RpcClientFactory#getInstance` method, as explained in "Building Flume RPC Clients" on page 169. When an RPC client is returned to the application by the `RpcClientFactory`, it is fully configured and ready to be used. RPC clients can send either a single event or an entire batch of events in an RPC call. The batch size is configurable via the `Properties` instance that was passed to the `RpcClientFactory` when this RPC client instance was created. Example 7-3 shows a simple class that generates events using random strings and then writes batches of events via RPC to a Flume agent. We will use `UsingFlumeRPCApp` as the base class when we discuss the various RPC Clients.

*Example 7-3. Flume RPC client usage example*

```
package usingflume.ch07;

public abstract class UsingFlumeRPCApp {
```

```
private static final Logger LOGGER = LoggerFactory.getLogger(
  UsingFlumeRPCApp.class);

private RpcClient client;
private final Properties config = new Properties();
private final ExecutorService executor
  = Executors.newFixedThreadPool(5);
private int batchSize = 100;

protected void parseCommandLine(String args[])
  throws ParseException {
  setClientTypeInConfig(config);
  Options opts = new Options();

  Option opt = new Option("r", "remote", true,
    "Remote host to connect " +
      "to");
  opt.setRequired(true);
  opts.addOption(opt);

  opt = new Option("h", "help", false, "Display help");
  opt.setRequired(false);
  opts.addOption(opt);

  opt = new Option("b", "batchSize", true, "Batch Size to use");
  opt.setRequired(false);
  opts.addOption(opt);

  opt = new Option("c", "compression", false, "If set, " +
    "data is compressed before sending");
  opt.setRequired(false);
  opts.addOption(opt);

  opt = new Option("l", "compression-level", false,
    "The compression level " +
      "to use if compression is enabled");
  opt.setRequired(false);
  opts.addOption(opt);

  opt = new Option("s", "ssl", false,
    "If set, ssl is enabled using keystore supplied by argument k");
  opt.setRequired(false);
  opts.addOption(opt);

  opt = new Option("k", "keystore", true,
    "Keystore to use with SSL");
  opt.setRequired(false);
  opts.addOption(opt);

  opt = new Option("d", "keystore-password", true,
    "Password for keystore");
```

```
opt.setRequired(false);
opts.addOption(opt);

opt = new Option("t", "keystore-type", true,
  "Type keystore");
opt.setRequired(false);
opts.addOption(opt);

opt = new Option("i", "maxIoWorkers", true,
  "Set the maximum number of " +
    "worker threads to use for network IO");
opt.setRequired(false);
opts.addOption(opt);

opt = new Option("o", "backoff", false,
  "Backoff failed clients?");
opt.setRequired(false);
opts.addOption(opt);

Parser parser = new GnuParser();
CommandLine commandLine = parser.parse(opts, args);

if (commandLine.hasOption("h")) {
  new HelpFormatter().printHelp("UsingFlumeDefaultRPCApp", opts,
    true);
  return;
}

parseHostsAndPort(commandLine, config);

if (commandLine.hasOption("b")) {
  String batchSizeStr = commandLine.getOptionValue("b", "100");
  config.setProperty(CONFIG_BATCH_SIZE, batchSizeStr);
  batchSize = Integer.parseInt(batchSizeStr);

}

if (commandLine.hasOption("c")) {
  config.setProperty(CONFIG_COMPRESSION_TYPE, "deflate");
  if (commandLine.hasOption("l")) {
    config.setProperty(CONFIG_COMPRESSION_LEVEL,
      commandLine.getOptionValue("l"));
  }
}

if (commandLine.hasOption("s") && commandLine.hasOption("k") &&
commandLine.hasOption("d")) {
  config.setProperty(CONFIG_SSL, "true");
  config.setProperty(CONFIG_TRUSTSTORE, commandLine.getOptionValue("k"));
  config.setProperty(CONFIG_TRUSTSTORE_PASSWORD, commandLine.getOptionValue("d"));
  if (commandLine.hasOption("t")) {
    config.setProperty(CONFIG_TRUSTSTORE_TYPE, commandLine.getOptionValue("t"));
```

```
      }
    }

    if (commandLine.hasOption("i")) {
      config.setProperty(MAX_IO_WORKERS,
        commandLine.getOptionValue("i"));
    }
    backoffConfig(commandLine, config);
  }

  protected abstract void setClientTypeInConfig(Properties p);

  protected abstract void parseHostsAndPort(CommandLine commandLine,
    Properties config);

  protected abstract void backoffConfig(CommandLine commandLine,
    Properties config);

  @VisibleForTesting
  protected void run(String[] args) throws Exception {
    parseCommandLine(args);

    final UsingFlumeRPCApp app = this;

    for (int i = 0; i < 5; i++) {
      executor.submit(new Runnable() {
        final int total = 100;
        @Override
        public void run() {
          int i = 0;
          while (i++ < total) {
            app.generateAndSend();
          }
        }
      }).get();
      app.closeClient();
    }

    // Set a shutdown hook to shutdown all the threads and the
    // executor itself
    Runtime.getRuntime().addShutdownHook(new Thread(new Runnable() {
      @Override
      public void run() {
        executor.shutdown();
        try {
          if (!executor.awaitTermination(60, TimeUnit.SECONDS)) {
            executor.shutdownNow();
          }
        } catch (InterruptedException e) {
          LOGGER.warn(
            "Interrupted while attempting to shutdown executor. " +
              "Force terminating the executor now.", e);
```

```
          executor.shutdownNow();
        }
        app.closeClient();
      }
    }));

  }

  private synchronized void reconnectIfRequired() {
    if (client != null && !client.isActive()) {
      closeClient();
    }
    // If client is null, it was either never created or was closed by
    // closeClient above
    if (client == null) {
      try {
        client = RpcClientFactory.getInstance(config);
      } catch (Exception e) {
        e.printStackTrace();
        LOGGER.warn("Client creation failed. Source may not have been started yet");
      }
    }
  }

  protected synchronized void closeClient() {
    if(client != null) {
      client.close();
    }
    client = null;
  }

  protected void generateAndSend() {
    reconnectIfRequired();
    List<Event> events = new ArrayList<Event>(100);
    for (int i = 0; i < batchSize; i++) {
      events.add(EventBuilder.withBody(
        RandomStringUtils.randomAlphanumeric(100).getBytes()));
    }
    try {
      client.appendBatch(events);
    } catch (Throwable e) {
      e.printStackTrace();
      LOGGER.error(
        "Error while attempting to write data to remote host at " +
          "%s:%s. Events will be dropped!");
      // The client cannot be reused, since we don't know why the
      // connection
      // failed. Destroy this client and create a new one.
      reconnectIfRequired();
    }
  }
}
```

As you can see, the UsingFlumeRPCApp is an abstract class, whose concrete implementations will be presented in following sections. The same class will be used to write data to more complex RPC clients, like the *load-balancing RPC client* by implementing the setClientTypeInConfig method, which will set the required parameter in the configuration to instantiate the correct type of RPC client. Implementations of the parseHostsAndPort method converts the hostname parameter into the required format for each RPC client, and the backoffConfig method enables backoff based on the command-line input.

The parseCommandLine method reads several arguments, including the hostname(s) and port(s) to connect to, whether to use compression and SSL, whether to backoff on failure, etc., as command-line arguments. The arguments are then mapped to the corresponding configuration parameters for the RPC client and inserted into a Prop erties instance that is passed to the getInstance method to create the client. A safe way to correctly specify the parameters is to use the RpcClientConfigurationConst ants class that defines all configuration parameters as static final strings. In this example, these strings are imported statically and used to specify the configuration parameters when they are passed to the Properties instance.

The RPC client methods are thread-safe, though multithreaded applications are likely to do some thread synchronization by themselves to ensure that one thread does not close a client, or set it to null while allowing another thread to try to write data, leading to a NullPointerException.

In the application shown in Example 7-3, if any thread hits an exception while writing data to the remote host, the client is immediately closed and a reconnect is forced. If at this point there are other threads using this client, they will also hit an exception —which is fine, because Flume's default RPC client is considered dead as soon as it throws an exception.

At this point, one of the threads has to create a new connection. Having all threads reconnecting will lead to multiple clients being created one after the other, even though only one is needed. Therefore, we create the new connection in a synchronized method, reconnectIfRequired, that forces the reconnect only if the client is no longer active or is null (by virtue of never having been created). By doing this, we ensure that once a new RPC client is created and is available for use, the other threads will not create fresh connections. When asked to shut down, in addition to shutting down the executor and the threads, the application also closes the RPC client instance to clear up resources.

The run method generates a fixed number of events and sends them in batches to remote Flume agent(s) using the RPC client instance. For simplicity, this example simply uses byte array representations of randomly generated strings as the event body.

## Default RPC Client

The *default* RPC client instance uses the Avro RPC protocol and can connect to exactly one Avro Source. For Java programs writing data to exactly one Flume agent, this is the recommended client. To create the default RPC client, the RpcClientFac tory provides a couple of convenience methods that can be used:

```
public static RpcClient getDefaultInstance(String hostname, Integer port);
public static RpcClient getDefaultInstance(String hostname, Integer port,
Integer batchSize);
```

Since the default RPC client writes to exactly one Avro Source, the parameters required to connect to this Avro Source are only the hostname and port information, which can be passed in to the first method shown here as the first and second parameters, respectively. The second method takes an additional parameter, which is the batch size—the maximum number of events this client sends out in a single RPC call. Since the first method does not take a batch size, the RPC client created by that method simply uses the default batch size of 100 events per batch. No further configuration of the RPC client is required before using it.

In addition to the parameters discussed in "Configuration Parameters Common to All RPC Clients" on page 170, there are several more parameters that can be used to encrypt data being sent to the agent or to compress it. Table 7-2 describes these parameters.

*Table 7-2. Default RPC client configuration*

| Parameter | Default | Description |
| --- | --- | --- |
| connect-timeout | 20 | The timeout, in seconds, to wait for the initial connection to complete. |
| request-timeout | 20 | The timeout, in seconds, to wait for a batch to successfully complete writing a batch of events. |
| compression-type | - | The compression algorithm to use. The value can be deflate or not set at all. |
| compression-level | 6 | The compression level to be used if compression is enabled using the compression-type parameter. Valid values are 1–9. The higher the number, the better the compression. |
| ssl | false | If set to true, SSL is enabled. |
| trust-all-certs | false | If set to true, all SSL certificates are trusted. |

| Parameter | Default | Description |
|---|---|---|
| truststore | - | The trust store to use. This is a required parameter if SSL is enabled. |
| truststore-password | - | The password to use to open the trust store. |
| truststore-type | JKS | The type of trust store that is being used. |
| maxIoWorkers | 10 | The maximum number of threads to use for communication with the remote machines. |

Many of the parameters shown here are common to the Avro Sink and the RPC client. The reason for this is that the Avro Sink is actually a channel- and transaction-aware wrapper around the default RPC client. Therefore, all features supported by the default RPC client may be supported by the Avro Sink (though they may not be exposed to the user).

To pass in these parameters, the RpcClientFactory methods that accept the Proper ties instance (shown in "Building Flume RPC Clients" on page 169) must be used.

To use the default RPC client with more advanced configuration, the value of the cli ent.type parameter must be set to default in the Properties object (or use RpcClientConfigurationConstants.DEFAULT_CLIENT_TYPE).

The batch-size parameter specifies the maximum number of events that should be sent per RPC call. If the number of events passed to a single appendBatch call is greater than the batch size, then the events are sent in multiple RPC calls.

The connect-timeout parameter specifies the time period to wait for the initial connection setup to complete; if this is exceeded, the client will throw an EventDeliver yException. This is done only when the first batch of events is being sent. The request-timeout parameter specifies the time period to wait before a single RPC call is assumed to have failed. If an RPC call takes more than the number of seconds specified by this parameter, an EventDeliveryException is thrown.

The RPC client can compress data while sending data to agents that are expecting compressed data. To send compressed data, set compression-type to deflate. The compression level can be set using the compression-level parameter, whose value can range between 1 and 9. As the compression level increases, the compression ratio also improves, as does the time taken to compress the data. You can read about deflate compression and compression levels in the zlib manual [zlib-manual].

**Compression Type Mismatches**

If the RPC client is configured to use compression, the Avro Source receiving the events must have `compression-type` set to `deflate`.

To enable SSL, set `ssl` to `true`. The client can be set to trust all SSL certificates by setting `trust-all-certs` to `true`—this should not be done in production, to avoid security issues. A *trust store* is a file that contains information about which public keys to trust. Unless instructed otherwise, Flume will use Java's default JSSE certificate authority files, *jssecacerts/cacerts*, to determine if the Avro Source's SSL certificate should be trusted.

If a custom trust store is to be used, set the value of the `truststore` parameter to the path to the respective trust store file [truststore]. The user running the agent should have read access to the file. The `truststore-password` parameter must be set to the password that can be used to open the trust store. The `truststore-type` parameter is optional and can be set to an alternate keystore type, if needed [truststore-type].

It is possible to limit the number of worker threads that the RPC client spawns by setting the value of the `maxIoWorkers` parameter. By default, this is set to `10`, which means a maximum of 10 workers are used to perform network I/O.

To configure `UsingFlumeRPCApp` to use the default RPC client, we override the `set ClientTypeInConfig`, `parseHostsAndPort`, and `backoffConfig` methods as shown in Example 7-4.

*Example 7-4. Default Flume RPC client usage example*

```
package usingflume.ch07;

public class UsingFlumeDefaultRPCApp extends UsingFlumeRPCApp {
  private String remote;

  @Override
  protected void setClientTypeInConfig(Properties p) {
    p.setProperty(CONFIG_CLIENT_TYPE, DEFAULT_CLIENT_TYPE);
  }

  @Override
  protected void parseHostsAndPort(CommandLine commandLine,
    Properties config) {
    config.setProperty(CONFIG_HOSTS, "h1");

    remote = commandLine.getOptionValue("r").trim();
    Preconditions.checkNotNull(remote, "Remote cannot be null.");
    // This becomes hosts.h1
    config.setProperty(CONFIG_HOSTS_PREFIX + "h1", remote);
```

```
  }

  @Override
  protected void backoffConfig(CommandLine commandLine,
    Properties config) {
    // No op
  }

  public static void main(String args[]) throws Exception {
    // Outsource all work to the app.run method which can be tested
    // more easily
    final UsingFlumeDefaultRPCApp app = new UsingFlumeDefaultRPCApp();
    app.run(args);
  }
}
```

For the default RPC client, the `client.type` is set to `default` in the `setClientTypeIn Config` method. The `parseHostsAndPort` method simply reads the host and port from the command line and then sets the `hosts` parameter with value `h1`, to indicate that the host is identified by the alias `h1`. The value of `hosts.h1` parameter is set to the hostname and port in the hostname:port format.

To enable SSL or compression, or specify the batch size, connection timeout, request timeout, etc., all parameters for the default RPC client can be passed in to the load-balancing RPC client or the failover RPC client.

## Load-Balancing RPC Client

The load-balancing RPC client works similarly to the load-balancing sink processor. The load-balancing RPC client can be configured to send events to several clients. For each `append` or `appendBatch` call, the load-balancing RPC client selects one of the agents it is configured to send data to, in either *random* or *round-robin* order based on configuration.

When the application calls `append` or `appendBatch`, the load-balancing RPC client attempts to send events to Flume agents one after another, until the data is actually sent out successfully. If a remote agent fails and this RPC client tries another host, the application will not know of the failure or get an exception until all hosts have been tried and all of them have failed. If all remote agents have failed, then `append` and `appendBatch` will throw an `EventDeliveryException`.

All parameters that can be passed to the default RPC client (shown in Table 7-2) can also be passed to the load-balancing RPC client, which results in the same behavior as the default RPC client. For example, SSL and compression can be enabled using the same parameters as the default RPC client.

To configure load-balancing RPC clients, the parameters in Table 7-3 can be passed in via the `Properties` instance (in addition to the ones shown in Table 7-1 and Table 7-2).

*Table 7-3. Load-balancing RPC client configuration*

| Parameter | Default | Description |
|---|---|---|
| backoff | false | If set to `true`, a failed host will not be reconnected for an exponentially increasing backoff period. |
| maxBackoff | - | The maximum time, in milliseconds, to back off a failed agent. |
| host-selector | round_robin | The order in which to select hosts to send data to. |

As we discussed earlier, the load-balancing RPC client can select one of many hosts to write events to. When a host it is connected to has failed and is not accepting data (or is too slow, or the network connection has failed), the load-balancing RPC client can blacklist this host for an exponentially increasing backoff period (similar to the load-balancing sink processor). Each time the backoff period expires, the load-balancing RPC client tries to write to that host, and if it fails the backoff period is doubled; otherwise, it is reset to zero and the host is considered active. If the `backoff` parameter is set to `true`, this exponential backoff is enabled. There is no default maximum ceiling for the backoff period, but this can be set using the `maxBackoff` parameter. Once the backoff period for a host has reached this value, the backoff period for trying the host is not increased any further.

The `host-selector` parameter specifies the policy by which the client selects hosts to send events to. If this is set to `random`, a host that is not backed off is selected at random. If set to `round_robin`, active hosts are selected in round-robin order based on the order in which they are specified in the `hosts` list. This can also be set to the FQCN of the class that implements `LoadBalancingRpcClient$HostSelector`. "Writing your own host selector*" on page 183 explains how to write a custom host selector.

Example 7-3 can be easily modified to use the load-balancing RPC client by changing the way hosts are accepted into the application and then parsing this host list and setting them as hosts named `h1`, `h2`, `h3`, etc. For each of these aliases, the address of the host is specified in hostname:port format, which is set as the value of parameters named `hosts.h1`, `hosts.h2`, `hosts.h3` etc.

The client is set to `default_loadbalance`. To switch to the load-balancing RPC client, the `setClient` method should be modified to the following:

```
  protected void setClientTypeInConfig(Properties p) {
    p.setProperty(CONFIG_CLIENT_TYPE, "default_loadbalance");
  }
```

This is shown in Example 7-5.

*Example 7-5. Load-balancing Flume RPC client usage example*

```
package usingflume.ch07;

public class UsingFlumeLBRPCApp extends UsingFlumeRPCApp {

  private String host;
  private String port;

  @Override
  protected void setClientTypeInConfig(Properties p) {
    p.setProperty(CONFIG_CLIENT_TYPE, "default_loadbalance");
  }

  protected void parseHostsAndPort(CommandLine commandLine,
    Properties config) {
    host = commandLine.getOptionValue("r").trim();
    Preconditions.checkNotNull(host, "Remote host cannot be null.");
    StringBuilder hostBuilder = new StringBuilder("");

    String[] hostnames = host.split(",");
    int hostCount = hostnames.length;

    for (int i = 1; i <= hostCount; i++) {
      hostBuilder.append("h").append(i).append(" ");
    }
    config.setProperty(CONFIG_HOSTS, hostBuilder.toString());

    for (int i = 1; i <= hostCount; i++) {
      config.setProperty(
        CONFIG_HOSTS_PREFIX + "h" + String.valueOf(i),
        hostnames[i - 1]);
    }
  }

  @Override
  protected void backoffConfig(CommandLine commandLine,
    Properties config) {
    if (commandLine.hasOption("o")) {
      config.setProperty(CONFIG_BACKOFF, "true");
    }
  }

  public static void main(String args[]) throws Exception {
    // Outsource all work to the app.run method which can be tested
    // more easily
```

```
    final UsingFlumeLBRPCApp app = new UsingFlumeLBRPCApp();
    app.run(args);
  }
}
```

Since the load-balancing RPC client supports backing off failed hosts, the `backoffCon fig` method sets this in the `Properties` instance based on the command line configuration.

As mentioned earlier, the load-balancing RPC client also accepts the parameters that are passed to the default RPC client. Therefore, all of the parameters passed to the default RPC client in the `parseCommandLine` method are also used in the configuration of the load-balancing RPC client.

## Writing your own host selector*

Round-robin or random selectors satisfy most use cases for selecting the sink that should be chosen to pull data out of the channel. But there are always cases where it might make sense to write your own algorithm to select the sink that should be active. To write a selector, the `LoadBalancingRpcClient$HostSelector` interface must be implemented. The interface is shown in Example 7-6.

*Example 7-6. HostSelector interface*

```
public interface HostSelector {
  void setHosts(List<HostInfo> hosts);
  Iterator<HostInfo> createHostIterator();
  void informFailure(HostInfo failedHost);
}
```

When Flume starts the sink processor, it creates the host selector and calls the `setHosts` method, to which it passes a list of `HostInfo` instances [hostInfo] that contain information about hosts to which events should be sent. For each `append` or `appendBatch` call coming from the client, the load-balancing RPC client calls `create HostIterator`, which must return an iterator of `HostInfo` instances that must return the hosts in the order in which the client should try to send events. When the events can be sent successfully to one of the hosts, this iterator is discarded and `createHos tIterator` is called again. If a host has failed or sending data to that host fails, the RPC client calls the `informFailure` method, passing in a `HostInfo` instance describing that host. This can be used to temporarily blacklist the host.

When building a host selector, add the `flume-ng-sdk` artifact to your project's *pom.xml* file's dependency section as shown earlier.

## Failover RPC Client

The failover RPC client works exactly like the failover sink processor, connecting to agents based on priority. The RPC client connects to the agent with the highest priority first. If this agent fails, the client connects to the agent with the next highest priority. Unlike the failover sink processor, the failover RPC clients don't need priorities to be set explicitly. Instead, the priority is based on the order of hosts in the hosts parameter. The host specified first in the hosts parameter has the highest priority, followed by the second host in the list, and so on. Table 7-4 lists the failover RPC client configuration parameters.

*Table 7-4. Failover RPC client configuration*

| Parameter | Default | Description |
| --- | --- | --- |
| client.type | default_failover | |
| max-connections | 5 | The maximum number of hosts to attempt to connect to before throwing an exception. |

The client.type for the failover RPC client is default_failover. The only parameter in addition to the ones specified in Table 7-1 and Table 7-2 is the max-connections parameter. This is the number of times the RPC client must fail over within a single append or appendBatch call. For example, if this is set to 5, then up to five connections are attempted if there are five or more hosts. If there are fewer hosts, only that many attempts are made.

The setClientTypeInConfig method from Example 7-3 must be overriden to use the failover sink processor:

```
protected void setClient(Properties p) {
  p.setProperty(CONFIG_CLIENT_TYPE, "default_failover");
}
```

## Thrift RPC Client

Apache Thrift is a data serialization and RPC framework that can be used to serialize and deserialize data from various languages. Thrift supports this by having a language-neutral specification of the data format. The Thrift compiler can then generate the code in various languages that can be used to read and write this data. To send data from applications in different languages to Flume, the Flume Thrift spec [flume-thrift] can be used to generate the code that can be used in the specific language. The Flume Thrift spec is shown in Example 7-7.

*Example 7-7. Flume Thrift specification*

```
namespace java org.apache.flume.thrift

struct ThriftFlumeEvent {
  1: required map <string, string> headers,
  2: required binary body,
}

enum Status {
  OK,
  FAILED,
  ERROR,
  UNKNOWN
}

service ThriftSourceProtocol {
  Status append(1: ThriftFlumeEvent event),
  Status appendBatch(1: list<ThriftFlumeEvent> events),
}
```

More details on generating Thrift code for different languages can be found in the Apache Thrift tutorial [thrift-doc].

We will not discuss the Thrift RPC client in detail, since this client should only be used when there is a Thrift Source already running on the agent to receive data from applications written in another language (simply to avoid running an Avro Source as well). If the data being sent is only Java, then the Avro Source should be used with the default, load-balancing, or failover RPC clients.

# Embedded Agent

One very obvious issue with using Flume RPC clients in applications is that the applications have to buffer the data in the case of failures and retries. This means that downstream failures can have a direct impact on the applications, even if load-balancing or failover RPC clients are used (which may impact latency as well). Applications that cannot afford to lose messages would now have to buffer events. Buffering events in such a way that they survive process or machine failure is time-consuming and painful to implement. Buffering, sending data without affecting the application—sounds like a problem already solved, doesn't it? Flume was designed to solve this very problem!

To solve this issue, Flume provides the *embedded agent*. The embedded agent is a very restricted Flume agent that can be deployed within a third-party application. The advantage of using an embedded agent rather than an RPC client is that an agent has a channel—a buffer that the application does not need to manage—which can be on disk as well. This allows the application to survive failed downstream agents for longer; basically, until the channel is full.

Embedded agents also allow the application to buffer events while waiting for a downstream HDFS failure and the resulting full Flume channels to get resolved, by buffering data within the application. Since each application process often produces only a small fraction of the data being handled by a first-tier Flume agent, having a much smaller Flume channel size within each application's embedded agent will suffice.

Figure 7-1 shows a typical embedded agent architecture. The embedded agent is configured and then started by the application. Since the agent is embedded within the application, it resides within the application's process address space and creates and runs threads within the application. Therefore, the application will consume more resources than if it simply used the RPC client. That is the cost to be paid for the additional buffering time that the embedded agent provides.

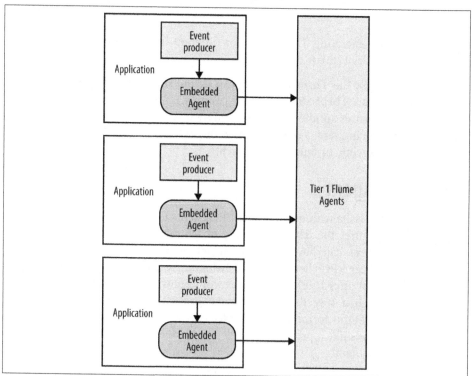

*Figure 7-1. Embedded agent architecture*

Embedded agents also support using the File Channel, which can help persist events even if the application dies or the machine is restarted. This can increase the I/O performed by the application and can lead to more load on the machine, and specifically the disks that are being used by the File Channel. Also, as discussed in Chapter 4, File Channels perform well when there are no other processes using the disks. In this case, even the application embedding this agent should preferably not be using the same disk, to avoid unnecessary seeks.

The embedded agent exposes a very simple API that starts the agent and then operates by itself until it is stopped. It is represented by a class aptly named Embedded Agent. An embedded agent has the same lifecycle as any other Flume agent. It is first created by creating an instance of the EmbeddedAgent class via the public constructor that takes a name, which is the name used to refer to this specific agent. Exceptions and log messages will contain the name of this agent, so the user can identify the agent that is in trouble if more than one embedded agent is being deployed within a single application instance.

**Whitespaces in Embedded Agent Name**

Be aware that the name of an embedded agent cannot currently contain whitespaces. Whitespaces in the name will cause the embedded agent to not start throwing an Exception stating that the configuration is bad.

Once it is created it is configured using the configure method, which is passed a Map containing the configuration of the agent. If configuration fails, this method will not return, but will throw a FlumeException.

The agent can then be started using the start method. A failed start will result in a FlumeException being thrown by this method. This method initializes all the configured components and starts them.

Events can be written to the agent using the put or putAll methods, which accept individual events and event batches, respectively. If the events cannot be written to the channel for any reason, including but not limited to the channel being full, an EventDeliveryException will be thrown.

When the agent is ready to be shut down, it can be stopped using the stop method, which may throw a FlumeException if the stop fails. The Embedded Agent API is shown in Example 7-8.

*Example 7-8. Embedded Agent API*

```
public class EmbeddedAgent {
    public EmbeddedAgent(String name);
    public void configure(Map<String, String> configuration) throws
    FlumeException;
    public void start() throws FlumeException;
    public void put(Event event) throws EventDeliveryException;
```

```
        public void putAll(List<Event> events) throws EventDeliveryException;
        public void stop() throws FlumeException;
}
```

## Configuring an Embedded Agent

An embedded agent can contain only one source, one channel, and one sink group (technically, the limit is on the number of sink runners), though the sink group may contain multiple sinks. Table 7-5 list the configuration parameters for an embedded agent.

*Table 7-5. Embedded agent configuration*

| Parameter | Default | Description |
| --- | --- | --- |
| source.type | embedded | The only source that an embedded agent can use is the embedded source. |
| channel.type | - | The channel type to use. |
| channel.* | - | The configuration parameters to pass to the channel. |
| sinks | - | Names of the sinks in this agent. This is equivalent to the `<agentname>.sinks` line in the active set of normal agents' configuration. |
| <sinkname>.type | - | Embedded agents can contain only Avro Sinks, so this must be set to avro. |
| <sinkname>.* | - | The configuration parameters to pass to each sink. |
| processor.type | - | If there are multiple sinks specified, the sink processor to use for selecting the active sink. |
| processor.* | - | The configuration parameters to pass to the sink processor. |

It is not required to specify the source to be used—the agent is automatically set to use the embedded source. Even if the source is set through the configuration, it *must* be set to embedded. No configuration is necessary for the embedded source.

Each embedded agent can have only one channel, either the File Channel or the Memory Channel, so the channel.type parameter accepts file or memory as its value. Any parameters to be passed to this channel can be passed using the channel. prefix.

An embedded agent can have multiple sinks. If an embedded agent has multiple sinks, the sinks *will be* grouped into a single sink group, as an embedded agent has only one sink runner. Since the embedded agent can have multiple sinks, they are named using the sinks parameter, where their names are specified. Any parameters are passed in to the sinks using the sink's name as a prefix. Only Avro Sinks can be used in an embedded agent, so the type parameter for all sinks *must* be set to avro. If there are multiple sinks specified, the sinks are automatically grouped into a sink group, whose sink processor can be configured by the processor.type; any configuration can be passed to it via the processor. prefix.

Since there is only one channel in an embedded agent, the source and sinks do not have to specify the channels or channel parameter explicitly—the agent will automatically set the source to write to the only channel and the sinks to read from it. Example 7-9 shows an application that uses the Embedded Agent API and can write data to several Flume agents via load balancing.

*Example 7-9. Embedded agent example*

```
package usingflume.ch07;

public class UsingFlumeEmbeddedAgent {
  private static final Logger LOGGER = LoggerFactory.getLogger
    (UsingFlumeEmbeddedAgent.class);
  private final EmbeddedAgent agent = new EmbeddedAgent(
    "UsingFlume");
  private int batchSize = 100;

  public static void main(String args[]) throws Exception {
    UsingFlumeEmbeddedAgent usingFlumeEmbeddedAgent = new
      UsingFlumeEmbeddedAgent();
    usingFlumeEmbeddedAgent.run(args);
    int i = 0;
    while (i++ < 100) {
      usingFlumeEmbeddedAgent.generateAndSend();
    }
  }

  public void run(String args[]) throws Exception {
    Options opts = new Options();

    Option opt = new Option("r", "remote", true,
      "Remote host to connect " +
        "to");
    opt.setRequired(true);
    opts.addOption(opt);

    opt = new Option("p", "port", true, "Port to connect to");
    opt.setRequired(true);
    opts.addOption(opt);

    opt = new Option("b", "batchSize", true, "Batch Size to use");
    opt.setRequired(false);
    opts.addOption(opt);

    Parser parser = new GnuParser();
```

```java
    CommandLine commandLine = parser.parse(opts, args);

    if (commandLine.hasOption("h")) {
      new HelpFormatter().printHelp("UsingFlumeEmbeddedAgent", opts,
        true);
      return;
    }

    Map<String, String> config = new HashMap<String, String>();
    parseHostsAndPort(commandLine, config);
    config.put("source.type", "embedded");
    File dcDir = Files.createTempDir();
    dcDir.deleteOnExit();
    config.put("channel.type", "file");
    config.put("channel.capacity", "100000");
    config.put("channel.dataDirs", dcDir.toString() + "/data");
    config.put("channel.checkpointDir", dcDir.toString() + "/checkpoint");
    agent.configure(config);
    agent.start();
    Runtime.getRuntime().addShutdownHook(new Thread(new Runnable() {
      @Override
      public void run() {
        agent.stop();
      }
    }));
  }

  private void generateAndSend() {
    List<Event> events = new ArrayList<Event>(100);
    for (int i = 0; i < batchSize; i++) {
      events.add(EventBuilder.withBody(
        RandomStringUtils.randomAlphanumeric(1024).getBytes()));
    }
    try {
      agent.putAll(events);
    } catch (Throwable e) {
      LOGGER.error(
        "Error while attempting to write data to remote host at " +
          "%s:%s. Events will be dropped!");
      // The client cannot be reused, since we don't know why the
      // connection
      // failed. Destroy this client and create a new one.
    }
  }

  private void parseHostsAndPort(CommandLine commandLine,
    Map<String, String> config) {
    String host = commandLine.getOptionValue("r").trim();
    Preconditions.checkNotNull(host, "Remote host cannot be null.");

    String port = commandLine.getOptionValue("p").trim();
    Preconditions.checkNotNull(port, "Port cannot be null.");
```

```
        String[] hostnames = host.split(",");
        int hostCount = hostnames.length;
        final String sinkStr = "sink";
        StringBuilder stringNamesBuilder = new StringBuilder("");
        for (int i = 0; i < hostCount; i++) {
          stringNamesBuilder.append(sinkStr).append(i).append(" ");
        }
        // this puts sinks = sink0 sink1 sink2 sink 3 etc...
        config.put("sinks", stringNamesBuilder.toString());
        final String parameters[] = {"type", "hostname", "port",
                                "batch-size"};
        final String avro = "avro";
        for (int i = 0; i < hostCount; i++) {
          final String currentSinkPrefix = sinkStr + String.valueOf(i) +
            ".";
          config.put(currentSinkPrefix + parameters[0], avro);
          config.put(currentSinkPrefix + parameters[1], hostnames[i]);
          config.put(currentSinkPrefix + parameters[2], port);
          config.put(currentSinkPrefix + parameters[3],
            String.valueOf(batchSize));
        }

        if (hostnames.length > 1) {
          config.put("processor.type", "load_balance");
          config.put("processor.backoff", "true");
          config.put("processor.selector", "round_robin");
          config.put("processor.selector.maxTimeout", "30000");
        } else {
          config.put("processor.type", "default");
        }
      }
    }
}
```

This application reads the hostnames and port from the command line in the parse HostsAndPort method, and configures Avro Sinks to connect to each of them. If several hosts are specified on the command line, a load balancing sink processor is added to the configuration to make sure data is sent to all hosts that this application connects to. It also configures a File Channel with a capacity of 100,000 and the checkpoint and data directories to use. These parameters are all set in a Map, which is then passed to the configure method of the EmbeddedAgent class.

Once configured, the agent is started by calling the start method, after which the agent can accept events from the application via the put and putAll methods. In this case, a predefined number of randomly generated events are passed to the agent using the putAll method.

When the application is done sending data, the agent is shutdown by calling the stop method.

The Embedded Agent API is contained in the `flume-ng-embedded-agent` artifact, which can be added to your application's *pom.xml* file's dependency section as follows:

```
<dependency>
  <groupId>org.apache.flume</groupId>
  <artifactId>flume-ng-embedded-agent</artifactId>
  <version>1.5.0</version>
</dependency>
```

# log4j Appenders

Apache log4j is an extremely popular logging system that supports plugging in custom loggers. Flume provides two log4j appenders that can be plugged into your application: one that can write data to exactly one Flume agent and another that can choose one of many configured Flume agents in a round-robin or random order. To use Flume's log4j appenders, *flume-ng-log4jappender-1.5.0-jar-with-dependencies.jar* [flume-log4j] should be put in the classpath of your application. It is not required when building your project, but during deployment.

log4j appenders are configured via the *log4j.properties* files. To learn more about log4j configuration, please refer to the log4j documentation [log4j-doc]. The log4 appenders support log4j layouts, which can be specified using the `layout` parameter in the appender configuration.

Both of the log4j appenders accept the parameters in Table 7-6.

*Table 7-6. Configuration parameters common to both Flume log4j appenders*

| Parameter | Default | Description |
| --- | --- | --- |
| UnsafeMode | false | If set to `true`, the log4j appender will not throw any exception if a log message could not be committed into the Flume agent's channel. |
| AvroReflectionEnabled | false | If set to `true`, the appender will attempt to parse the content of the message as an Avro datum. |
| AvroSchemaUrl | - | The URL where the Avro Schema is stored. |

The `UnsafeMode` parameter can be set to `true` to ignore failure when log messages sent to the Flume agents fail. This should only be set if it is acceptable to lose log messages quietly. If this is not set or is set to `false`, and log messages time out or fail to be committed to the Flume agent's channel(s), logging methods may throw an exception.

Both log4j appenders can serialize data using Avro serialization. If the incoming data is an instance of an Avro Generic Record or Specific Record, the log4j appender will serialize it using Avro serialization. If `AvroReflectionEnabled` is set to `true`, the appender serializes any arbitrary data to Avro as well. Note that this should be used only when the data must be serialized to Avro. If the `AvroSchemaURL` parameter is set, then the appender sets in the Flume event with key `flume.avro.schema.url` whose value is the value of the `AvroSchemaURL` parameter. If this is not set, then the entire JSON-ified schema is written to a header with the key `flume.avro.schema.literal`.

Both log4j appenders insert additional headers into Flume event headers, which give additional information about the events. They are shown in Table 7-7.

*Table 7-7. Headers added by Flume log4j appenders*

| Header | Description |
| --- | --- |
| `flume.client.log4j.logger.name` | The name of the logger instance that inserted the event. |
| `flume.client.log4j.log.level` | The level at which this message was logged. |
| `flume.client.log4j.message.encoding` | The encoding of the message (currently it is always UTF-8). |
| `flume.client.log4j.timestamp` | The timestamp at which the message was appended. |

The log4j appender takes two additional configuration parameters, listed in Table 7-8.

*Table 7-8. Flume log4j appender configuration*

| Parameter | Default | Description |
| --- | --- | --- |
| `<appender-name>` | - | Must be `org.apache.flume.clients.log4jappender.Log4jAppender`. |
| `Hostname` | - | The hostname where the Flume agent is running. |
| `Port` | - | The port where the Flume agent's Avro Source is listening. |

The name of the appender is the key for specifying the FQCN of the log4j appender. In this case, it must be set to `org.apache.flume.clients.log4jappender.Log4jAp` `pender`. The Flume log4j appender referred to as `flumeAppender` can be configured by using the following line in your *log4j.properties* file:

```
log4j.rootLogger = INFO, flumeAppender
log4j.appender.flumeAppender = \
org.apache.flume.clients.log4jappender.Log4jAppender
log4j.appender.flumeAppender.Hostname = usingflume-srv-1.domain.com
log4j.appender.flumeAppender.Port = 3343
log4j.appender.flumeAppender.UnsafeMode = true
```

This configuration writes any messages at INFO level or above to the flumeAppender and passes the data to the Flume agent at usingflume-srv-1.domain.com:3343.

## Load-Balancing log4j Appender

Similar to RPC clients, log4j appenders also can be configured to load balance between multiple Flume agents, using a round-robin or random strategy. This is configured using the additional parameters in Table 7-9.

*Table 7-9. Load-balancing log4j appender configuration*

| Parameter | Default | Description |
| --- | --- | --- |
| `<appender-name>` | - | Must be `org.apache.flume.clients.log4jappender.LoadBa` `lancingLog4jAppender`. |
| Hosts | - | A list of hosts specified in hostname:port format, where Flume Avro Sources are listening. |
| Selector | ROUND_ROBIN | Can be ROUND_ROBIN, RANDOM, or the FQCN of a class that implements Load `BalancingRpcClient.HostSelector`. |
| MaxBackoff | - | The maximum time (in milliseconds) to back off while connecting to a Flume agent that may have failed. |

The load-balancing log4j appender can load balance over several hosts, similar to the load-balancing RPC client. The list of hosts must be specified as a comma-separated list in the format hostname:port as the value of the key Hosts.

Just like the load-balancing RPC client, this log4j appender can select the hosts in round-robin or random order by setting ROUND_ROBIN or RANDOM as the value of the Selector parameter. To use a custom strategy, the FQCN of a class implementing LoadBalancingRpcClient$HostSelector can be specified. Also like the load-balancing RPC client, a log4j appender can blacklist a failed Flume agent for an increasing period of time up to a maximum backoff using the MaxBackoff parameter:

```
log4j.rootLogger = INFO, flumeAppender
log4j.appender.flumeAppender =
org.apache.flume.clients.log4jappender.LoadBalancingLog4jAppender
log4j.appender.flumeAppender.Hosts = usingflume-srv-1.domain.com:5545,
usingflume-srv-2.domain.com:3133,usingflume-srv-3.domain.com:4454
log4j.appender.flumeAppender.UnsafeMode = true
log4j.appender.flumeAppender.Selector = RANDOM
log4j.appender.flumeAppender.MaxBackoff = 120000
```

This configuration uses a LoadBalancingLog4jAppender that connects to three different hosts in a random order and blacklists failed Flume agents for 120 seconds.

# Summary

In this chapter, we covered the APIs Flume provides to get the data out from applications to Flume agents reliably. We also covered the log4j appenders that come bundled with Flume that allow the user to send data to Flume without actually writing any code, using some simple configuration.

In the next and final chapter, we will look at how to plan and deploy Flume, and how to monitor a Flume cluster once it's deployed.

# References

- [truststore] Oracle trust store documentation, *http://bit.ly/1oprwQn*
- [truststore-type] `KeyStore` types, *http://bit.ly/1wxll6y*
- [thrift-doc] Apache Thrift tutorial, *http://thrift.apache.org/tutorial/*
- [flume-thrift] Flume Thrift specification, *http://bit.ly/1oprwjc*
- [hostInfo] `HostInfo` class, *http://bit.ly/1opryrq*
- [zlib-manual] zlib manual, *http://www.zlib.net/manual.html*
- [log4j-doc] log4j manual, *http://logging.apache.org/log4j/1.2/manual.html*
- [flume-log4j] Flume log4j appender on Maven Central, *http://bit.ly/1oprCav*

# CHAPTER 8

# Planning, Deploying, and Monitoring Flume

Up to this point, we've discussed the architecture of Flume and the various components and their configuration. In this chapter, we will discuss how to plan a Flume deployment and how to deploy and monitor Flume agents. We will also discuss the various tools available outside of the Flume project itself that make deployment and monitoring of Flume easier.

## Planning a Flume Deployment

Planning a Flume deployment can be tricky. In this section, we will discuss the steps involved in planning a Flume deployment for your requirements.

### Time to Repair

Most production deployments define a *mean time to repair* (MTTR) for systems that have gone down, which is usually a good estimate of how long systems will take to come back online. In this section, we will assume that the MTTR for servers hosting the various services is available and that in most cases the time required for recovery does not exceed this. In simple terms, let's consider this to be the time taken for servers to recover from failure in most cases. This will vary between deployments, and if a *maximum time to repair* (maximum time in which a failed system recovers) is available, that should be considered instead. In this chapter, we assume that this is available; we'll call it *MaxTTR*.

Now that the user already has information on (or has calculated) the maximum time that each machine can go down for, we also assume for the purposes of this chapter that any planned or unplanned downtime for the storage or indexing system (the system as a whole, not just one machine) has a known upper bound—let's call it *maximum time to storage repair* (MTSR).

Summarizing, we have two types of upper bounds: the MaxTTR, which is the maximum downtime of a single server, and the MTSR, which is the maximum downtime of a storage or indexing cluster. For the sake of simplicity, let's also assume that these values are measured in seconds.

### Validity of These Calculations

If client applications cannot write to all agents in the first tier and the first-tier agents cannot write to all agents in the second, these values no longer have any meaning, since it is does not make sense to combine capacities when one agent cannot write to another (if the second agent goes down, the capacity of the path from the client via the first agent will be reduced). So, all numbers in this chapter are valid only when a load-balancing or failover strategy is deployed between client applications and the first tier, and between tiers.

In the following sections, we will discuss ratios between the number of agents in different tiers and between the final tier and HDFS. These numbers are based on experimentation and not necessarily scientifically valid for every scenario. When the servers in question are really powerful, with several cores and a lot of RAM, newer OS optimizations, etc. can improve the performance a whole lot.

The ratios presented here might vary wildly based on a number of factors including, but not limited to, the hardware, the network configuration, the OS used, and the optimizations made for the deployment. *The idea here is to present the technique used and not to provide absolute ways of doing this planning.* The real ratios will vary for each deployment, based on all the factors mentioned earlier. Use these numbers as guidance, but do not depend on them blindly. Use them as a starting point and then come up with values based on experimentation that reflect the actual hardware and network the deployment is going to be on.

## How Much Capacity Do I Need in My Flume Channels?

This is one of the most common questions faced by teams deploying Flume. The capacity of Flume channels is what provides a buffer between the applications producing data and the storage system. The maximum time that the storage system is not accessible is equal to the MaxSTR, according to our earlier definition. This means that for a period equivalent to the MaxSTR (plus a buffer period), the application must still be able to produce and write data to Flume, while Flume buffers the data.

Calculating the total buffer capacity is simple. Assume that the combined production of events from all application servers at peak hours is $p_{max}$ events per second. The total number of events that are produced in this period can then be represented as:

$$T_{max} = p_{max} \times MaxTSR$$

This is the total number of events that should be buffered in the entire Flume deployment. But this does not consider the fact that machines hosting Flume agents can also fail, which means any buffering provided by them will be unavailable. To account for this, it is important to also add an additional buffer in the Flume cluster. A reasonable buffer to add is an additional 25% of the $T_{max}$. So, a good overall channel capacity over the entire Flume deployment would be represented by:

$$T = 1.25 \times T_{max}$$

# How Many Tiers?

Now that we know how much overall capacity the Flume deployment needs to have, we need to understand how to split the Flume deployment into multiple tiers. When designing a tiered Flume deployment, start calculating capacity from the tier that talks to HDFS.

The number of machines that directly write to an HDFS cluster should be very limited, since the HDFS cluster must also support applications that read and process data, like MapReduce, Impala, Spark, etc. It is usually a good idea to limit the number of Flume agents writing data to Flume to a few tens of agents. Depending on the servers used for the HDFS cluster, how loaded the cluster is, and the network, your deployment may be able to handle more clients writing at any point in time.

### HDFS and Avro Source Scaling

In general, keeping the number of agents writing to an HDFS cluster low is a good idea. The number of sinks required and number of agents required vary based on specific use cases.

Since Avro Sources that receive data from other Flume agents really are servers running within a JVM that does a lot of additional work —buffering to the channel, sinks running several threads pulling data out of the channel and writing to the storage system, etc.— Avro Sources eventually will reach a point where they cannot scale any further. It will end up taking too long for Avro Source worker threads to push data into the channels, causing timeouts on the Avro Sink in the previous tier. At this point, more agents running Avro Sources need to be added to that tier.

The goal is make sure that there is at least a capacity of $T$ in the Flume cluster channels. To do this, we add agents between the application and the HDFS cluster. Once the tier writing to HDFS is full, it pushes back on the previous tier or the application. Since it is not a good idea to be pushing back on the application, an additional tier between the application and the tier writing to HDFS is a good idea when the total capacity of the agents writing to HDFS is more than $T$, and the number of HDFS tier agents has increased to more than eight agents.

The idea is to start adding agents to the tier writing to HDFS to increase the overall channel capacity. Once the number becomes large and the HDFS cluster starts facing hiccups due to too many open files or too many clients writing to it, this indicates more capacity needs to be added. At this point, a tier between the application and the HDFS tier becomes necessary—let's call this tier $T_n$.

Once the ratio between the number of agents in $T_n$ and the tier writing to HDFS reaches 32:1 (remember, these numbers need to be tested for individual deployments), an additional tier between the application and $T_n$ may be necessary to add more capacity. The same logic can be applied further to add more capacity between the application and currently existing tiers.

Similar logic needs to be applied to scale the number of agents receiving data from the application. Add agents to increase capacity and decrease the ratio of application servers to the first-tier agents to less than 32:1. If the number of Flume agents in the first tier is small (of the order of tens of machines), write directly to HDFS from these machines; otherwise, add a second tier such that the ratio is less than 32:1 between the first tier and the second. Now keep increasing the number of agents in tiers such that the ratio between consecutive agents is less than 32:1. Additional tiers become necessary because of the ratio between the final tier and HDFS, since the final tier cannot have more than around eight machines.

### How do you know if Flume is not scaling or if the destination storage system or index is slow?

The previous ratios give a good starting point for your cluster deployment. But once you have deployed Flume, how do you know if you can write more data via Flume? In most cases, if you are not seeing exceptions in the logs consistently, and your channel sizes are not growing out of control (some growth is fine, provided they eventually go down in size), it means all is well and more data can be sent. Once you start seeing exceptions consistently or your channel sizes are simply growing, then action is required on your part.

If Flume sinks are not clearing the channels fast enough, and there are no timeouts in the logs, adding more sinks will help—until the maximum number of threads that the JVM can support is reached, at which point the rate at which the channel is being cleared starts flatlining (and there are still no timeouts in the logs). If the channels are still not being cleared fast enough, and the channel sizes are creeping up, it means all the sinks combined are not clearing the channels as fast as the sources are writing to them, indicating that more Flume agents are needed on this tier. Adding more agents on this tier distributes the load, thus reducing the gap between the rate at which sources are writing and the rate at which sinks are clearing. This should ensure that channel sizes stay consistent and don't keep growing.

There is another possibility, though—your storage or indexing system may be under-deployed for all the write load from Flume combined with the already heavy processing you are doing on the cluster. An indication of this is timeouts happening on the sink, usually indicated by `TimeoutExceptions` in the logs. If this is the case, adding more sinks won't help as the storage system itself is unable to keep up with the load.

For HDFS, this can happen if there are several MapReduce or Impala jobs running on the same cluster and the cluster's I/O devices are getting overwhelmed.

For HBase, this can happen for multiple reasons, like too many writes going to the same regions or scans happening too often, locking up rows. Either way, this needs to be fixed by scaling up the storage system.

For each system, how this is done depends on the system itself. You can add more data nodes to an HDFS cluster or add more region servers to an HBase cluster, or distribute the writes to hit multiple regions.

## Sending Data over Cross–Data Center Links

Cross–data center links are usually much slower and much less reliable than intra-data center links. If the application producing data is in one data center and the HDFS cluster is in another, it is always a good idea to have a Flume tier in each data center, since cross–data center links are more likely to fail or have a higher latency than local links. To keep the application from seeing these higher latencies or failures on these links, it should write to Flume and have Flume deal with the latency or failures. The application writes to one tier, which writes data across the WAN to another tier, which writes to HDFS. This works better because Flume *autoregulates* by adjusting the backoffs when writes fail. This allows the application to continue working despite failures or slowdowns in the cross–data center links, relying on Flume to do the buffering, retries, and backoffs to reduce the congestion on these links.

It is not a good idea to have Flume write directly to HDFS across a WAN, since failures are more likely. When failures happen, Flume might not be able to close files or ensure data was reliably written to the HDFS cluster. This can cause a huge number of duplicates, and/or small files getting written to HDFS as Flume will close a file as soon as a single write to that file times out or fails.

If the responsibility to write across WANs is given to Flume, it is less likely that failures will cause duplicates and small files in HDFS, as the RPC sink–source combo takes care of delivering data reliably across the WAN. Of course, timeouts will have to be adjusted based on the level of latency across the WAN, but a few failures every now and then will not stress the Flume agents a whole lot. This is shown in Figure 8-1.

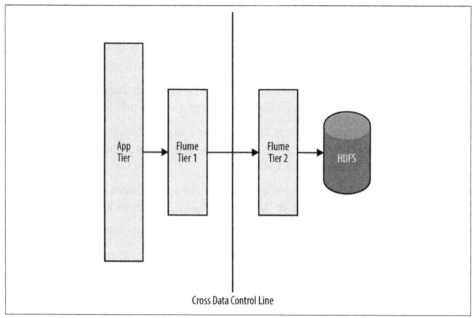

*Figure 8-1. Cross–data center communication using Flume*

## Sharding Tiers

Adding tiers makes sense in order to scale the number of events that need to be buffered. But with each agent in one tier opening connections to every agent in the next, the number of connections still coming into each Avro Source on the second tier is as many as the number of agents in the first tier. Such high absolute numbers still put some stress on the resources on those servers because sockets use up file descriptors and TCP buffers, even though their use might be limited since the agents in the previous tier write to so many agents. To avoid this, a good idea might be to *shard* tiers.

Let's take an example where tier 1 has 380 agents, which means tier 2 must have at least 12 agents to keep the ratio below 32:1. Each one of the 12 agents in tier 2 will end up having 380 incoming connections open. (You could substitute this with 380 application servers and 12 Flume agents as the first and only tier as well.) This gives the agents in the first tier 12x failure tolerance, but this also means that each of the 12 agents allocates TCP buffers for 380 sockets. Often, 12x failure tolerance is not necessary at all. You could easily get away with something like 3–4x failure tolerance. If each of the tier 1 agents sent data to only four tier 2 agents, they would still have 4x failure tolerance.

Therefore, you could essentially partition tier 1 and tier 2 into three shards, each handling a subset of the total data being sent from the application to HDFS. If each of these tiers were sharded, tier 1 would have three shards, each with approximately 128 agents, and tier 2 would have the same number of shards with 4 agents each. All shards from tier 2 could either write directly to HDFS or to another tier, which need not be sharded since the number of agents in tier 2 is small.

This technique is shown in Figure 8-2.

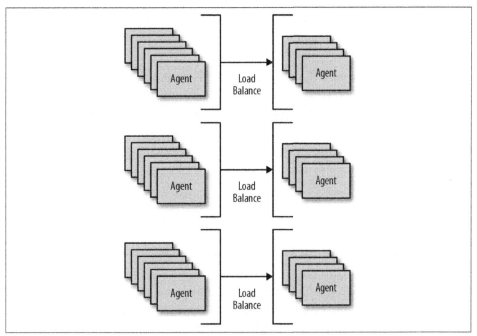

*Figure 8-2. Sharding tiers to reduce load on individual servers*

# Deploying Flume

Now that you have planned a Flume deployment, you need to deploy the software and configuration to these machines to get them running. Flume does not have a centralized deployment or management service, but there are systems available in the market that can do this for you. One example is Cloudera Manager [cm]. Cloudera Manager can deploy Cloudera's Flume distribution to various servers, in addition to deploying custom code for plug-ins and also configuration files.

Another option is Apache Bigtop [bigtop]; it provides packages in native formats for various operating systems, like RPM for Red Hat (and derived systems), deb for Debian, etc. These packages are generally based on the current Apache release of Flume. They can be used for easily deploying Flume to various machines and even installing and removing Flume using native package management systems.

## Deploying Custom Code

Custom code is often deployed with Flume. Custom code may be written for interceptors, serializers, deserializers, HTTP Source handlers, etc. Flume provides an easy way to deploy custom code: the *plugins.d* framework. The *plugins.d* directory is automatically added to the Flume classpath, and hence this does not need to be added to the FLUME_CLASSPATH explicitly. To add custom code to the *plugins.d* framework, you must understand the way Flume adds plug-ins to its classpath from the *plugins.d* directory.

The directory structure of the *plugins.d* directory is shown in Figure 8-3. For each custom component, you create a new subdirectory in *plugins.d* (the name really does not matter). In each of these subdirectories, Flume expects three directories:

*lib*
> This directory contains the actual JAR files that contain the plug-in classes and builders that go into the configuration file and are to be instantiated by Flume.

*libext*
> This directory contains external dependencies that the plug-in depends on.

*native*
> This directory contains any native libraries that are to be loaded via the Java Native Interface (JNI).

The directories are added to the Flume classpath in no specific order, so no ordering should be expected in the JAR files being added in any of the directories.

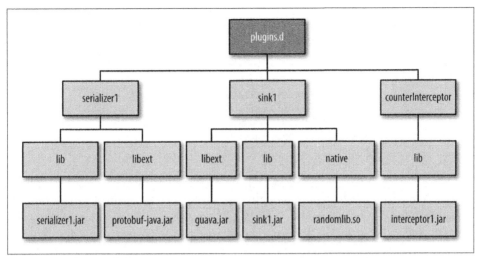

*Figure 8-3. plugins.d directory structure*

# Monitoring Flume

Flume has a metrics framework that can expose metrics via Java Management Extensions (JMX) or HTTP, or to a Ganglia server. For each of the components, there are multiple metrics that are exposed. Table 8-1, Table 8-2, and Table 8-3 show the various metrics exposed by channels, sources, and sinks.

All metrics are exposed in all cases via JMX. Since JMX can be used to start or stop Java applications, it is not recommended to allow JMX to be accessed from remote machines. This is disabled by default, and it is best not to enable this for security reasons.

To report metrics to HTTP, pass -Dflume.monitoring.type=http to the agent while starting it:

```
bin/flume-ng agent -f flume.conf -n agent -c conf -Dflume.monitoring.type=http \
  -Dflume.monitoring.port=5653
```

This will cause Flume to start an HTTP server on port 5653. Accessing the */metrics* web page returns the metrics in the following JSON format (the URL used to access the metrics would be of the form *http://usingflume.oreilly.com:5653/metrics*):

```
{
"type1.component1" : {"metric1" : "value1", "metric2" : "value2"},
"type2.component2" : {"metric3" : "value3", "metric4" : "value4"}
}
```

For the previous source, the type is SOURCE (CHANNEL is the type for a channel, SINK for sink, etc.). Here's an example of how metrics are represented:

```
{
"CHANNEL.ch1":{"EventPutSuccessCount":"6645",
              "Type":"CHANNEL",
              "StopTime":"0",
              "EventPutAttemptCount":"6887",
              "ChannelSize":"434",
              "StartTime":"1455782222341,
              "EventTakeSuccessCount":"45200",
              "ChannelCapacity":"600000",
              "EventTakeAttemptCount":"45100"
              }
}
```

Flume can also send metrics information to Ganglia, which can be used to monitor Flume. Only one of Ganglia or HTTP monitoring can be enabled at any point in time. The same metrics shown in Table 8-1, Table 8-2, and Table 8-3 are exposed via HTTP and Ganglia. Flume reports metrics to Ganglia periodically—the default is once per minute, though this can be configured to report more often. To start Ganglia reporting, start Flume with the following command line (replacing the arguments with their corresponding values in your deployment, of course):

```
bin/flume-ng agent -f flume.conf -n agent -c conf \
-Dflume.monitoring.type=ganglia \
-Dflume.monitoring.pollFrequency=45 -Dflume.monitoring.isGanglia3=true
```

To report metrics to Ganglia, you pass -Dflume.monitoring.type=ganglia to the agent while starting it. By default, Flume reports metrics in Ganglia 3.1 format. To report in Ganglia 3 format, pass -Dflume.monitoring.isGanglia3=true to the Flume agent on startup, as in this command line. To change the reporting interval, use the -Dflume.monitoring.poll Frequency command-line argument. The value passed is the period between two consecutive reports from Flume (in seconds).

*Table 8-1. Channel metrics*

| Metric | Description |
| --- | --- |
| ChannelSize | The total number of events currently in the channel. |
| EventPutAttemptCount | The total number of events the source(s) attempted to write to the channel. |
| EventPutSuccessCount | The total number of events that were successfully written and committed to the channel. |
| EventTakeAttemptCount | The total number of times the sink(s) attempted to read events from the channel. This does not mean that events were returned each time, since sinks might poll and the channel might not have any data. |
| EventTakeSuccessCount | The total number of events that were successfully taken by the sink(s). |
| StartTime | Milliseconds since the epoch when the channel was started. |

| Metric | Description |
|---|---|
| StopTime | Milliseconds since the epoch when the channel was stopped. |
| ChannelCapacity | The capacity of the channel. |
| ChannelFillPercentage | The percentage of the channel that is full. |
| Type | For channels, this always returns CHANNEL. |

*Table 8-2. Source metrics*

| Metric | Description |
|---|---|
| EventReceivedCount | The total number of events that the source has received until now. |
| EventAcceptedCount | The total number of events where the event was successfully written out to the channel and the source returned success to the sink/RPC client/system that created the event. |
| AppendReceivedCount | The total number of events that came in with only one event per batch (the equivalent of an append call in RPC calls). |
| AppendAcceptedCount | The total number of events that came in individually that were written to the channel and returned successfully. |
| AppendBatchReceivedCount | The total number of batches of events received. |
| AppendBatchAcceptedCount | The total number of batches successfully committed to the channel. |
| StartTime | Milliseconds since the epoch when the source was started. |
| StopTime | Milliseconds since the epoch when the source was stopped. |
| OpenConnectionCount | The number of connections currently open with clients/sinks (only an Avro Source currently exposes this). |
| Type | For sources, this always returns SOURCE. |

*Table 8-3. Sink metrics*

| Metric | Description |
|---|---|
| ConnectionCreatedCount | The number of connections created with the next hop or storage system (like when a new file is created on HDFS). |
| ConnectionClosedCount | The number of connections closed with the next hop or storage system (like when a file on HDFS is closed). |

| Metric | Description |
| --- | --- |
| ConnectionFailedCount | The number of connections that were closed due to an error with the next hop or storage system (like when a new file on HDFS is closed because of timeouts). |
| BatchEmptyCount | The number of batches that were empty—a high number indicates that the sources are writing data slower than the sinks are clearing it. |
| BatchUnderflowCount | The number of batches that were smaller than the maximum batch size this sink is configured to use—this also indicates sinks are faster than sources if it's high. |
| BatchCompleteCount | The number of batches that were equal to the maximum batch size. |
| EventDrainAttemptCount | The total number of events the sink tried to write out to storage. |
| EventDrainSuccessCount | The total number of events that the sink successfully wrote out to storage. |
| StartTime | Milliseconds since the epoch when the sink was started. |
| StopTime | Milliseconds since the epoch when the sink was stopped. |
| Type | For sinks, this always returns SINK. |

These metrics can be used to keep an eye on the health of the Flume agents. There are systems like Cloudera Manager that can take these raw metrics provided by Flume and provide more meaningful metrics, like how long until the channel is filled. Such systems also provide time-bucketed graphs of these metrics. These systems can alert operations engineers when metrics hit critical situations, which are indicative of downtime in the HDFS cluster or underplanned capacity of Flume agents.

## Reporting Metrics from Custom Components

Custom components such as sources, sinks, or channels can expose metrics directly to the Flume framework using the SourceCounter, SinkCounter, and Channel Counter classes, respectively, which provide methods to update any of the previous metrics for sources, sinks, and channels.

Other components, like interceptors, serializers, etc., can also expose metrics, but there are no convenience classes that make this direct, since each component might expose very different-looking metrics. Such components can report metrics directly to JMX using the MonitoredCounterGroup class. Custom components should create a counter class that inherits this class, and have public getter methods for the various metrics. To add, update, or increment metric values, the counter class can expose methods that can be used by the custom class implementation.

# Summary

In this chapter, we discussed how to plan, deploy, and monitor Flume. Flume can be planned and deployed in a scalable and flexible way if issues such as cluster downtime and the desired buffering are considered before actually deploying Flume. You should also make sure that there is enough buffering to ensure HDFS downtimes do not affect the application writing data to Flume.

Flume can be deployed and monitored using simple techniques built into Flume or using third-party systems that allow for the deployment and configuration of Flume from a single location.

# References

- [cm] Cloudera Manager, *http://bit.ly/1opzYiz*
- [bigtop] Apache Bigtop, *http://bigtop.apache.org*

# Index

HADOOP_PREFIX directory, 30
HBase (Apache), 5
    client API, 5
    client-side security configuration, 139
    HTTP API, 10
    master server, 6
    operations, 5
    regions in, 6
    Shell, 6
    shell commands for, 5
    Thrift API, 6
    timeouts in, 201
    versions, 121
HBase Sinks, 114-121
    configuration, 114
    performance of, 95
    Puts, translating events into, 117-121
    serializer, location of, 120
    translating events into Puts, 117-121
HBase: The Definitive Guide, 6, 115, 139
HDFS (Hadoop Distributed File System), 1-5, 7
    calculating tier capacity for, 200
    data formats in, 3
    data processing in, 4
    immutability of data in, 1, 2
    replication factors, 2
    shell commands for, 3
    source scaling for, 199
    SQL interfaces for, 4
    timeouts in, 201
    write constraints on, 8
    writing across a WAN, 201
    writing to, 96-114
HDFS Sink, 96-114
    buckets, 97-100
    configuring, 100-108
    data format, controlling, 108-114
    Hadoop support for, 96
    multiple, configuring, 104
    performance of, 95
    serializers and, 108-114
headers
    generated by interceptors, 147
    generated by log4j appenders, 193
hidden files, writing to, 96
Hive (Apache), 4, 7, 99
    Avro container format, 112
    HDFS Sinks and, 103
host information, replacing, 97

host interceptors, 143
host selector, custom, 183
host-selector parameter (load-balancing RPC
    client), 181
hostHeader parameter (interceptors), 143
HostInfo class, 183, 195
Hostname interceptor, 97
hosts parameter (RPC client), 171, 184
HostSelector class (LoadBalancingRpcClient),
    183, 194
HTTP Source, 43-49
    as event-driven source, 74
    configuring, 43
    custom handlers configuration, 44
    custom handlers for, 44-49
    exception handling in, 45
HTTP, exposing metrics via, 205
HTTPBadRequestException, 45, 47
HTTPHandler interface, 49
HTTPServletRequest, 45
HTTPSourceHandler interface, 44
HTTPSourceXMLHandler, 46

# I

IANA Time Zone Data, 139
idle timeouts, triggering, 106
idleTimeout parameter (HDFS Sink), 104
ignorePattern parameter (Spooling Directory
    Source), 51
immutability of data, 1, 2
increments (HBase), 5
    translating events into, 117-121
indexName parameter (Elastic Search Sink),
    130
indexType parameter (Elastic Search Sink), 130
inflight pointers (File Channel), 91
informFailure method (RPC client), 183
informSinkFailed method (sinks), 162
ingest format, 113
initialContextFactory parameter (JMS Source),
    65
input format for MapReduce, 4
intercept method (interceptors), 148
Interceptor interface, 147
interceptor parameter (source), 142
interceptors, 11, 141-150
    configuration, 142
    configuring for sources, 35
    custom, 147-150

readChar method, 53
readEvent method (deserializers), 54
records (Morphline Solr Sink), 125
regex filtering interceptors, 144
region server (HBase), 6
regions (HBase), 6
replicating channel selectors, 151
replication factors, 2
reporting metrics from custom code, 208
request-timeout parameter (RPC client), 178
ResettableInputStream instances, 53
restart parameter (Exec Source), 63
rollCount parameter (HDFS Sink), 104
Rolling File Sink, 134
    configuration, 134
rolling timeouts, triggering, 106
rollInterval parameter (HDFS Sink), 104
rollTimerPoolSize parameter (HDFS Sink), 106
round-robin sink selection, 160
row key (HBASE), 5
RPC clients, 169-185
    batching and, 27
    building, 169
    closing, 170
    compression and, 38
    configuration parameters for, 170-176
    creating, 171
    default, 177-180
    failover, 184
    interface, 169
    load-balancing, 180-183
    reconnecting, 176
    sending data over, 169
    SSL and, 38
    Thrift, 184
RPC sinks, 121-125
    agent to agent communication and, 17
    Avro Sink, 121-124
    batching and, 27
    sink groups and, 157
    Thrift Sink, 124
    transaction handling by, 24
RPC sources
    agent to agent communication and, 17
    failure handling, 42
    Thrift, 40-42
    transaction handling by, 24
RpcClientConfigurationConstants class, 176
RpcClientFactory class, 171

creating default clients with, 177-180

# S

SANs (storage area networks), 2
scalability
    of Avro Source, 36
    of Flume agents, 9
    SolrCloud and, 128
Scribe (Facebook), 7
security
    Avro Sink, 123
    Avro Source, 39
    for Avro Sink, 39
    for RPC clients, 38
    HBase Sink and, 116
    in RPC clients, 179
    Kerberos, 105
    keystores, SSL, 38
    SSL, 38
    SSL keystores, 38
    Thrift and, 41
Selector parameter (log4j appenders), 194
sequence files, 4
serializers, 4
    controlling data format with, 108-114
    custom, metrics for, 208
    specifying for HDFS Sinks, 105
    translating events into increments with,
        117-121
    translating events into puts with, 117-121
server types (HDFS), 2
setClient method (RPC client), 184
setHosts method (host selector), 183
shell commands
    for HBase, 5
    for HDFS, 3
shell parameter (Exec Source), 63
shell, running Exec Source in, 63
sink groups, 12, 157
    component-type parameter for, 14
    multiple, 158
Sink interface, 135
sink processors, 12, 158-164
    failover, 162-164
    load-balancing, 159-162
sink runner thread, 12, 94, 135
sink-to-source communication, 36-43
    Avro Source, 36-39
    failure handling, 42

## About the Author

**Hari Shreedharan** is a Software Engineer at Cloudera where he works on Apache Spark, Apache Flume, and Apache Sqoop. He's also a committer and a PMC member on the Flume Project and helps make decisions on the project's direction. He regularly presents at various Big Data–related conferences and meetups. Hari completed his Masters in Computer Science from Cornell University in 2010.

## Colophon

The animal on the cover of *Using Flume* is a burbot (*Lota lota*), a fish of northern waters that is often found in clean, large rivers and deep, cold lakes. Also known as mariah, the lawyer, and eelpout, the burbot is closely related to the marine common ling and the cusk.

Burbot are unusual looking, with a head like a catfish, a body like an eel, and very small scales that make it smooth and slimy to the touch. They are marked by a single barbel on their chin (the fish's name comes from *barba*, the Latin word for "beard"). They are aggressive predators and primarily fish eaters but, at times, burbot will also eat insects and have been known to eat frogs, snakes, and birds.

Burbot are the only freshwater fish to spawn in midwinter. Spawning takes place when water temperatures are between 32° and 40°F, often under ice cover. They are difficult to study, due to their deep habitats and reproduction under ice, but they provide great fishing opportunities for winter anglers. In fact, the town of Walker, Minnesota, holds an International Eelpout Festival every winter on Leech Lake.

Many of the animals on O'Reilly covers are endangered; all of them are important to the world. To learn more about how you can help, go to *animals.oreilly.com*.

The cover image is from Meyers Kleines Lexicon. The cover fonts are URW Typewriter and Guardian Sans. The text font is Adobe Minion Pro; the heading font is Adobe Myriad Condensed; and the code font is Dalton Maag's Ubuntu Mono.

# Get even more for your money.

**Join the O'Reilly Community, and register the O'Reilly books you own. It's free, and you'll get:**

- $4.99 ebook upgrade offer
- 40% upgrade offer on O'Reilly print books
- Membership discounts on books and events
- Free lifetime updates to ebooks and videos
- Multiple ebook formats, DRM FREE
- Participation in the O'Reilly community
- Newsletters
- Account management
- 100% Satisfaction Guarantee

### Signing up is easy:

1. Go to: oreilly.com/go/register
2. Create an O'Reilly login.
3. Provide your address.
4. Register your books.

Note: English-language books only

**To order books online:**
oreilly.com/store

**For questions about products or an order:**
orders@oreilly.com

**To sign up to get topic-specific email announcements and/or news about upcoming books, conferences, special offers, and new technologies:**
elists@oreilly.com

**For technical questions about book content:**
booktech@oreilly.com

**To submit new book proposals to our editors:**
proposals@oreilly.com

**O'Reilly books are available in multiple DRM-free ebook formats. For more information:**
oreilly.com/ebooks

## O'REILLY®

CPSIA information can be obtained at www.ICGtesting.com
Printed in the USA
BVOW08s2343181214

380121BV00001B/2/P